THE OARSMEN

THE
OARSMEN

THE REMARKABLE STORY OF THE MEN WHO ROWED
FROM THE GREAT WAR TO PEACE

Scott Patterson

Hardie Grant

BOOKS

Published in 2019 by Hardie Grant Books,
an imprint of Hardie Grant Publishing

Hardie Grant Books (Melbourne)
Building 1, 658 Church Street
Richmond, Victoria 3121

Hardie Grant Books (London)
5th & 6th Floors
52–54 Southwark StreetLondon SE1 1UN

hardiegrantbooks.com

 A catalogue record for this
book is available from the
National Library of Australia

The Oarsmen
ISBN 978 1 74379 549 1

10 9 8 7 6 5 4 3 2 1

Cover design by Nada Backovic
Typeset in 10.5/15 pt Sabon LT Std by Megan Ellis and Graeme Jones
Cover images: Photograph courtesy of University of Melbourne Archives,
1976-0013-00126 Strathfieldsaye Estate Collection; 1919 Rowing Section
emblem, featuring the Third Pattern Rising Sun badge, used with permission
from the Australian Army

Printed by McPherson's Printing Group, Maryborough, Victoria

To hear the faint sound of oars in the silence as a rowboat
comes slowly out and then goes back is truly worth
all the years of sorrow that are to come.

Jack Gilbert

Contents

Part 3 – The Regatta

PROLOGUE

Rowing into war

On 23 April 1915 in Mudros Harbour, the Allied troopship HMT *Ionian* weighed anchor and steamed out to sea from the small island of Lemnos in the Aegean Sea. It was carrying the men of the Australian Imperial Force (AIF) 10th Battalion, heading into their first active deployment, one that would be perhaps the largest amphibious landing ever attempted in modern war.

Running to a tight timetable, during the afternoon of 24 April the HMT *Ionian* rendezvoused with the Formidable-class battleship HMS *Prince of Wales* and two escort torpedo destroyers. B and C companies of the 10th Battalion transferred to HMS *Prince of Wales* and the remaining A and D companies boarded the torpedo destroyers HMS *Scourge* and HMS *Foxhound*. Men, administrative staff, weapons, ammunition and equipment were carefully issued, checked and stowed. Already the 10th Battalion was fatefully split into separate companies, with orders to reassemble upon landing. They would have to find each other once they made landfall on hostile terrain of which they knew very little except that there was a beach – Beach Z – and distant rugged heights: known by the Turks as Sari Bair.

At 3 am on Sunday 25 April, the first wave of scouts and signallers of the 10th Battalion clambered down the cargo nets into cutters, launches or rowboats tethered to steam pinnaces. At carefully timed intervals, sections of men clambered over the rails and tightly gripped the cargo net as they descended. Everything was carried out in complete silence except for the noises of anxious men clambering from ship to rowboat, knocking railings, weapons and equipment dully clunking, and the odd muttered curse as a foot, buckle or rifle muzzle was caught in the net, or as the deck of the rocking rowboat threw them off balance and into the arms of one of their mates.

Once each rowboat was fully loaded with men and cast off, the sailors aboard each of the steam pinnaces took up the slack and pulled away from the safety of the heavily armed HMS *Prince of Wales* and began towing a line of three tethered smaller cutter rowboats towards the darkened shore. The first wave of men landing in the predawn light would, of course, possess the element of surprise, which would not extend its tactical advantage to those in the following waves for very long. From onboard the destroyer HMS *Foxhound*, now off the island of Imbros, a fair-haired man anxiously awaited his turn. Private Thomas Whyte of A Company, 10th Battalion, watched as the larger battleships disappeared into the distance.

Whyte was an oarsman, with a handsome, weather-beaten face that conveyed intense discipline, and a muscular body in the peak physical condition necessary at the highest levels of competition. But as many sportsmen in those days did, he was no doubt sneaking a cigarette, cupped within his calloused hands to calm his steadily increasing last minute nerves.

Thomas Anderson Whyte was from South Australia. Born in Unley, he attended St Peter's Anglican College, Adelaide, and grew into a tall (5 foot 11 inch), robust young man who was very good at sport, including lacrosse, but especially rowing. His oarsmanship, physicality, spiritedness and competitive edge were quickly identified by rowing officials in South Australia and he represented the state time and again in competition in the years leading up to the great war.

Whyte had enthusiastically enlisted within weeks of the declaration of war, along with several clubmates from Adelaide Rowing Club, which he had recently joined, and old St Peter's College schoolmates including Arthur Blackburn, who would later be awarded the Victoria Cross.

At twenty-nine, Whyte had life experience and was already engaged to be married to his beautiful young fiancée, Eileen Champion. In his letters, Tom frequently signed off with 'Goodnight, my wife' – in his mind they were as good as married. Eileen had a steady job as a stenographer and still lived with her parents in Unley Park. Tom and Eileen's love and affection for each was very real. In his love letters Tom wrote about his voyage from Australia, the military training and the sights of Egypt, where he was stationed prior to active service, and spoke of their longed-for reunion:

> The 3 months I have been away seem more than 12. I build
> castles in the air every day about our reunion. When I get back,
> I am not going to think of work for a month and you will have to
> have a month's holiday even if it means the sack.[1]

After weeks of apprehension, when word came that the 10th Battalion were to finally embark for the peninsula, Whyte tried to imagine what the upcoming deployment against the Turks would be like:

> Won't it be eerie in the dark creeping towards an enemy. What
> tricks our nerves will play and then in the morning with their
> artillery harassing us and our ships … guns flying overhead.
> I wonder what it feels like … If I get through alright well and
> good if not well it's the Buddhist's nirvana for me and you bear
> the sorrow. That's the cruellest part of war those that are left.
> Still it is the greatest sorrow that heals in time.[2]

On the day before the landing, from onboard the HMS *Foxhound* as it cruised the peninsula beside the battleships, Whyte wrote to Eileen about his growing anxiety and unease about the uncertain days ahead.

My Dear Sweetheart, I thought of writing this in case I went
under suddenly ... May this letter never be necessary. But the
thought that hurts worst of all is of you and your sorrow ...
Just think of me as non-existent in spirit, blotted out completely
... It would soften the last thoughts if I knew you would be really
happy again ... Goodbye my love, may you get all the happiness
you deserve, that will be my last wish.[3]

The story of Gallipoli has been told well and perhaps too often.
What occurred in the predawn hours of 25 April 1915 and throughout
the remainder of that manifestly Australian 'longest day' is mythic.
Troops arrived in a steady stream throughout the morning, afternoon
and well into the evening, conveyed from transports to steam pinnaces
to rowboats, before splashing into the water and stumbling over the
slippery pebbles of Anzac Cove or North Beach.

There, they either dumped gear on the beach before racing up
narrow, treacherous ravines blindly following the shouts and tumbling
loose gravel of others; or they huddled on the beach in confused groups,
cowering under intense Turkish shrapnel, waiting for comrades and
orders before anxiously following the steady stream of men up the
slopes of Sari Bair, believing there was now some kind of order to
the madness.

It is worth acknowledging how the first Anzacs in their first
major engagement of the Great War met their destiny: with the skills,
courage, sweat and blood of trained oarsmen, who rowed their way
into Australia's national psyche and collective identity.

In the days and weeks stationed aboard the HMT *Ionian* at
Mudros Harbour, the oarsmen had practised boarding and rowing the
boats around the anchored troop ships and destroyers, getting a feel
for the weight of these clunky metal and wooden boats. The naval
midshipmen spent hours coaching them from the boat, issuing orders
such as 'oars up' and 'easy' and working on the timing of their strokes.
Thomas Whyte and his experienced band of 10th Battalion volunteer
oarsmen became the 'uber' oarsmen around Mudros Harbour. They
water taxied top brass from ship to shore, rowed errands and messages

between transport ships, delivered supplies and ferried troops ashore to camp. Sometimes the conditions in Mudros Harbour were rough, but Whyte and the oarsmen were expected to row in any conditions.

> The wind increased so those heavy gigs needed some pulling
> against the headwind. It took us nearly 2 hours solid pulling to
> get to the newly constructed 9th jetty. We got back to the ship at
> 2:30am. We have been off all duty to-day as a reward.[4]

The upside was that there was always some cruising or sightseeing to be done. Sometimes the oarsmen just went out for a row because the water looked so good, and they were always curious about the increasing military build-up in Mudros Harbour as the Anzac invasion force prepared for war. One day, Whyte and mates taxied the brigadier ashore and then, with a few hours to kill, and the brigadier's permission, rowed out to ogle the impressive British dreadnought battleship HMS *Queen Elizabeth*, anchored miles offshore. As they rowed around the 'Eliza', encircling the monolithic dreadnought dozing in the harbour, Whyte and his band of oarsmen gazed up aghast, Whyte later wrote,

> at the great floating mass of armoured steel and guns. What a
> personification of power she looked. Think of it 8 immense long
> 15-inch dealers in death capable of throwing shells weighing
> a ton, 15 miles ... and yet to think that floating fort costing
> 2 million (pounds) and its thousand souls could be blotted out
> by one little mine. War is cruel.[5]

As the weeks went on, the training schedule for Whyte and his oarsmen in Mudros Harbour gathered pace. They progressed to practising beach landings by rowing fully laden boats with infantry, rifles and packs onto the Mudros Harbour shore. These practice landings progressed to dress rehearsals held both under the cover of darkness and actual naval gunfire, to prepare the oarsmen for the real world peninsula experience.

The programme this morning was practising landing under cover of a warship's guns. B Coy was the covering coy. and had to be landed first to hold the position while the other landed. They started at 3:30am ... It was very dark, the shore not visible until within 100 yards making it very difficult to pick up any direction. There are no prominent landmarks around the bay and the boats being anchored forward only, swing around to each change of wind. It is most perplexing at night time. I think it was more luck than anything that we hit the right spot. After landing our passengers we came back and met several boatloads wandering about. Just after we got aboard the rain started, only half could have got ashore when it was cancelled. They came back like drowned rats. Naturally the whole thing was a failure which the ship's officers expected.[6]

The primary lesson for these oarsmen from their dress rehearsals was to expect the unexpected. It would turn out to be be uncannily like the real thing, with all the tactical complications of loud naval bombardment, darkness, lack of distinguishing landmarks, strong winds, unknown coastal tides, no accurate visual description of the landing zone and incoming shrapnel and machine gun fire.

During the dummy runs, just before the boats scraped the bottom, an 'oars up' command was given and Whyte and the oarsmen would deftly pull in their oars and swing them into an upright position between their knees, both hands gripping them around the collar and oar handles placed firmly on the bottom. The oars needed to be upright so that when the landing force disembarked, they wouldn't be awkwardly hurdling sets of oars protruding from the sides of the boats. This was important stuff and they rehearsed it over and over again. But these oarsmen were used to this type of repetitive training; it was just like preparing for a big regatta back home, except this event was somewhat more lethal.

It was pretty obvious to the oarsmen that during the invasion they would be in a very dangerous position. Whyte's old schoolfriend Arthur Blackburn later wrote:

The most dangerous position of the lot was that of the men who were rowing, as they of course could take no shelter. They could not even crouch down in the boat but were compelled to sit up and row. The dangers of such a task were so apparent that officers hesitated to order men to expose themselves to the work of rowing. Tom immediately grasped the situation, and, as everyone knew he would, volunteered his services as a rower.[7]

Not only did the oarsmen have to sit bolt upright but, due to the unique quirk of rowing, they also had to sit with their backs to the direction they were heading. As all rowers know, it is one of very few sports where one competes by racing to the finish line backwards. Sitting in the boat watching where you set out from rather than looking towards where you are heading adds a singular perspective to which only rowers are privy. In addition, clocking the faces of the men peering wild-eyed past you towards the action must have added to the anxiety.

On the evening before the landing, after days of briefings, lectures, checking of equipment and playing dominoes below deck on the HMT *Ionian*, the diggers bunked down for the night. In the quieter hours, Thomas Whyte once again put pencil to paper, writing about what was to come. Ever the competitive oarsman, Whyte wrote:

> Personally, I feel exactly like I used to on the morning of an important boat race. Perhaps when we are creeping through the scrub or waiting to land the reality of our risk will come home to us.[8]

In the very early hours of 25 April 1915, on the darkened deck of the ship, Thomas Whyte scrawled a last pithy entry on page 169 of his scrapbook of love letters to Eileen:

> 2.30. left Mudros Bay April 24th Sat Imbros Is about 8, just after dark. Waited for several hours. Aboard Foxhound 11.30. Parted Ionian midnight. 3.30 got into small boats.[9]

Whyte clambered down the cargo net from HMS *Foxhound* and took his place in a small rowboat. Without a word, and like clockwork, Whyte and other volunteer AIF oarsmen dumped their backpacks under the benches, took their seats, picked up their oars and held them upright so the rest of D Company could squirm their way aboard. There were naval ratings and midshipmen manning the boats, with space at a premium and required for the infantry, who were going to provide the boots on the ground. Once Whyte and the volunteer oarsmen had rowed each crammed and very heavily laden boat to shore, the skeleton crew of naval ratings was only required to row a much lighter and near-empty lifeboat back to the waiting troopships, load up again and deliver their next set of boots to Beach Z. It was to be an endless procession that would go on throughout the day and night, and long into the following days.

The steam pinnaces slowly pulled away and with a sudden jolt the tethered rowboats moved off and sliced through the water at a steady 6 knots.

Whyte, along with the other oarsmen, sat on his fixed bench seat and held his wooden oar tight. One can imagine that he knew this was going to be a completely different style of rowing from his days on the River Torrens. These rowboats weren't long, slim boats with little freeboard, built for speed, like the eight-man racing shells used in the Interstate Rowing Championships. In fact, they were simple ship's lifeboats designed to float, carry as many souls as possible and primarily save lives. They had no outriggers bolted to the sides of the gunwale and the oars were slipped into rudimentary rowlocks with no 'gate' or twine to keep them locked in position. An important distinction between 'paddling' and 'rowing' is that rowing relies on a fulcrum at the fixed point of the rowlock to lever the boat through the water and produce increased drive. These oars were also much heavier and longer than a racing eight's oars. Their 'blade', the tip of the oar which dips into the water, was pencil or 'square' shaped, a design feature which had literally not changed for thousands of years, since the Greeks, Carthaginians and Phoenicians had plied these very same waters.

The oars in the rowboat had to reach the water from a much higher freeboard and thus the oarsmen sat higher above the waterline. If the oars were too short, the angle of the handles would be too high for the oarsmen perched on their bench seats to 'find' the water with the end of the oar and draw the handle efficiently into their chest. At the sluggish speed that they would be rowing to Beach Z there was also no need to 'feather' the oars – turn the blades parallel to the water when coming back for another stroke – as they did when competitively racing to reduce wind resistance. Instead, the oarsmen would row 'square' blade and simply catch the water and put their backs into it.

There is a saying in rowing: 'It's the coxswains who win the races and the rowers are just the horsepower.' These rowboats were no different. At the stern of the boat a young midshipman gripped the tiller and acted as coxswain, calling out orders to sound the depth, directing the men to pull harder on one side or the other to keep a steady course, and quietly giving the oarsmen feedback on their timing and effort.

By about 4.30 am on 25 April, as Whyte and the second wave of Anzac rowboats neared the shore, the crackle of gunfire grew louder and now bursts of shrapnel exploded overhead. The element of surprise had long gone. The flotilla of rowboats was encircled by a spray of hundreds of small but vicious fountains of white water as pieces of exploding shrapnel and bullets draped the second wave. As they came within 100 to 50 yards offshore of Beach Z (known by the Turks as Ari Burnu), still in deep enough water, the steam pinnaces cast off the rowboats and turned back out to sea under full steam. Now it was Whyte's moment to thread his oar through the rowlock and, on a single command from the coxswain, start rowing. The naval oarsmen in the stern of the boat set the pace for those behind them in the forward section.

In rowing, to move the boat at the fastest possible speed and maintain a steady course, the timing of the oarsmen is everything and each stroke must be in sync, both in and out of the water. At this point, within the final 100 yards to the beach, Turkish machine gun fire originating from the hills above Ari Burnu started to rain down on the boats.

One account said that 'two men to every oar we rowed like — for the shore'.[10] Racing crews on calm flat water in a final 100 yards dash to the finish line often 'lose it' – fade or panic. To say that rowing this final dash, maintaining boat speed and keeping in time all the way into Beach Z under these somewhat hostile conditions, would demand an enormous degree of composure and self-discipline would be more than a mild understatement.

As the second wave of the 10th Battalion Anzacs rowed to within 15 yards of the beach, the boat scraped the stony bottom of Beach Z and ground to a halt, the men of the 10th Battalion already leaping over the sides. They found 3 feet of water on a seabed of rounded, slimy stones and many officers and men 'slipped on them and fell in the water' under a perfect hail of bullets.[11] Hardly a clean and tidy start to an invasion. Scrambling, splashing and stumbling ashore, the attackers paused on Beach Z, fixed bayonets, and the race to the heights of Chunuk Bair was on.

Whyte didn't even start. He slumped into the bottom of the boat, his blood mixing with seawater, shot through the pelvis from somewhere high above the beach.

Whyte wasn't the first shot or 'knocked'[12] by shrapnel. The boats were so crammed with men that some casualties remained sitting, jammed upright alongside their comrades, only slumping forward as the landing boats emptied. The invading rowboats, cutters and pinnaces instantly returned to their original purpose – as lifeboats. The midshipmen and naval ratings who manned the rowboats now either shuttled back out to sea to collect a fresh load of invading Anzacs or waited bravely on shore till the first walking wounded or men laid out on stretchers were hoisted back on board. Once each boat was loaded with enough casualties, these dedicated seamen pushed the lifeboats back out to sea and manned the oars to row them back to the hospital ship, HMT *Gascon*, for immediate medical treatment. Thomas Whyte didn't need to be loaded onboard. Arthur Blackburn later wrote:

> the poor fellow was killed before he had fired a single shot,
> but there is no doubt that it was largely due to the courage and

endurance of Tom and his fellow-rowers in all the boats that
everyone was landed with the minimum of loss.[13]

Not quite. Whyte was bleeding out but still alive when he arrived
on board the HMT *Gascon*. Despite receiving the best possible medical
treatment on the ill-equipped hospital ship, Whyte died on 25 April,
during the full steam ahead voyage back to Alexandria. Sitting beside
him as he lay dying was Sister Katherine Lawrence Porter, who wrote
to Eileen some months later:

> I remember Private Tom Whyte very well ... He had an
> abdominal wound and was taken to the operation room almost
> at once and everything possible was done for him ... the only
> thing he was worried over was some package being delivered
> to his friend ... I feel certain that there must have been some
> message for you in it ... It was a terrible day for us all and I saw
> so much that was awful that day.[14]

Arthur Blackburn, who had been specially chosen as a scout and
landed in the very first wave, had advanced for inland while the fateful
landings on Beach Z were taking place. It was only when Blackburn
stumbled exhausted down the rugged slopes of the Sari Bair range out
of the fight four days later that he heard of the tragic death of his old
schoolfriend Tom. Blackburn wrote some months later to Eileen:

> officers and other men who were with him have told me that
> no one was more cheerful than he. He was joking and laughing
> all the way to the shore, and our battalion has lost one of its
> best soldiers.[15]

Thomas Whyte was buried at sea, probably as part of a mass funeral
service conducted by Commander Hanley of the HMT *Gascon*.[16] His
and other shrouded Australian bodies, with due military precision
and centuries of requisite British naval protocol, were ceremoniously
slipped over the side of the hospital ship into the Mediterranean Sea.

His safety razor, wristlet, photos, letters, pen and cigarette case were safely parcelled up and dispatched back to Australia months later via the HMAT *Argyllshire*.[17] Eventually they found their way to Eileen, who treasured these precious reminders of Tom for the rest of her life.[18]

It is generally accepted that Private Thomas Anderson Whyte, No. 47, A Company, 10th Battalion, was the first Australian oarsman to be killed in action at Gallipoli in the Great War. He would not suffer the trauma, indignities and horror that his fellow Australian oarsmen would for the next few years, nor would he live to see their finest hour, which came well after the guns fell silent, far away from that fateful beach, on the genteel River Thames at Henley, England.

PART 1

The War

Nevertheless I long to reach my home and see the day of my
return. It is my never-failing wish. And what if one of the gods
does wreck me out on the wine-dark seas? I have a heart inured
to suffering and I shall steel it to endure that too. For in my day
I have had many bitter and painful experiences in war and on the
stormy seas. So let this disaster come, it only makes one more.

Homer, *The Odyssey*

1

The game is worth the candle

On 3 August 1914, as hostilities in Europe escalated, Australia's prime minister, Joseph Cook, convened an urgent meeting in Melbourne, then the seat of Federal parliament in Australia. While only five of the possible ten members of Cabinet attended, Cook resolutely offered Britain an initial expeditionary force of 20,000 men to be sent to any destination required, at Australia's expense.

This initial deployment was diverted to Egypt to take part in the Gallipoli landings, and formed the basis for the Australian Imperial Force, which would incrementally grow to 332,000 serving men and women by the time of the Armistice in 1918. Throughout the war, the AIF was to remain uniquely a purely volunteer military force and certainly not every man or woman fit for service rushed to volunteer at once.

The enthusiastic calls for enlistment and rallying of potential reinforcements (read 'replacements') ebbed and flowed dramatically throughout the war as public opinion swung and Australian military successes or failures were reported. Within days of the Gallipoli landings, on 30 April 1915, the first sketchy and hopelessly incomplete casualty lists from Gallipoli were being published in newspapers back home. They appeared alongside patriotic editorials and filtered reports from the Gallipoli front extolling the dashing and manly fighting virtues of the Australian soldier against the 'moribund Ottoman Empire'.[1] By Monday 3 May 1915, the Melbourne *Argus* editorial proclaimed:

> The war is beginning to take its toll of our bravest, and as the fatal lists come in they cannot but bring grief to the sorrowing hearts of many; but it will, we doubt not, be a grief tempered with that noble pride which old Spartan fathers and mothers felt when their loved ones fell in obedience to their country's call upon the field of battle. Australians have all the high patriotism and self-control of a ruling race, and they will not let their private sufferings dim their eyes to the glory of wounds and death incurred in their country's cause by its gallant sons … It is not, however, upon the sadness of the inevitable cost of war that we should dwell, but upon the stirring story of duty manfully performed and undying fame won by courageous self-sacrifice.[2]

The Adelaide *Advertiser* also joined in early with a rousing chorus of patriotism and propaganda, conjuring up Homeric exultations of Troy, with the Anzac landings having take place 'on classical ground'.[3] The so-called tactical brilliance of the Gallipoli operation was elaborated upon with a report (at best speculative) of '1000 baggage mounted donkeys loaded with air guns' being used as a 'comic ruse' to divert a strong German force from the actual landings. Fortunately for the war effort, the donkeys had been purchased for 'a song' but not so fortunately for the donkeys they 'were annihilated by the gun fire'.[4]

Like-minded editorials were pumped into newspapers from one end of Australia to the other throughout late April and early May 1915. One can only imagine what effect it had on the average reader – descriptions of massive naval firepower and stirring accounts of Aussie derring-do seemed to dim the raw statistics of brutal casualty lists. The physical prowess of the rugged Australian male was exalted, and comparisons drawn between the sporting ability of the nation and its participation in 'the great game', the largest theatre of war the world had ever known.

At various stages of the war, campaigns were waged to recruit recreational sportspeople, either as part of the larger effort or in specialist battalions, culminating in a drive to recruit an AIF 'Sportmen's 1000'. In the prime minister's words: 'As you have played the game in the past, we ask you to play the greater game now. This is your day. Its success or failure rest on you.'[5]

The reasoning was sound; athletes were already at peak fitness, ready to transfer their stamina and lightning reflexes to the field of battle. Even better, in a sports-mad nation like Australia, having young sporting heroes volunteer to serve their country was an invaluable propaganda boost. There was almost rivalry between Australian sporting codes and administrative bodies as to who could respond more enthusiastically to the patriotic call and pit their members' competitive mettle against the Turks.

Among the many rugby footballers, cricketers, golfers, track and field athletes, tennis players, AFL footballers, lacrosse players, boxers and swimmers – just to name a few – the administrators of the sports codes continued to endorse the government's patriotic call of the day. The subeditors of weekly newspapers such as the aptly named *Referee* also did their patriotic bit, calling sportsmen to volunteer as if it was as simple as switching sporting codes, with headlines like 'Sportsmen, representing all branches, answer Empire's call'.[6] No sporting code was safe.

> We want players, not barrackers, in this big test match, and the man who helps the wounded is as good a player as we have.[7]

Many sportsmen who were high-profile recruits became poster boys for Empire's big call to 'play the greater game'. Glib subheadings targeted specific sports: 'Flannels give place to khaki' or 'Abandon beaches, shoulder rifles.'[8] One who wore flannel was the well-known cricketer Albert 'Tibby' Cotter, who had toured England with the Australian cricket team and notoriously bowled a full toss at the legendary Dr

W. G. Grace, hitting him square on in an early example of 'bodyline' bowling. Another who swapped the beach for a rifle was the surf and swimming icon Cecil Healy, who, in an incredible display of true sportsmanship, famously refused to swim in the 100-metre finals at the 1912 Stockholm Olympics unless the great American swimmer Duke Kahanamoku was readmitted after he accidentally missed the semi-finals. The Duke won gold and Cecil took away the silver.

It was difficult for the state rowing associations not to succumb to such persuasive rhetoric and many oarsmen from across Australia swapped rowing blades for bayonets and dutifully answered the Empire's call.

The patriotic calls certainly seemed to have worked on one strapping, ambitious sportsman, Syd Middleton.

Sydney Albert Middleton was born in Pyrmont on 24 February 1884, the fifth of nine children and one of seven boys and two daughters born to James Middleton and Charlotte (nee Stephens): William (Bill) James (b. 1874), Ethel (b. 1876), Louisa (b. 1878), Victor (b. 1880), Arthur (b. 1881), Sydney (b. 1884), George (b. 1889), Ernest (b. 1891) and Cecil (b. 1893). Syd's father James had been born in Hadley in Shropshire, England but had migrated to Australia with his parents when he was three years of age. James and Charlotte Middleton settled at 63 John Street, in the heart of Pyrmont, a tough waterside suburb just a stone's throw from Darling Harbour and the thriving commercial business district of Sydney.

Pyrmont was like the corner hardware store for Sydney's rapidly growing central business district, with its shameless pursuit of commerce, graft and profit. From the mid to late 19th century Sydney was flexing its economic and commercial muscle. This economic power derived from the opening up of vast, rich, agricultural runs of cattle and wool in the New South Wales interior; the mid 18th century gold rush and other sprouting mining operations further west; and a harbour that was the centre of Australian commerce, trade, shipping and industry.

The other distinguishing feature of Pyrmont was its cannibalism: the suburb was literally eating itself into non-existence. Pyrmont had four major sandstone quarries, each between 50 and 80 yards deep into prime golden sandstone bedrock, called 'Paradise', 'Purgatory', 'Half-Way' and 'Hell Hole'. These quarry pits were filled with choking clouds of dust from steam-driven sawing engines, cutting through solid layers of foundation sandstone and to create large building blocks. The work was hard, noisy and dangerous. These open-cut quarries became the source of quality yellow sandstone for the many grand government buildings taking shape in Sydney, for example the GPO, the Queen Victoria Building, the Treasury, Sydney Town Hall and the hallowed residential colleges, Quadrangle and Great Hall of Sydney University, dating from 1859.

The peninsula of Pyrmont was bounded by Darling Harbour to the east, Johnson's Cove to the north and Blackwattle Bay to the west and was teeming with wharves, warehouses, wool stores and waterside workers, referred to as 'watersiders'.[9] A busy steam engine freight rail network transported the livestock, raw materials and wool from across New South Wales through Pyrmont to Darling Harbour.

In essence, Pyrmont was a mecca of manual labour, hard-living artisans and daily survival. But amidst the dust, smoke, grime and long hours of back-breaking work the 'watersiders' did find time to build a community and, as in East London, the working oarsmen of Pyrmont were part of the fabric of work, life, play – and death.

James Middleton lived all his life there, and fondly remembered the early days of Pyrmont as a child during the late 1850s, when he mixed with and played among the watersiders. He recalled seeing many 'grown men chalking their greasy fingers on the way from the workshop to the marble ground'.[10] It's difficult at first to imagine the tough workers of Pyrmont heading to the rings to play such a childish game as marbles – but the flick of a marble could have meant a little more income from side bets and wagers. James Middleton spent much of his early years also working in the sandstone quarries of Pyrmont, eventually becoming a quarry foreman for the Saunders family–owned quarries when they supplied the sandstone for the construction of the GPO in Sydney.[11]

Ringed by a bustling maritime industry, Pyrmont was also home to rough and ready watermen, their hands calloused from a firm grip on the oar handle, plying the trade of rowing on the waters around Darling Harbour. When packet steamers and mail ships sailed through the heads and arrived in Sydney Harbour, a system of flags shot up that could be seen from the heights of Pyrmont announcing their arrival. James Middleton found work on the waters of Sydney Harbour, and he and his fellow Pyrmont watermen would take to their skiffs and wherries and race to collect the first mailbags from the arriving ships. In a way, competitive rowing in Australia was born of men earning a living by collecting the mail on the protected waters of Sydney Harbour. Eventually, James Middleton must have proved himself an able oarsman and moved his way up to the position of clerk. At heart, though, the Middleton family were proud watersiders, dismissive of affectation; fierce battlers in work and play.

Pyrmont was the natural place for rowing to flourish as a sport and spectacle in Sydney, and Pyrmont Bridge was the perfect site for spectators to watch the start and finish of sculling races. Soon, as the sport of rowing grew, thousands of spectators watched the professional local derby sculling races, held every summer Saturday at Pyrmont. All 'the old timers who were expert with the use of the short or long handled sculls' were involved. 'Most races were rowed for £10 a side.' The scullers would start at Pyrmont Bridge and race out to and around Goat Island and back to the bridge to finish, a distance of two and a half miles. The racing oarsmen came from 'the boatsheds, the shipyards, quarries or the iron working establishments', such as Joe Donnelly; or were boilermakers by trade, such as Harry Smith or Geordie McBride. Many of these oarsmen crafted their own skiffs with Joe Donnelly building his own clinker 'without a mould and relying on his eye'.[12]

Syd's brother Bill, who was ten years older, was the first to join the local Glebe Rowing Club and Glebe Rugby Club in the adjoining Blackwattle Bay precinct, in 1894. Bill was an exceptional athlete, both on the rugby pitch and in the boat, but he didn't possess Syd's natural athletic talent, nor did he have the towering height, bulky physique or natural competitive aggression. As a member of the Glebe Rowing Club, Bill represented New South Wales in the Interstate Eight-oared Rowing Championships in 1902–1903 and took Syd down with him to the club to learn to row as an eighteen-year-old. Syd, by then, would have finished his education at Fort Street Model School. Bill then set his sights on elite rowing and representative opportunities and transferred to the moneyed and prestigious Sydney Rowing Club in Woolloomooloo Bay, under the auspices of Mr Q. L. Deloitte, the general manager of the Colonial Sugar Refinery (situated near their family home in Pyrmont) from 1903.

At Sydney Rowing Club, Bill mixed with the top end of Sydney town, representing New South Wales again in 1904 and 1906 as a stocky bowman in the club's 'light blue' colours. He had made sure that his talented and physically much larger younger brother trained hard and learned to row and play rugby well, so that in no time, his tall, fair-haired brother Syd joined him in the 1904 and 1906 NSW Interstate Eight-oared crews. Syd was a natural oarsman and Bill ensured a strict training regime continued: 'From 1907 William and Sydney never stopped training. A typical day was to run to the baths, swim, run home, have breakfast, run to work, work, run to either football or rowing training with or without tea, run home, have a meal and go to bed.'[13] Syd quickly proved himself to be both an exceptional and aggressive Sydney club rugby player and a powerful oarsman.

Syd Middleton was thirty-one years old, living a quiet, middle-class life, when he volunteered. Maybe his job as a clerk at the Australian Mutual Provident Society felt dull in comparison to the heroic deeds going on at Anzac Cove. He enlisted with the AIF on 5 May 1915. Possibly the life and death game against the Turk or the Hun appealed to Middleton's competitive instinct, even though he had been retired from representative sport for some years.

Like all Australians who enlisted, Middleton signed his attestation paper stipulating the term of service as 'until the end of the war and a further period of four months'. It didn't sound too bad.

There is a note in his papers to the effect that Middleton had joined the AIF in December 1914 but was possibly waiting for a commission as an officer. His commission as a second lieutenant in the 19th Battalion was gazetted on 15 May 1915 – both his commission and placement within that battalion were very likely due to his reputation as sportsman:

a champion rower and former Wallaby rugby captain who tackled with the ferocity of 'a grizzly bear'.[14] Middleton was well over 6 feet tall, but his sedentary job had seen his weight creep up to 14 stone and 12 pounds (94 kilograms), a little heavier than his previous rowing racing weight.

Middleton's former NSW rowing crewmate and close friend, Tasmanian Keith Heritage, had already enlisted in the AIF, in July 1914. They'd rowed together in the 1911 NSW Interstate, 1912 Henley Royal Regatta (HRR) Grand Challenge Cup and 1912 Stockholm Olympics, and when war was declared, Heritage had been among the first to volunteer. Possessing education and experience as a traffic manager in the shipping industry, he received a commission as a lieutenant in the first Australian Naval and Military Expeditionary Force (AN&MEF). The AN&MEF sailed north from Australia to seize the German colonies of New Guinea and destroy German wireless stations from September to November 1914.[15]

After this tropical deployment to New Guinea, Lieutenant Heritage returned to Australia on 17 February 1915 and some of the AN&MEF veterans were integrated into the 19th Battalion, which reunited Heritage with his old Sydney Rowing Club mate, Syd Middleton.

The 19th Battalion was soon getting a reputation as a 'sportsman's' battalion, but probably with no more official imprimatur than any other battalion. By the time the war lingered into 1917, there were moves from certain quarters and organisers to enlist as many sportsmen as possible through the 'Sportsmen's Reinforcement Unit No. 2' into the 19th Battalion. The men 'need not necessarily be of tremendous physique, expert athletes, or top-notch players ... so long as they are clean, game, real Britishers, they will be welcomed.'[16] All they had to do was apply on the fifth floor of the Commonwealth Bank in Sydney.

It seems possible that through Middleton's personal network, which included various alumni, sports clubs and sports associations, a few strings may have been pulled to organise transfers from one unit to another, or to give volunteers with a sports background preference for joining the 19th Battalion. The secretary of the NSW Rugby Union, and another close friend of Syd Middleton, W. W. 'Bill' Hill, did chair a committee with the intent of uniting the old sporting friends in the same unit. The war was still seen as the adventure of a lifetime, and who better to share it with?

On 25 June 1915, Second Lieutenant Syd Middleton and Lieutenant Keith Heritage, as part of the 2nd Reinforcements, 5th Brigade, 2nd Division, embarked from Sydney onboard the HMT *Ceramic* and arrived at Camp Heliopolis on 23 July 1915.[17] Middleton wrote home from Cairo:

> I am not given to romancing as you know, but these fellows with a little more training are bound to do well. I met Hector Clayton at Suez ... and he has no end of praise for the pluck and fighting qualities of our troops but reckons they have a tremendously tough task before them when the time comes to force their way forward.[18]

Middleton was always up for a challenge, and this drove him to keep moving and to embrace every opportunity – a relentlessness which took him, inevitably, to Gallipoli.

Under pressure from Winston Churchill, the recently appointed Vice-Admiral John de Robeck, Winston's man in the Dardanelles, was ordered to send the battleships into the strait to fight their way up the narrows and knock out the Turkish guns. On the morning of 18 March, British and French battleships entered the straits and launched their attack. The Allies initially had the upper hand, bombarding the Turk forts and gun emplacements. Several French ships were hit but the intensity of the Ottoman fire was eventually reduced. As the battleships turned to starboard to bombard the opposite shore, they ran into the string of undetected mines laid by the Turkish naval ship *Nusret*. The French vessel *Bouvet*, one of the fastest battleships in the world, struck a mine at speed. She took on tonnes of water, capsized and was gone in a matter of minutes, with a huge loss of life; of her complement of 710, only seventy-five men were rescued. Later in the afternoon, the

British battle cruiser HMS *Inflexible* hit a mine but managed to beach itself. Soon after, the pre-dreadnought battleships HMS *Irresistible* and HMS *Ocean* also hit mines, and both were quickly abandoned.

It was a bad day at the office for de Robeck. Confusion reigned, with reports of the ships also being sunk by enemy submarines. Later, when a destroyer was sent in to retrieve (or sink) the floundering battleships, they had both mysteriously disappeared. With half of his fleet out of commission, Vice-Admiral de Robeck ordered a withdrawal.

Churchill wanted his commander to press on, but de Robeck insisted on waiting for army support forces and the whole Dardanelles operation crucially lost the advantage. The Turks were now well aware that the Gallipoli peninsula was prime real estate for the Allies and further work was hastily carried out shoring up its land defences on all sides. Ironically, the first lord of the admiralty's ambitious plan to seize the Dardanelles by sea was now drastically altered to an amphibious invasion, with the support of the Royal Navy, and the somewhat drier option of a hard footslog land campaign across the peninsula's incredibly rugged terrain.

When Middleton was in Egypt, before he had embarked for the peninsula, he wrote home:

> To get to matters of greater interest, I regret that I cannot talk
> as fully as I would like to, or send you what I know. We are not
> supposed to, and you must play the game ... I understand from
> the wounded that the Turks are good, game and fair enough
> fighters. They like a scrap, but don't relish bayonet charges ...
> One becomes more imperialistic in one's mind over this way.
> We are now in touch with the real men who are fighting in the
> same cause and realise better what the British Empire means.[19]

He was now undoubtedly aware of the life and death stakes, but determinedly kept his game face on.

> I am feeling fine and was never more contented now that I have
> something worthwhile to do. I am looking forward to some hard

work and hard fighting, but the game is worth the candle, and I
am lucky to be free to come along.[20]

After a few weeks of desert training, the 19th Battalion sailed for
Gallipoli and by 1300 hours on 21 August 1915, Sydney Middleton
(now newly promoted to lieutenant) and Lieutenant Keith Heritage
of the 19th Battalion came ashore at Anzac Cove and bivouacked in
Reserve Gully.

The legendary horror and mass slaughter that resulted from
forcing 'their way forward' in August 1915 was pretty much over
by the time of Syd Middleton and Keith Heritage's arrival at Anzac
Cove. The ambitious dawn landing, the grim truce in May to bury the
dead in no-man's-land, the bloody hand-to-hand melee that was the
Battle of Lone Pine, and the immortalised suicidal charges at the Nek
were now part of history.

The 19th Battalion did participate in the poorly planned and hastily
arranged attack on Hill 60, the day after their arrival. This attack was
aimed at linking up a coastal strip with the recently arrived British
forces allegedly 'sitting drinking cups of tea'[21] at Suvla Bay. The 19th
Battalion's losses at Hill 60 were nothing like the 2500 Australians
who had either been killed in action or died of wounds during those
bloody first few days of August.[22] In fact, at Hill 60 the 19th Battalion
were comparatively lucky. Their close comrades in the 5th Brigade,
the 18th Battalion, copped the worst of the attack and suffered more
serious losses.

For Middleton and the 19th Battalion, life in the trenches around
Pope's Hill soon settled down to a regular routine of 'defending the
line'. The prospect of death and danger, however, was present every
minute of the day. On 5 September, a Turkish shell claimed the life
of the second-in-command of the 19th Battalion, Major James W. F.
McManamey, Middleton's good friend and mentor during his rugby
days. Major McManamey had gone to the rear lines to supervise the
building of defences around a much-needed well that had become a
regular target for keen-eyed Turkish artillery. He was fatally struck
by a burst of shrapnel during his inspection of the well – the only man

hit. The next day Middleton wrote to his friend and rugby associate
W. W. 'Bill' Hill:

> The position is very trying for all concerned as we are losing
> men without being able to answer back, and it was through this
> that poor old Jim met his end ... He was struck in the side with a
> piece of shrapnel or shrapnel bullet, which pierced the abdomen,
> and he fell, practically killed outright, for those who were
> standing near rushed up, but he never spoke again, and groaned
> and expired as he was carried to the dressing station.[23]

The death of Jim McManamey reminded Middleton and many
others at Anzac Cove just how close death could be when living,
working and fighting in such close quarters with the Turks. There were
eyes everywhere and everyone had to take extreme caution, whether
manning dugouts, on carrying fatigue or going for a drink of water.

> ... and so passed one of my best friends and one of the finest
> soldiers on the Peninsula ... and though we have become
> accustomed to see our men kicked over, his loss has affected
> soldiers and officers alike.[24]

It was not uncommon for soldiers to achieve a promotion in the field
due to the invaliding or demise of the man ranked immediately above
and on 9 October, Middleton was duly promoted to acting captain.[25]

General Ian Hamilton's infamous order of 'dig, dig, dig until you
are safe' – issued on the day of the landings so long, long ago – was
by September 1915 the routine. The daily tasks of the 19th Battalion
at Pope's Post was chiefly keeping the trenches in good condition and
fighting order. Getting a good feed beyond standard rations was also
a top priority. Meanwhile, the Turks would often riddle the sandbags
perched on the parapets (the forward edge of a trench) with machine gun
fire, causing the sand to leak out and necessitating immediate repair,
refilling and replacement of the sandbags. Middleton wrote to his good
friend and well-respected rugby administrator, J. R. Henderson:

We peg along in the same old routine order – trench warfare.
It gets colder every day. Our casualties are about the same, and
we look forward to what is next to be done. Now that we have
settled down some time, and the wolves have learned to know the
district a bit, it's quite possible to get a feed sometimes. We send
one of the 'hard heads' out with a pound, and he generally comes
back with something better than bully beef. But apart even from
these extras, the tucker is not too bad. There are no olives, but it
is good enough for the job.[26]

The conflict at Pope's Post had turned into a sniping, bombing
and harassing game of cat and mouse, anything the Turks could do to
make life untenable for the men. At times the conflict was reduced to
farcical name-calling. The Australians would crudely call the Turks
'Abdul' and the Turks called the Australians 'Johnny'.[27] Most of the
time Middleton and Heritage (and their men) just kept their heads
down to protect themselves from stray bullets, shells and bombs; the
foul odour of the rotting dead permeated no-man's-land. Middleton
lamented:

I haven't killed a Turk yet, but they have gone pretty close to
me far too often. The damage we do one another in the style of
warfare is mainly from shells and bombs, and we never see the
results in these cases, but there's plenty of evidence of former
willing hand-to-hand goes lying all round us, far too close to be
pleasant if one's at all delicate.[28]

The call to withdraw finally came after British Secretary of State for War
Lord Kitchener visited Anzac Cove on 13 November 1915. Kitchener,
accompanied by General Birdwood, wanted to see for himself what
all the fuss, frustration and bother was about. An imposing figure,
Kitchener strode up around the Sphinx and came within 30 yards of the
Turk trenches at Lone Pine. He immediately saw what the Australians
had known from day one and was out of there. Once the word was
given, the newly promoted Brigadier-General Cyril Brudenell White

was immediately set the task of planning and supervising one of the truly great military feats of the whole Gallipoli campaign, one which is only now assuming its rightful place in Australian military history – the evacuation of Anzac Cove.

Nine months after landing tens of thousands of soldiers and thousands of tonnes of weapons, ammunition and materiel at Anzac Cove and North Beach, the evacuation was successfully carried out in secret, in silence and in subtle stages. The Australians shipped what supplies they could offshore and either dumped, buried or set fire to what they couldn't carry. By 18 December, the Anzac deployment at Ari Burnu was reduced from 41,000 men to 26,000 men. The final two nights of the evacuation, from 18 to 20 December, required hundreds of volunteers in small 'C. Parties' from the AIF 1st and 2nd Divisions to man their frontline positions, pretend that there was ongoing activity in the trenches (including via the use of improvised self-firing timed rifles) and then, on a strict timetable, make their way to the waiting boats as quickly and quietly as possible, without arousing enemy suspicion. It would demand discipline, stamina and the ability to keep watch over a sleepless night. Middleton volunteered for this role, as he was unmarried, had no dependants and was very probably determined to play it out till the final whistle. Captain Middleton and Captain Keith Heritage were both chosen to stay behind with other bands of 'diehards' or C. Parties from the 2nd Division, 5th Brigade under the command of Colonel J. Paton, and were part of the very last remaining C.3 Party.

They spent the long night shuffling from one end of the forward galleries of trenches to the other, firing off bursts of rifle fire to cover the sounds of the Anzacs' withdrawal. The C. Parties began destroying any artillery pieces that couldn't be moved (though breech locks and gun sights were salvaged), constructed trench barricades and placed wire entanglements and trap lines attached to the pins of Mills bombs. Silence was paramount. Men wore two pairs of socks on top of their boots, or tied hessian sacks over them. No lights or smoking was allowed; nor was the use of the order 'Retire'.

There was a lot involved in the evacuation, some of it terrible and traumatic work. Many guns were to be thrown into cesspits and all animals that couldn't be embarked were destroyed 'without noise either by pithing or some other means'.[29] From the heights of Pope's Hill, Middleton saw 'a wonderful sight of hundreds of ships and small craft' on the calm Aegean Sea.[30] The last lighter to leave Anzac Cove and rendezvous with the British ships waiting offshore under cover of darkness was to depart at 0400 hours. At 0330, as one last covering ploy for the withdrawal, three underground mines were exploded under the infamous Nek, and then began the final thirty-five minute scramble down the hills from Quinn's Post to Walker's Pier on Anzac Cove. Keith Heritage was especially mentioned for good conduct and service throughout the evacuation. In a letter to his parents, Keith wrote:

> We were jolly pleased to make the landing stage and jetty and tumble in steel lighters, and an hour later all the beach staff and remainder of guard were off ... The old 5th Brigade has done noble work really all the while here and had the honour of forming the last guard ... had things gone awry, well there wouldn't have been much a Brigade left.[31]

Middleton later described that last eerie night at Anzac Cove as lit by 'a most lovely moon light' and how keen he was, once he had clambered up a ladder from the lighter and onboard a waiting warship, to look back one last time at that mythic landscape, with the Sphinx illuminated by the moonlight; to quietly take stock and soak up the wretched exhilaration of the evacuation.[32] But, overcome with exhaustion and physically played out, as soon as Middleton clambered over the ship's rail and sat down on the deck, he fell fast asleep and slept soundly through the whole thing.

2

Hauenstein

In the aftermath of Gallipoli, the weary Anzacs regathered and regrouped in Egypt. All fully laden troop ships from Gallipoli, Sydney, Melbourne, Adelaide and Fremantle eventually came to Egypt via the Suez Canal. The veterans of Anzac Cove disembarked in various stages at Alexandria and rendezvoused at Camp Heliopolis, mixing with the fresh, eager reinforcements who had been training for several months in the desert. These 'wet-behind-the-ears' soldiers had heard snippets of the exploits of their comrades, from newspapers and sketchy official reports; through 'furphies' passed down the bush telegraph; from the many ill or wounded soldiers recovering in hospital; and direct from those able-bodied survivors lucky enough to be rotated out of the peninsula for much-needed R and R.

The battle-hardened Gallipoli veterans and the uninitiated Anzac reinforcements converged and underwent a complex and major military reorganisation. Original AIF battalions were split into two, and 'sister' battalions created, composed half of experienced Gallipoli veterans and half of fresh recruits.

In January 1916, as Middleton, the 19th Battalion and the Anzac corps were being rested, reinforced and reorganised in Cairo and Mena Camp – Middleton having exhausted himself physically and emotionally to get his men away from the worst of the war – an old acquaintance of his was rowing towards it, all the way across the world, off the coast of Fremantle, Australia.

Henry 'Harry' Hauenstein was a very different kind of soldier to Middleton. A giant of a man, fond of a drink, loyal to his friends, terrifying to his enemies, he was not afraid to stand up for himself in sport, in battle, or to his superior officers.

On 16 January 1916, the HMAT A7 (*Medic*) had anchored off Fremantle Harbour on its last Australian stop to a destination unknown to the men of the AIF 12th Reinforcements of the 2nd Battalion. The voyage from Sydney had taken nearly two weeks and the *Medic* had been a dry ship. All the diggers on board were now looking forward to a day's shore leave where they could do some sightseeing and enjoy a farewell ale at one of the many watering holes in Perth, a short train ride away. On 17 January, Lieutenant Edward Justelius relayed orders to the dour and imposing Corporal Harry Hauenstein that his section of men (nine in total), granted shore leave, were to be back onboard the *Medic* by 6 pm, saying, 'I will hold you responsible for the return of your party.' With that final warning, Hauenstein's section departed the ship for shore.

Corporal Hauenstein and his party did not make it back by 6 pm. As it was reported, 'He did not return to the Ship till after midnight.'

Hauenstein was charged with being absent without leave and drunkenness. At the district court-martial held on board the *Medic* on 22 January 1916 as it steamed toward the Suez, Hauenstein testified that his party had planned to meet opposite the Railway Hotel in Perth to return together to Fremantle. Three of Hauenstein's party did not show. Knowing he was responsible for the return of all the men, Hauenstein, who had himself enjoyed five or six shandies throughout the afternoon, sent the six men who had turned up to the troopship and went searching for the missing three. One of them, Collins, was found drinking in Fremantle and evaded Hauenstein by running off. When

Hauenstein eventually returned to Fremantle wharf after midnight with Kelly and Graham and was challenged by Lieutenant Errol Knox, Knox reported that he displayed insubordination 'in no uncertain manner'.

Lieutenant Knox testified that Hauenstein was drunk. When cross-examined by Hauenstein as to how he could tell that he was drunk, Knox replied, 'You were decidedly hilarious.' Corporal Arthur Annesley, who had been sober, testified for the defence: 'Judging by the way he rowed the boat I should think he was not drunk.' Hauenstein had singlehandedly rowed the boat from Fremantle docks to the waiting troopship – a feat seemingly impossible for a drunk to manage. Private Charles Kelly, also a witness for the defence, testified that as Hauenstein rowed the boat away from the shore he had not noticed any effects of drink. Hauenstein pleaded not guilty to both charges, but the officers of the court found him guilty on both counts, and he was disciplined.[1]

Hauenstein was likely inebriated as he rowed away from Australia and to war. But being a three-time NSW Interstate Eight-oar rowing champion, Henley Royal Regatta Grand Challenge winner and 1912 Olympic oarsman, even drunk he could probably still row a boat gracefully.

On the day of his enlistment in the AIF, 5 August 1915, Harry, aged thirty-two, had married Eva Charlotte Loaney at St Stephen's Church, Newtown, in Sydney. Eva, twelve years Harry's senior, was a single widowed mother to three girls. Even before the marriage they had lived together in a small semi-detached house at 11 Leamington Street in the working-class suburb of Macdonaldtown, adjacent to the elevated brick railway line that ran like a river of steam to the screaming hub of Central Railway Station.

Hauenstein had embarked from Sydney aboard the HMAT *Medic* on 7 January 1916. On deck, he would have been a hard man to miss, standing at 6 feet 2½ inches and a fighting fit 13 stone 4 pounds (84 kilograms). With his dark complexion, dark hair and fierce brown eyes, he was the antithesis of the fair-haired, fresh-faced, gangly but physically robust twenty-something youngsters we stereotypically associate with our Anzac heritage.

Harry's father, Carl Herman August Hauenstein, was a Swiss German immigrant who had come to Australia in 1881 via South Africa, married Australian Elizabeth Annabella Field and settled in Barmedman in the Riverina district of New South Wales. This was hard, flat, dry country but a number of German settlers had been drawn to the Riverina by the prospect of a small gold rush in the 1880s. Carl and Elizabeth worked a holding of 319 acres of unirrigated land. Farming was tough so Carl had to work as a carpenter and as a coach driver on the run to West Wyalong during the gold rush, to supplement the income from his property. In 1883, Carl and a team of prospectors worked two deep shafts near Conway but after persistent flooding came back almost empty-handed. The Hauensteins worked hard to make the property profitable but the odds were against them. In 1904, his excellency the governor directed that under the Crown Lands Act of 1895 'through non-payment of rent, survey fees, and value of Crown improvements' their land holding was forfeited.[2]

The Hauensteins packed up and moved to Sydney, finally settling in James Street in the inner-city suburb of Leichhardt, nestled along the waters of Long Cove and Iron Cove. Harry was the eldest. He had three sisters – Susan, Henrietta and Frances – and two brothers: Dennis, known as 'Paddy', and William. All three Hauenstein brothers were tall and ruggedly built, but Harry towered.

The change from the dry flat interior of New South Wales to the sparkling waters of Sydney Harbour held an immediate fascination for the boys. The Hauenstein brothers joined Leichhardt Rowing Club, situated near the Hawthorn Canal on Long Cove, and learned how to row. For work, Harry soon entered into an apprenticeship with J. Fenwick & Co., a tugboat company situated in East Balmain. Harry's younger brother Paddy was also a 'reasonably' accomplished oarsman but Harry's talent was far superior. He had taken to rowing like a duck to water and spent hours and hours training, often on his own, from the waters of Long Cove to Manly Cove – a return distance of more than 25 miles, 'crossing the Heads on more than one occasion against a north-easter'.[3] Perhaps as a way to make their respective sporting marks the younger Hauensteins took up rugby union and both Paddy and William became formidable rugby footballers.

The three Hauenstein brothers enlisted in the AIF and served on the Western Front from 1916 to 1918. They fought in some of the most ferocious battles of the war, were wounded in action and served with considerable distinction against their ancestral home. During the early years of the war, Australian settlers of German heritage were, at times, viewed with suspicion and several internment camps were set up, one at Holsworthy near Liverpool, which is ironically where Harry enlisted. Despite this, the Hauenstein family didn't seem to need to hide their German heritage.

Hauenstein, owing much to his size, proved himself an exceptional oarsman for several rowing seasons. As a youth he won many maiden rowing events (a lighter weight division) with Leichhardt Rowing Club before maturing into a powerful giant of a man and transferring to the Balmain Rowing Club. With a dour Germanic disposition, he had almost singlehandedly been the engine room of the NSW State Representative Eight from 1907 to 1911.

Harry Hauenstein and Syd Middleton, when Middleton was not on international rugby duties, had been a perfect combination of raw power sitting in the middle of an eight in the number 5 and number 6 seats, driving the boat through the water. Both men were aggressive in the boat, had good reach of the arms and upper body, and razor-sharp rowing technique. When it came to applying pressure in the water, both Hauenstein and Middleton delivered simple but elegant brute force. It was no surprise that both oarsmen were selected in the Australian eight-oared crew that toured England to compete in the prestigious 1912 Grand Challenge Cup at the Henley Royal Regatta, and then later in the 1912 Olympic Games in Stockholm.

But rowing didn't pay the rent, and Harry found another calling. The NSW police had minimum height restrictions in the early 20th century and Harry was naturally well-qualified. In 1903, he joined up and was gazetted as probationary constable #8217 on 26 January 1904[4] and then as a full constable on 1 July 1905.[5] Harry served for several years 'on the beat', patrolling the mean streets of Sydney where life was rock-bottom hard and desperate for many. This was an era of governmental social neglect, where the underclasses and poor were left to their own devices and relied on church or social charities to ease their hunger or help them pay the rent. Wives and children were abandoned and many subjected to violent assault. There were many instances of 'water babies' and infants found floating in the harbour or abandoned on doorsteps or in back lanes, a significant number of whom were already deceased. Life as a beat cop was no bed of roses.

After his return from the Henley Royal Regatta and the Stockholm Olympics in October 1912, Harry made a living as a contractor, picking up work where he could and hawking the carpentry skills gained from his early apprenticeship at Fenwick's tug company. In 1915, without the weekly pay of the NSW police force, providing for his instant family was likely tough going. Perhaps Harry joined the AIF for financial reasons. On the attestation paper, there was a section allowing an enlistee to nominate how much of their pay could be withheld for wives and families. For whatever reason, Harry was on his way to the war.

By January 1916, after his brief but comic run-in with military law in Fremantle and Perth, Harry Hauenstein had arrived in Egypt, precisely at the time that the A & NZAC was being split into two corps, I ANZAC and II ANZAC, and standby deployed to defend the Suez Canal.

During the first few months of 1916, Cairo, Mena Camp, Suez, Giza and Heliopolis teemed with Australians and New Zealanders from many sports codes, many of them oarsmen. There was now much debate back home about whether regional or national rowing competitions should be suspended for the duration. There were reasonable arguments both for and against. In one of the last local rowing regattas in Brisbane, the Baynes Diamond Jubilee Regatta, the official Mr J. N. Devoy was reported as saying that:

> it was necessary that they should provide some sport for those
> who were too old to go to war and for the younger generation ...
> In reference to the Empire's call for men, he was pleased to
> say that the Toowong Rowing Club had sent 70 per cent of

its members to the front, Brisbane R.C. more than half, and Commercial R.C. two-thirds. This showed that oarsmen had fully realised their duty to the Empire.[6]

Competition was soon suspended.

After arriving in Alexandria in March 1916, Harry perhaps thought the infantry wasn't tough enough because in May 1916 he transferred to the 1st Pioneer Battalion. The Pioneers were a mobile subsidiary of the Engineers Corps, and their work could be described as a tad crazy – a little like Harry. Equal parts tradesman, repairman and soldier, a Pioneer could wield a hammer or entrenching tool and, at the same time, efficiently thrust a bayonet and squeeze the trigger of a Lee Enfield .303 rifle. The Pioneers fought like infantry and were often in the front line, but their primary job was construction and reconstruction.

A key task for the Pioneers was to 'reverse' captured enemy trenches by removing and rebuilding the 'fire steps' that soldiers stood on while firing, essentially moving them to the opposite side, in preparation for the inevitable counterattack. This was essential to consolidating a captured position and was almost always done while under fire.

They also established strongpoints, excavated dugouts and built deep bomb-proof bunkers. The Pioneers did almost everything the regular infantry didn't want to do. If something had to be dug, drained, duckboarded, revetted, repaired, reinforced or just slapped together under fire, the Pioneers did it. It was often grim, thankless and backbreaking work.

When they were out of the front line, the Pioneers would lay and bury telecommunication wires; dig, support and supply trenches; dig, clear and construct roads; and build spectator stands, canteens or huts for brigade race days. Basically, the Pioneers dug, dug, dug their way into war, built something, rebuilt it and then dug their way out the other side. They were the toughest, most bloody-minded of the diggers who finally found themselves at one of the most nightmarish military engagements Australia has ever seen – the Battle of Pozières.

Pozières, a maelstrom of death and mud, was described by historian and journalist Charles Bean as 'more densely sown with Australian sacrifice than any other place on earth'. The village had finally been captured and secured by the AIF 1st Division by daybreak on 23 July 1916.

The AIF assault on the village of Pozières had been almost completely against the standard playbook of offense. The attack required just two companies of the 9th and 10th Battalions to frontally engage superior numbers of Germans in what were called the OG1 and OG2 trenches, accompanied by artillery and mortar fire. The main attack of the Gallipoli veteran 9th and 10th Battalions, however, went against military orthodoxy and ran parallel to these same OG1 and OG2 trenches toward Pozières, which in itself was a very heavily fortified outpost of the German line. This meant that the 1st Division were under constant enfilading fire from the Germans in OG1 and OG2 as they fought their way to the village, hopping over sodden sandbags and scrambling over open, sloppy, pitted and churned-up ground. The attack on Pozières was nothing short of crazy, but it worked, albeit with huge Australian casualties.

Hauenstein entered the battle like everyone in the AIF 1st Division – bent over, through a narrow, rutted and muddy maze of disintegrating communication and support trenches. After what remained of the village of Pozières had been secured on 23 July 1916, the AIF turned toward Thiepval. German artillery fire was already ranged onto Pozières, and harassing fire aimed to make life miserable and severely reduce any movement across open ground. The Pioneers were constantly clearing the maze of support and communication trenches that zigzagged around Pozières and repeatedly revetting the front-line trenches that were either blown away or just crumbling back into the soil. One of the most impregnable German strongpoints just outside Pozières was Mouquet Farm. The AIF needed to take it if they were to join up with the British at Thiepval. The heavily fortified farm was a labyrinth of German tunnels and bunkers that concealed enemy movement, stored huge dumps of ammunition and allowed the Germans to pop out almost anywhere to rain machine gun fire down onto any diggers scrambling across exposed terrain below. Almost every inch of no-man's-land between Pozières and Mouquet Farm was under constant fire and enemy observation. Fighting up to Mouquet Farm was like trying to swim up a wall of breaking water before you were ploughed back into the soggy ground.

Hauenstein entered this maelstrom and went about his work, incessantly digging and rebuilding trenches and strongpoints. The sound of exploding shells and cracking gunfire went all day and night. Anything that moved or looked like it might move was ruthlessly targeted. The noise of mechanical battle was peppered with shouts, curses, moans and screams. Pozières was about feeding a meat grinder and seeing who would run out of cattle first. Dead bodies and wounded men were scattered everywhere and throughout the battle many simply degraded and disintegrated into the dirt.

Perhaps Harry couldn't stand the sounds of the badly wounded men. And if you couldn't sleep, it was best to keep busy. Over a number of sleepless days and nights, in between building work, digging and shoring up crumbling fire-steps, Harry followed the persistent cries and moans and crawled out across exposed ground at night. His face blackened and helmetless, he crawled through ditches, depressions and dips, zeroing in on the desperate cries. Not just once but again and again, copping scrapes and cuts from the tangled barbed wire.

Harry eventually rescued ten men, singlehandedly dragging or carrying them back to the tenuous safety of the trenches, which at least obscured them from German observation. From there they could be carried by a chain of stretcher bearers down the narrow, forever crumbling trenches to a regimental aid post (RAP), and perhaps then further back to a casualty clearing station (CCS), then even further back to a base hospital at Le Tréport or Le Havre, and, with a bit more luck, ultimately back to Blighty, as England was then affectionately known.

To crawl out into the death zone once would be heroic enough, but to do so another nine times could be described as driven, or crazy, or both. Exactly what drove Harry to do so is hard to say but it was definitely his own choice. Harry's heroic actions over those harrowing sleepless nights between 15 and 22 August 1916 did not go unnoticed.

In October 1916, he was awarded the Military Medal, issued for bravery to men below commissioned rank. But no medal for bravery would ever cleanse Harry, or anyone else who was there, of the horror of Pozières. In a press release of the day, Harry's citation in the *London Gazette* read:

At Pozières, France, 15th to 22nd August 1916 Cpl Hauenstein was engaged in the frontline construction in the direction of Ferme Mouquet having one nights [sic] sleep only. He was constantly under fire and by his courage and example greatly helped the work. Corporal Hauenstein is a man of great physical strength and repeatedly left the trenches going to shell craters and carrying in wounded under fire when but for this they must have remained. He at different times brought in ten men in this manner each under very hazardous conditions.[7]

Hauenstein's conduct in the war shows he was an exceptional man. Whatever drove him forward – courage, compassion, determination, a touch of madness – also made him a relentless oarsman.

By some quirk of fate, or perhaps because of this quality particular to competitive rowers, Hauenstein was just one among several heroes of Pozières who happened to be oarsmen. These men would part ways after the slaughter and reunite to test their mettle on an entirely different battleground, under the leadership of legendary oarsman Syd Middleton.

By 25 March 1916, Middleton and the AIF 5th Brigade had arrived in the French port of Marseilles. In the hustle and bustle of the fresh Anzac troops marshalling on the wharves, collecting equipment and lining up for kit inspection, Leichhardt R.C. oarsman Sergeant Jack Hoskins came across two clubmates:

The rowing boys are putting up a good race here, and they handle their guns just as well as they handled a pair of sculls on the Iron Cove or the Parramatta River. When we landed at Marseilles … I strolled along the line looking for familiar faces, and I struck Tom McGill and young Jack Lewis. I watched them for a while; they moved like clockwork. It was here I pictured old

Tom and that broad smile grafting in the old eight at the shed.
He is just as serious as ever. When the order came, 'Stand easy,'
I had a long yarn to them.[8]

From Marseilles, I ANZAC entrained through the peaceful green
fields of the south of France to the many railheads in the grim north-
east. Syd Middleton's 5th Brigade arrived in Thiennes in the far-off
French department of Pas du Nord. Once in battle order, the 5th
Brigade route-marched for tens of miles down pleasant winding
country roads and through untouched villages. As they drew closer to
the front, the sounds of war grew louder; village steeples were pock-
marked, town squares revetted with sandbags or barricades, buildings
blown apart, the roads were heavier with military traffic, and there
were fewer welcoming French locals. Eventually they arrived at the first
of an endless procession of billets and bivouacs and trenches on the
Western Front.

3

The dying days

In 1917 Middleton was transferred to England as a 'temporary' major and second-in-command of the 63rd (training) Battalion, 16th Brigade, based on the desolate Salisbury Plains from 19 May 1917 till 15 September 1917. Middleton understood teamwork intimately and knew a good commander had to lead bullishly at all times from the front. However, this headstrong approach, which he ably displayed on the rugby field or in a boat, was immediately at odds with his infamous commanding officer, Brigadier-General John Macquarie Antill, the commander who had ordered the notorious and tragic third wave charge at the Nek at Gallipoli in August 1915. Antill wrote a scathing report of Middleton's character and military leadership abilities.

> He appears wanting in energy, initiative, powers of command
> and general supervision, especially in the field, among the
> Officers and in general support of the Battalion Commander
> in the important work of Training.[1]

It was obvious that an attachment to a 'training' battalion did not suit Middleton at all. Middleton was transferred back to duty in the field with the 17th Battalion on 18 November 1917. Six weeks later, however, Middleton was sent back to Senior Officers' School at Aldershot on 2 January 1918 with a view to him commanding an infantry battalion of his own. Middleton was still not one easily pushed around and was often determined to stand up for himself and hold his ground. If he disagreed with trivial routines, he could arc up and display a darker side that could be both a benefit and an impediment.

> You know I was very much nearly thrown out of the Senior
> Officers School at Aldershot for refusing to make a bloody fool
> of myself at playing games which was part of a day's work.[2]

Despite Middleton's bouts of stubbornness, his greater leadership qualities and commitment to teamwork were soon recognised and valued. This time his officer school syndicate commander, Lieutenant-Colonel G. K. Sullivan, glowingly wrote in his final assessment on 3 March 1918 that Middleton was

> A capable and reliable Officer with plenty of determination, tact
> and energy. Good physique … Even tempered; goes about his
> work in a quiet methodical way and gets things done …
> He should prove a very efficient Battalion Commander.[3]

In the heat of conflict, he had led men at all levels and in various arenas, from a rugby pitch to platoon commander and now all the way to battalion commanding officer.

In France Middleton served throughout the 17th, 18th and 19th battalions of the 5th Brigade. After completing officer training school at Aldershot in England from 8 January until 16 March 1918, he arrived back in France on 7 April with the 17th Battalion, just in time to catch the full force of the German Spring Offensive that tore through British lines during the dark, desperate days of March and April 1918. The Germans made a savage push for the large railhead at Amiens that fed a radiating network of rail lines toward Paris and beyond. On 14 May 1918, Middleton was in command of the 17th Battalion at Heilly, near Amiens, when the Germans, desperate for one last big play in the war, hammered away at the Australian front line to break through to this vital rail hub.

Middleton – perhaps recalling the 1910 Test rugby series, in which he led the Wallabies to their first win over the terrifying All Blacks – rallied his men, one of many bold Australian leaders determined to stop the German offensive. His Distinguished Service Order (DSO) recommendation letter read, in part:

> he has al [sic] all times shown, by his resolute leadership and courageous conduct, that he possesses the confidence of those under his command ... when the enemy made a very determined attack on the front held by the 17th Battalion and the manner in which he handled the situation and quickly restored the line showed great initiative and leadership.[4]

Middleton and the 5th Brigade were then heavily involved in what Anzac commander General Sir John Monash would later call the 'final victories of 1918'. Like the dying seconds of a rowing race or rugby match, desperate moves were made wide of the battlelines or rushed through the centre as grim efforts redoubled to clinch a victory.

There was a growing sense that things were coming to an end, but no one could be completely sure. Years of vicious fighting for ground won and lost and then won back again meant that many imagined that such a day would never come at all.

At the beginning of 1918, there had been a growing confidence that hardship and civil unrest in Germany, combined with the massed arrival of American forces eager to show their 'Yank' know-how, would break the entrenched deadlock. Still, there was no tangible assurance for the British that it would be the last year of the war.

At dawn on 29 August, in the dying days of the war, Middleton's fellow 1912 Olympic teammate, good friend and Olympic gold and silver medallist, lifesaver and all-round Australian swimming legend Cecil Healy was in action during the push on the village of Mont St Quentin. The 19th Battalion's attack was held up by intense German machine gun fire. Lieutenant Healy was in his very first 'stunt', leading his company into the firing zone. With another officer he gamely took his company forward and mopped up a machine gun nest. Then, as he led his men further up the hill, he was hit by a lethal burst of enfilading machine gun fire emanating from Ticker Copse near the villages of Halles and Omiécourt-lès-Cléry.

Major Syd Middleton duly reported:

> during the early stages of the attack on Mont St. Quentin and Peronne, Cecil was doing gallant work, leading his platoon, and met his death by rushing a machine gun … as we would expect of him, but he was shot through the neck and fell, when a further burst of machine gun fire went through his chest.[5]

The death of Healy hit Middleton hard. There was no getting used to friends dying, especially when one felt, as Middleton did, that the Allies now had the upper hand in the game. A heartbroken Middleton, showing a rare glimpse of emotion, wrote:

> By Healy's death, the world loses one of its greatest champions, one of its best men. Today, in the four years I have been at the front, I wept for the first time.[6]

The loss of sportsmen such as Healy was always hard on morale and often made the news back home. They were media darlings, poster boys for enlistment. Cecil Healy embraced the true amateur ethos of sport as neither elitist nor specialist, but rather simply as an active participant. Lieutenant Cecil Healy remains the only Australian Olympic gold and silver medallist to be killed in action.

August to October 1918 were months of movement, both in the Middle East and on the Western Front. The somewhat diminished AIF had evolved into a nimble fighting force and, now enabled with lightweight rapid-fire Lewis guns, could be quickly deployed for hastily organised attacks and operations. Numerous small movements, attacks and 'straightening of the lines' were referred to ironically as 'peaceful penetration' – as if something so risky and deadly could ever be peaceful.

No longer entrenched in the mud, the AIF's peaceful penetration tactics often surprised the Germans and resulted in their taking small chunks of enemy ground, and then even more ground, leading up to the last vigorous set piece battles around Péronne, Le Verguier, Mont St Quentin and the very last battle (for the AIF) at Montbrehain on 5 October.

The last action, taking the defences of the Beaurevoir Line, produced simple but stark statistics: frontage of over 6000 yards taken; several guns and numerous machine guns; 1000 prisoners; 800 enemy dead; and 700 Australian casualties.[7] The ground still came at great cost. The body counts on both sides were still stacking up. By mid-October, the AIF finally moved out of the front lines for much needed rest and reorganisation.

When the final whistle blew and the crack of gunfire sputtered out from 11 am on 11 November 1918, time on the 'great game' was finally called. With the eerie silence, a deep sense of uncertainty and disbelief must have descended upon the combatants before one brave soul gingerly leaned his rifle against the parapet, took a deep breath and clambered up the fire step. His mates in the trench would have watched stunned as he disappeared over what must have seemed the edge of the world.

When dawn broke in Vignacourt on that day the weather was fine and clear. A new brigade major, Major J. Chapman, had reported for duty the day before to implement and oversee the new battalion disbandment policy. The diggers woke up in their comfortable billets, had breakfast and then started their daily pack drill routine. Initial rumours about the end of the war were no doubt discussed and then sworn away as a furphy. Major Chapman, leaving it as long as he could, perhaps to make sure the diggers kept it business as usual, called them to parade and at 10.45 am delivered the news that all hostilities were to cease at 11 am.

The village of Vignacourt underwent a magical transformation as rejoicing diggers, Allied troops and French locals decorated the streets with garlands of flowers and colourful banners. Not even a gathering overcast sky and afternoon drizzle could dampen such spirits. By 2.30 pm the Australian flag was hoisted outside the church, guards of honour presented arms to the mayor of Vignacourt, and military bands played national anthem after national anthem after national anthem.

Ending the war in pretty French villages far to the rear, with no gunfire or incessant artillery thundering overhead or showers of lethal shrapnel raining down must have felt strange to the diggers. War? What war? Over the next few days there were official speeches, church services, lectures, performances and concerts. The diggers were sent out into the fields around Vignacourt to fill in trenches and roll up wire so the locals could reclaim some semblance of their prewar lives.[8] All they really wanted now was to get home. But the complexities of demobilisation and repatriation of the AIF were enormous, the task full of contradictions.

Over the four years of war, starting with an initial deployment of 20,000 men, the AIF had grown into a lumbering war machine of more than 340,000 men serving across Europe, Egypt and the Middle East. Of those, approximately 60,000 men had ended up permanently 'settled' in foreign fields.

The AIF was a relatively small army compared to other grand armies such as the British, French or Americans. The British Army, for example, numbered close to 3 million men, but they only had a quick rail trip to Boulogne and a quaint ferry ride across a 40-mile-wide channel to step back into Blighty. The French, of course, were fighting in their own backyard; the remains of smashed buildings across hundreds of bloody battle sites were once their homes. The Americans had poured men and materiel en masse into France for well over a year and had imported a little bit of America with them. They were now comfortably spread out in France and seemed happy to indulge in a European vacation for a while. Besides, they had first dibs on any troopships to nip back across the Atlantic.

The Australians, however, were immediately faced with the monumental problem of what to do with as many as 200,000 idle men with no more war to fight and stranded 12,000 miles from home. The AIF volunteers had all signed up for the nebulous term of service: 'duration of war plus 4 months'. In the context of demobilisation, this proved hopelessly inadequate – either a major administrative underestimation or simply overly optimistic, but then few had actually thought that the war would stretch over the years it did. After the Armistice in November 1918, the volunteers of the AIF, by the terms of their attestation paper and original legal contract, should have expected to be discharged by March 1919 – basically an impossible task.

To their credit, the Australian government had, in fact, anticipated the enormous burden of an AIF demobilisation and repatriation. Prime Minister W. M. 'Billy' Hughes, a champion of the diggers, along with his Nationalist Party Cabinet, had actually started the administrative process as early as September 1917, when Senator Edward Millen was appointed the first Minister of Repatriation.

It was new ground for the government and would prove to be extremely complex and encumbered by many policy errors as government bureaucrats and administrators learned the hard realities and subtleties of repatriation on the fly. It was also going to be expensive – *very* expensive – costing the Australian government upwards of £20,000,000 to implement, funded through long-term loans from the British government. Due to the massive cost, the primary focus of the Ministry of Repatriation was on getting able-bodied men back to work and retraining the disabled or permanently wounded in new skills that would enable them to find work.

After implementing the innovative battlefield tactics and plans during 1918 that led to the final 100 days of victory, General Sir John Monash, commander-in-chief, Anzac and Scotch College, Melbourne old boy, was appointed the director-general of repatriation and demobilisation in Europe. General Monash immediately knew he had his work cut out for him. Some believe that the 'straightening of the line' at the Battle of Hamel was Monash's masterpiece, but his implementation of demobilisation and repatriation was his major work. Monash's incredible intellect, capacity to grasp logistics, legal understanding, endless planning conferences and engineering eye for detail – all the factors that had changed military strategy and tactics – were brought to bear on a repatriation program that would last well into 1920.

Underscoring Monash's ambitious and comprehensive repatriation plan was money. It was going to potentially cost the Australian government 'over £1,000,000 per week in central expenditure, quite apart from the loss of productivity of the men of the AIF'[9] and so there was an urgent need to complete the process as quickly and economically as possible. But Monash had at heart the needs of the men who had endured four years of war, in particular those 'originals' who had rowed ashore at Gallipoli and had managed, mainly through sheer bloody luck, to see the carnage through to the bitter end.

Monash set about implementing a vast program of repatriation with some emphasis on getting 'the 1915 men to go quite early', and with serious consideration given to marital condition and family responsibilities, length of service, the industrial needs of Australia, and assured future employment of the man.[10] A 'Wheel of Organisation' was drawn up to illustrate the core administrative duties of the AIF repatriation and demobilisation process. Sport wasn't specifically mentioned, but likely fell under the 'entertainment of troops' spoke of the wheel.[11] Monash was also concerned that the diggers be aware that their 'plus 4 months' contract had been renegotiated.[12]

Almost immediately Monash encountered the logistical and administrative nightmare that had been anticipated. Delays in decisions regarding repatriation priorities from Australia, ever-changing staff, shipping control difficulties and endless communications created a constant bureaucratic fog. A hastily convened conference held at AIF Administrative HQ in London on 12 November 1918 calculated that perhaps 10,000–15,000 Australians could be shipped home per month.[13] This meant that the repatriation of the whole AIF was going to take at least 18 months, and quite possibly two years. Class 'A' or 'B' men – including newlywed diggers with British or French wives and some already with children (estimated to be 10,000 in total) – were to be given priority.[14] Monash was particularly concerned about the impact that the war had had on the men and believed this needed to be converted into a 'reconstruction morale' before their return to Australia, 'to adequately equip them for their future industrial life'.[15]

The leaders of the AIF, and of every fighting force active in Europe, were anxious to keep their troops occupied. The unprecedented slaughter and sociopolitical and spiritual derangement of the Great War had reshaped the world forever. The world as people knew it had ceased to exist, and the rulers of that world, even those on the winning side of the war, were facing a new and real threat to their very existence.

PART 2

The Peace

I am no novice, as you suggest, but consider myself to have been in the first rank so long as I was able to rely on the strength of my youth. But as things are, all the misfortunes and hardships I've endured in warfare and in fighting my way through hostile seas weigh heavily upon me. All the same, and in spite of what I have gone through I'll try my hand at the sports.

Homer, *The Odyssey*

4

Occupy the men

On 30 October 1918, after four days of discussions between Ottoman and British representatives on board the British battleship HMS *Agamemnon* – anchored off the island of Lemnos in the Aegean Sea, exactly where the Anzacs had embarked for Gallipoli years before – Sultan Mehmed VI's official envoy signed the Treaty of Mudros, effectively ending Turkey's role in the war. The treaty also accelerated the beginning of the end for the crumbling Ottoman Empire and the House of Osman, which had been in existence since 1299.[1] Soon the once mighty empire would be carved up into colonial territories and protectorates by the victors – with disastrous consequences through the century to follow and beyond.

In Central Europe, during the same month, the Habsburg Empire had been unravelling at pace. The Italians launched two attacks on 24 October at Monte Grappa and Vittorio Veneto against the already depleted and badly demoralised Habsburg Army, and within five days the Austro–Hungarian Army was in full flight. The desperate Hungarian government decided on 1 November to withdraw its forces from the retreating shambles of the Habsburg Army and matters spiralled from bad to beyond redemption.

After two days of desperate negotiations between the Italian and Austrian military high commands, on 3 November, the Armistice of Villa Giusti was signed, to come into effect twenty-four hours later. On 4 November, the chief of staff and commander of the Italian Army, General Armando Diaz, triumphantly decreed:

> The Austro-Hungarian army is vanquished … the remnants of
> what was one of the world's most powerful armies are returning
> in hopelessness and chaos.[2]

After a war, there is no real peace. In Europe, in the shattered remains of the old-world imperial order, new ideologies took hold. Empires, nations and states broke down into vicious ever-multiplying splinter cells of radical political, social, religious or racial ideologies. Winston Churchill, deeply suspicious of the spread of Bolshevism, sarcastically remarked, 'When the war of giants had ended, and the wars of the pygmies begin.'[3]

In particular, in the broken empires, vast populations of impoverished, traumatised civilians, not a few of whom had been heavily armed soldiers just months earlier, were beginning to see the appeal of new, socialist philosophies. To paraphrase Karl Marx, the spectre of communism was haunting Europe, and it scared nobody so much as the leadership of the broken Imperial Germany.

Since November 1917, after Bolshevik revolutions in Russia, things hadn't been looking pretty back home in Berlin. There were severe food shortages, civil disturbances (read Bolshevik agitation), immediate enforced drafting of men, women and children, labour strikes, growing unrest and war-weariness. It was noted in the AIF 2nd Divisional HQ diary of Major-General 'Rosie' Rosenthal, who interrogated captured German soldiers, 'that Germany cannot win the war, and at best can only hope for a compromise.'[4]

Kaiser Wilhelm felt the full brunt of the growing national and public dissatisfaction. He lost the confidence of his Western Front commanders and on 28 October the German revolution began with a mutiny by German sailors which spread to the shipyard workers in the naval base of

Kiel. German political revolutionaries, now emboldened by the Russian Revolution, 'began to demand peace at any price and the immediate abdication of the Kaiser – demands that sounded uncomfortably similar to those articulated by Russian protesters in Petrograd in early 1917'.[5] No one had the iron will or resolve to quell the disquiet. Socialism at best, or Bolshevism at worst, was taking a firm hold in Germany.

Bolshevism was perceived as an ever-present threat to Europe, particularly to Germany. By January 1919, the new Soviet movement was making its presence felt through the Baltic states of Lithuania, Estonia and Latvia and spreading further west along the precious Baltic coast toward Germany. There, some disillusioned soldiers of the German Army 'Freikorps' were still engaged as a quasi-mercenary force fighting Bolshevik expansion in Riga, Latvia, throughout the early months of 1919.

On the morning before the Armistice was signed in a plush first-class parlour car shunted into the woods near the quiet village of Compiègnie, the Kaiser fled into exile, to the Netherlands. Upon the signing of the bottom line, the German-speaking territories of Alsace-Lorraine, annexed by Germany in 1871, were snappily handed back to France.

On 5 December, under orders from Brigadier-General Thomas Blamey at Corps HQ, the AIF quickly got to work, falling in with a collegiate 'Army of the Rhine' alongside other Allied forces to occupy what was effectively a field of shallow graves all the way to the waterway that contentiously divided France and the former Imperial Germany. Even though hostilities had ceased, there was still a great sense of uncertainty among the Allies. The German Army had been defeated in the field, but not in a manner that would allow a victorious Patton-esque rampage across the Rhine and all the way to the doorstep of Berlin. The Germans had stopped fighting but, as an army, were still angry.

In the closing days of the war, when the writing was on the wall for Germany, the last of the Central Powers still in the game, thoughts began to turn to life after the slaughter. The elite of the allied American and British and Dominion nations were acutely aware of the threat that socialism posed – particularly with vast bodies of armed, shell-shocked and idle troops cooling their heels while socialist agitators ran wild in Europe.

Britain itself was facing the prospect of demobilising about 3.5 million soldiers after the Armistice. They were all trained in firearms and hand-to-hand fighting and very eager to come home to their villages, shires and towns and rejoin their families and loved ones. Marching out of the army into the peacetime wasn't going to be easy for the Mother Country. If these demobilised servicemen didn't get a job or some sort of assistance to train for a job, the prospect of a Bolshevik Revolution was very real. The upside to the Russian Revolution in October 1917 hadn't been lost upon the vast British working class and the trade unionists.

As early as November 1918, the AIF soldiers, buoyed by the new-found peace and prospect of going home, were becoming very rowdy and excitable. There were serious incidents instigated by diggers that resulted in numerous disturbances at brothels; fracas between diggers and Portuguese troops; robberies; assaults at gunpoint; and theft of coal and rail bags.[6] In the aftermath of the Armistice, behaviour bordering on mutiny spread among the Allies, signalling the fragile nature of the peace even among the victors. It was only about a week before signs of dissent first appeared in North Wales at Kinmel Park, where the Australians and Canadians were encamped side by side in miserable conditions. The Canadians were just as edgy as the Australians – perhaps edgier – and sometimes Allied dominion brother turned on brother. As Lieutenant George Goddard related to his mother:

There was a serious riot in the Camp last week ... The 16th ... were having a dance and some of the Canadians invited themselves in, they were asked to go, but refused. Then the fight started. The Canadians mustered 300 & 400 of their crowd and, with fists, sticks, stones and bottles, made things merry. Then the 16th turned out with fixed bayonets, but when it came to the point, they were afraid to use them, and fell back every time the Canadians made a rush. We were turned out, also armed with rifles and bayonets, and with the Australians in the van, arrived on the scene. We soon got busy among them & they slipped back off to their camps like whipped dogs. We didn't do any damage with the bayonets, but our presence was a very potent force. They went away muttering and hurling all sorts of curses and threats at us ... This was one of the unofficial battles, fought away from the front line, which the world in general will never hear about.[7]

In early January 1919, the same sense of disorder and incivility steadily increased in England, France and central Europe. The new year meant brand new expectations, the men of the AIF were already getting restless and a growing number of 'thieves and scoundrels' among the AIF was leading to the fear of a major crime wave.

Throughout the Anzac Corps horse rustling was a thriving business, and clothing, rations, boots and blankets were falling off the backs of trucks at an alarming rate. Concerted efforts from Australian Corps HQ were directed at preventing this. The consensus was that the widespread theft of AIF property was either the fault of the local population, or the AIF soldiers had a nice little racket going selling much-needed supplies to the deprived locals – in all likelihood, the latter.

On the upside, the diggers probably thought the French locals, who had lost so much, needed the blankets, rations and supplies more than they did. Needless to say, this unruly entrepreneurial behaviour was not endemic among the AIF and the vast majority of diggers complied with regulations, waited in line for demobilisation and resisted the temptations of a five-finger discount.

However, the overriding concern was that the damaging activities of a few would tarnish the reputation of all. The fear of sullying the fine fighting reputation of the AIF was certainly enough to be noted all the way up the line of command. The new commanding officer of the Australian Corps in Europe, Lieutenant-General J. J. Talbot Hobbs, worried about the AIF's reputation during the peace, wrote:

I do urge on all concerned the vital necessity of doing everything that lies in our power ... to put an end to what is becoming not only a serious loss, but a grave scandal.[8]

In any event, the pressure to 'occupy the men' and rehabilitate them from crafty battleground scavengers and thieves to honest hardworking employees was increasing. One important consideration was that the positions in education and training programs were limited and the question of what to do for the rest of the diggers was of primary concern. The solution seemed obvious and, ultimately, was very popular. It was a commonly held perception that Australians loved their sport, and while it wouldn't be directly educating or training the men as per government policy, it would occupy the men, and ameliorate the growing repatriation frustration among the homesick diggers.

As Lieutenant George Goddard stated in the preface of his 1919 work, *Soldiers and Sportsmen*:

> The fact they were Australians, and that they loved their sport, more almost than their work … made the solution possible. Unlimited sport of the best kind varied and made as attractive as possible – therein lay the secret. No better method could possibly be devised. So it was that a widespread movement began.[9]

So Australian leadership, under the command of General Monash (in charge of repatriation) and Lieutenant-General Hobbs (in the role of commander of AIF Headquarters in Horseferry Road), began to comb the ranks of the Australian armed forces for talented sportsmen who could spearhead this ambitious reworking of martial aggression into good-natured sportsmanship. They did not have to look far.

5

Battlefield to playing field

On 13 September 1918, on a chilly, windswept, grassy field outside the small French village of Frise, Major Syd Middleton crouched on his haunches, dressed in an officer's uniform with polished Sam Browne belt, peaked cap, overcoat, tightly bound puttees and mud-splattered boots. He now looked very much older and grimmer, his face lined with loss and his complexion wan. Middleton had had his fair share of war and he now carried scars both physical and mental. When his old Wallaby and 1908 Olympic rugby teammate Tom Richards had run into him just two years earlier, in late 1916, he saw how battered Syd had already been by the battle at Pozières:

> Middleton was practically buried five times in one day, his stars were shot away from his shoulder on one side, the heel of his boot dinted and his foot wrenched, a piece of shell penetrated his side and made quite a gash ... He thought his time had come to die.[1]

After the failure of the German offensive Operation Michael and the arrival of the American military machine, there was a sense among the Allies that hostilities were coming to an end but no one could be completely sure. Nor did they want to assume it could be over all so easily. Years of fighting, over hard-fought ground that was won, then lost and then won back again, had basically meant that many imagined that such a day would never come at all. The possibility that the war could stretch into 1919 was also very real.

It was drizzling as Middleton drew a crude map in the mud with a stick, explaining the principles of attack to a muddy, bedraggled circle of diggers. He described how to spearhead a drive through a defensive line; stressed the need for fast movement to the flanks, to outflank the opposition, and for constantly backing up your attack by being there in support.

To the casual observer, Middleton was the hardened officer, dispensing vital, taciturn advice, but they were far from the booming guns and slaughter of the front – this time the conflict was peaceful; the inter-brigade rugby match, 'the game they play in heaven', between the 19th and 17th Battalions – an exercise in keeping the troops occupied and morale up.

Throughout September, two months before hostilities ceased, Middleton had already been heavily involved in organising all types of sport in the 5th Brigade, which were crucial to maintaining morale by providing entertainment for those diggers out of the front line. On 9 September, Middleton had been appointed Officer Commanding of all the battalion sports teams, in order to select the best representative brigade squad for the upcoming 2nd Division sports carnival, to be held on 16 September. This was serious business indeed. On 11 September, battalion games had begun at 2 pm sharp, with Major Middleton as the senior judge and selector. Events contested included three-legged racing, boat races, sack races, tug of war, sprints, relays and bomb throwing (with a standing bowl).

Plans were also underway to use money from the 2nd Division canteen to look after the brigade's sporting interests and a divisional 'Tattersalls sur Somme' fundraising lottery was instigated to raise money for the 5th Brigade squad. For the deceptively cheap five francs per ticket, diggers had the chance to win a war saving certificate valued at £87 which would mature in three years to £100.

At the end of the war, the troops were dismayed to learn, that their battalions were to be disbanded and reformed. AIF battalions, with their unique colours and battle honours, had become sacred to the men within them. For the soldiers, the battalion had been home away from home over the last three to four years. Sport was a welcome distraction. The idea of channelling the aggression of the AIF into the wholesome pursuit of sport wasn't lost on a great leader of men like Middleton, nor on his commanding officer, General Monash.

Monash wrote in his 26 November address to his commanders in 1918 that:

> There is a most pressing necessity for some organisation to be set up at once to find the means of providing useful and beneficial employment for all these men, and that is what my chief business will be.[2]

At best, Monash anticipated that 150,000 men would still be in Europe in March 1919 and that by June 1919 there would probably still be '100,000 left in all theatres'. 'What unparalleled difficulties,' he wrote, 'to keep these masses of men in good heart and usefully employed!!'[3]

His primary aim now was to arrange a vast program of further education, apprenticeships, attachments to British trade unions, business internships, lectures and on-the-job training in industries such as iron, steel, chemicals and agriculture in both Europe and England.

But Monash faced many difficulties. Jobs were already scarce for the demobilising English soldiers in their own country; there was some opposition from local unionists, many with Bolshevist sympathies; and the lack of money to fund educational or industrial programs was always a consideration. As the diggers languished in Europe, Monash was focused on getting his diggers educated and finding them new jobs in a brave new postwar world. He knew that if they made no effort 'this feeling of uncertainty and unrest will in a few weeks develop into something much worse.'

Not all training was going to be educational, though. Monash and the British military authorities thought some recreational physical training would also be required and provide some vital downtime. It was a natural progression to take inter-brigade and inter-divisional sport to the next level of inter-Allied sport and an ersatz elite international competition. Sport would boost morale and would allow thousands of diggers to get behind their team, no matter the code, at multiple events across England and in France and Egypt.

At noon on 4 November, at Belloy-sur-Somme, Major Syd Middleton arrived in a staff car at the 2nd Division Headquarters and made his way up the chateau steps to report for an important briefing about – of all things – sport. Once ushered inside, 2nd Division General Officer Commanding Major-General Rosenthal likely offered Middleton a chair and an expensive French brandy – which Middleton would have politely waved away. Middleton had sworn off alcohol for the duration of the war. It was almost unheard of for a former Wallaby, Olympic oarsman and all-round sportsman not to drink.

Middleton had in fact given up alcohol before the war, after a drunken rampage with rugby teammates down the streets of Sydney following a momentous NSW rugby victory. Someone from the team had had the brilliant idea of shooting out streetlights as they careered along the main street on their pub crawl. It didn't take long for the NSW constabulary to arrive and the wayward band of intoxicated footballers, including Middleton, were apprehended and severely reprimanded. Middleton was so embarrassed by the incident that he made up his mind then and there to avoid alcohol for the following five years. It just so happened that a war started not long after, but he nonetheless resolutely stuck to his oath of abstinence.[4]

Major-General Rosenthal informed Middleton that word had come directly from Corps HQ, and General Sir John Monash himself, that someone with a reputation, know-how and an impeccable sporting pedigree was urgently required to keep the peace during the disbandment process and occupy the men. What was required was a sports program, to be held throughout the whole of the Corps, possibly on the scale of an Olympic Games. As an Olympic gold medallist in rugby, former captain of the Wallabies, heavyweight boxer of some repute, and NSW and Australian Olympic oarsman, Middleton's reputation had long preceded him. He had also been transferred at various times during the war from the 19th, and was also well-known and respected in both the 17th and 18th Battalions. He also personally knew many sportsmen scattered throughout the AIF, through his extensive pre-war sporting affiliations.

Major-General Rosenthal informed Middleton that his mission, of the highest importance, was to do with getting up and running an ambitious AIF sports program in both France and England.

Middleton was told to make them as varied and as 'attractive as possible'.[5] Without hesitation, he 'mapped out a scheme embracing a most extensive sports programme ... and no time should be lost in getting the best Australian athletes together.'[6]

This presented a difficult choice for Middleton. The majority of Australians who had travelled to the war had done so incrementally, as the conflict escalated, casualties grew and reinforcements arrived. Now, with the cessation of hostilities, there were too few troop-carrying ships available, and repatriation had to take place incrementally. The process allowed for Australian soldiers who had served the longest to be sent home as a priority. As an 'original' who had served at Gallipoli, and in various theatres of war since 1915, Middleton would be given preference and the chance to be sent home early. If he took on this role, he knew he would be forgoing the opportunity for early repatriation, and that there was no guarantee of how long it would be before he would see Australia again. But he must have judged that it was worth it; he accepted the opportunity to initiate and run the AIF sports program.

Middleton was Monash's middle-man and there was simply no one else who possessed the knowledge, nous or sporting pedigree across so many different codes of sport. If there had been, they had either been killed or invalided. Middleton perceived his duty to be clear, and spent the next few days at Divisional HQ, wasting no time getting started.

On 6 November 1918, a wire was sent saying that it was 'desired that Middleton be relieved from Corps' as soon as possible as he was required for upcoming training work as an acting commanding officer (CO) in the 17th Battalion. Before his orders had even arrived, Middleton was burning the midnight oil, sketching out his plans for a vast sports competition among the diggers deployed in England and across the continent. If the AIF were intent on putting on this show and doing it right, Middleton was determined to gather together the best of the best. He would show the world the cream of Australia's sporting talent, taking them from one test of mettle to another.

6

Syd and Marion

Major Syd Middleton had hit the ground running, preparing plans for sports competitions in France and England. Somewhere at the forefront of his ambition was a showcase of his beloved competitive rowing – a good, old-fashioned oarsmen's regatta.

The French had a long association with rowing, dating from 1838, and had developed a vibrant rowing community – sometimes established by English expats – along iconic rivers such as the Seine, Marne and Somme. In Paris, rowing was very popular, and spectators often gathered at the lake in the Bois de Boulogne to watch regattas or indulge in a recreational row. In Georges Seurat's famous 1886 work of pointillism, *A Sunday Afternoon on the Island of La Grande Jatte*, a coxed rowing four can be spotted through the trees, watched by the suited and parasol-bearing French bourgeoisie. France had had some success at the 1900 Olympic Games in Paris, with the men's coxed four winning gold and a local champion oarsman, Hermann Barrelet, winning in the single sculls.

Despite this, the prospect of staging a rowing regatta in France presented difficulties for Middleton, particularly on the Seine. Rowing, even at the best of times, is subject to more than its fair share of administrative complexities and practical considerations. In order to stage a multinational or major regatta, you have to find a stretch of calm water long enough and straight enough, without too many seen or unseen obstacles.

A rowing regatta also required numerous boat race officials at both the start and the finish lines. Officials at the start, after lining up crews, used a 'shotgun' start to the race. If the finish was in line of sight of the start, judges and timekeepers watched for a tell-tale puff of smoke from the starter's gun to begin their stopwatches. Other officials and timekeepers would then time and record the margin times between crews at the finish. When the finish line could not be seen from the starting point, timekeepers in the umpire's start and chase launch, huddled directly under the starter's gun, recorded the time and then relied on a flag system at the finish to signal the first crew to cross the finish line, with timekeepers recording the margins between crews.

Applying a bit of arithmetic to the times resulted in accurate finishing times for each of the crews. It was a very precise system that required officials who really knew what they were doing. The racing officials sat in powered launches so they could marshal crews on the water, follow a race and officiate over instances of boats fouling (colliding) or just plain foul play.

By the end of the war, the Allies didn't exactly associate the River Somme with the sleepy, meandering flat water its name implied. The Somme itself was often narrow, winding and perhaps more suited to a highly manoeuvrable single scull rather than a set-piece battle paddle between three or four timber racing eights. It was also the site of some of the bloodiest fighting of the entire conflict, had acquired a rather gloomy reputation and wasn't likely to attract the survivors of the war back in a hurry.

Other major obstacles included actually finding enough rowing eight- or four-man racing shells for competitors, as well as finding staging pontoons or portions of riverbank where crews could store their boats on racks or trestles, launch their boats and push off to row to the start.

Eight-man crew rowing was something the French hadn't quite embraced as thoroughly as the English, Americans and Australians had, and eight- or four-man racing boats were few and far between in France. There was also the issue of the quality of the boats. In Australia and England, rowing eights were beautifully crafted pieces made out of western red cedar, with steel outriggers and with the sliding seats on longer rails that were a recent innovation in rowing.

A lot of the rowing boats available in France after the war were clinker-style boats best suited for paddling along the Seine. These not-so-narrow clinkers were made from long, steamed wooden panels called strakes overlaid with each other, did not sport outriggers and had two pin rowlocks on the gunwale – sometimes with fixed bench seats. They were also seated diagonally along the boat, so if an oarsman was sitting, for example, on the port side, he rowed his oar fixed in its rowlock on the starboard side to get more leverage around the fulcrum. Good sleek racing boats were regarded as works of art and *très cher* – and resources were scarce.

Through the war years, precious resources could not be spared for an ambitious sport and recreation program. In the postwar world, though, with the offer of peace and hope in the new year of 1919, societies across the world were keen to get back to their comfortable and comfortably predictable prewar worlds, and forget the years of uncertainty, pain, grief and loss. Sport was a simple, popular and profound way to forget war and celebrate the peace.

Middleton pulled every string and called in every favour he could, and plans for the inter-brigade sports competition moved at a rapid pace. The idea of the sports competition was enthusiastically received at all levels, both in France and England, and not only by military authorities but also local clubs and sports associations desperate to revive competitions and restore genteel society with its gay summer calendar of racing, regattas and rugger.

But Middleton's busy schedule organising the AIF sports, and the sheer stress of the challenge of organising a fatigued, war-weary army, combined with the lingering effects of years of draining wartime living, quickly took a toll on his health. Searing gut pain, a jaded constitution and a slightly yellowing complexion were enough for the usually stoic Syd to seek medical assistance. On 15 November, Middleton was admitted to the 12th Casualty Clearance Station and then promptly transferred to the 10th British Red Cross Hospital, known as Lady Murray's Hospital, in the pretty seaside port town of Le Tréport, France, where many of the Allied forces had established army base hospitals.

He was diagnosed with catarrhal jaundice, an acute infectious viral disease of the liver characterised by fever, liver enlargement and jaundice. Maybe Middleton had got back into drinking a bit too quickly – but it was more likely simple burnout and exposure to diseases that thrived in unsanitary close quarters living in the postwar period. At this time, the deadly influenza pandemic known as the Spanish flu was sweeping through Europe and in a population run down by years of deprivation and poverty, the pandemic ended up killing far more millions than the Great War could manage.

Lady Murray's Hospital had originally been the quaint Golf Hotel, but had been converted into a boutique hospital with about fifty beds, which catered mainly to officers. Lady Margaret Murray was one of many titled ladies who had set up their own hospitals to tend to the sick and wounded. Middleton had been admitted, triaged and placed in a small room with another patient in need of rest and recuperation. As he arrived, Middleton no doubt saw any number of more serious cases: those with life-threatening wounds, gassing, serious illness and disease. He was relatively unscathed and had no obvious signs of trauma.

He woke early the next day when the orderlies, matrons, nursing sisters and Volunteer Aid Detachment members (VADs) commenced their rounds. He was sitting up in his iron-framed hospital bed when ward nurses – no-nonsense, with their blue dresses, distinctive aprons with a bright red cross on a white background, and white caps tied behind the napes of their necks – began to appear. Curtains were opened, trolleys rattled down halls, and the cheery banter of young nurses roused the sick and wounded from their fitful dreams. Middleton already wanted to be out of there and the thought of losing even more precious time was making him very agitated.

These tireless English nurses had seen the dreadful after-effects of war on a grand scale. After the horrors of the medical trains coming from the western front, tending to a big, grumbling, seemingly unscathed Australian officer was a walk in the park.

One young English nurse, with bobbed curly brown hair and at least a foot shorter than Middleton, approached his bed. He looked away, pretending not to notice her professional attention and ready to snap at any useless questions as to how he might be feeling or how he had slept. The nurse eyed Middleton and sized him up. Undaunted, she reached for the chart hanging above his bed and flipped through it without even casting a glance at him.

'Hmm ... So, you're an Aussie,' she said indifferently, sounding almost disappointed. Before Middleton could reply, she flipped the chart shut and said, 'Well, it looks like there's nothing much wrong with you and "Aussies" always make their own beds.'

And with that, Nurse Streatfeild, known by the officers as 'Streatty', hooked the chart back above the bed, threw Middleton a wan smile and briskly continued her rounds. Middleton was blindsided, stumped by her cheek and laconic bedside manner. He felt that he had just been dumped by the biggest hospital pass that anyone had ever flicked him, and he wasn't going to forget the girl who threw that pass so easily.

For the rest of his stay at Lady Murray's Hospital, Middleton could barely bring himself to speak to the nurse as she went about her duties. As she chatted and smiled with other recuperating British Army officers, all of whom seemed to fawn over her and flirt with her, Middleton quietly fumed. This was new ground for him. He was a straightforward and courageous man. He could tackle a man like a grizzly bear, stick his head into a rugby maul and rip the ball, race in an eight-man rowing crew or lead a company of men into battle. But this woman was an entirely different ball game. He spent his time trying to work up the courage to snatch a moment with her, but was for the first time completely at a loss for words.

7

The Sports Section

The year 1919 started with a bang for Major Sydney Middleton. On New Year's Eve, 1918, Middleton was mentioned in dispatches, a great honour for fighting men and a prerequisite for advancement. On New Year's Day he was awarded the Distinguished Service Order for his leadership skills in the field early in 1918. On 6 January, he was ordered by Brigadier-General Thomas H. Dodds to travel to London to attend a meeting of the British Army Sports Control Board as the AIF representative. The objective of this meeting was to convene a rugby competition presided over by Boer War veteran and General Douglas Haig's deputy chief of staff General Charles 'Tim' Harington Harington (by a quirk of family lineage his middle name and surname were the same).

In 1919, Harington was there to talk not ordnance but rugby. The sports conference soon expanded its brief to organising as many sports competitions for the Allied troops as possible. The aim was to encourage men to 'compete for the honour of their unit' and 'instil the root principle of true sport, viz.: "Play for your side and not for yourself."'[1]

Middleton had already been on the case organising a rugby match between the AIF and a French Armed Services rugby team hastily scheduled for 19 January 1919 and under the management of Sydney University rugby veteran Major 'Wally' Matthews. This was serious sports management, done on the fly. Rugby players had been gathered from units stationed throughout France and Belgium and quickly became known as the AIF 'Trench' Team.

Middleton's pedigree in rugby was impressive. As well as having been captain of the championship-winning Glebe Rugby Club and selected in 1908 for Dr Paddy Moran's original 'Wallaby' rugby tour of England, there was the Olympic gold in London 1908 and his captaincy of the Wallabies in a three-Test series against New Zealand in 1910. With this resume, everyone could see Middleton had more than just a passing interest in rugby. He was devoted to it, and to a great many other sports, displaying almost fanatical loyalty as he rucked, rowed, boxed or watched any sport for the sheer joy of it.

When Moran's famous 1908 Wallabies returned from their victorious tour to the UK, having won twenty-five of the thirty-one tour matches, over fifteen of them turned professional and signed up for the cashed-up upstart code of rugby league. Middleton was one of four or five of the squad who simply weren't interested in playing rugby for money, and it was said he wasn't even approached by the league's scouts.

Loyalty, in Middleton's mind, was the bedrock of sport, business and life. It was a quality he would apply to everything he undertook, then and in the years to come, whether it be work, family, colleagues, friendship, career, sport or love. Now, after four years of fighting loyally for their country, the men playing rugby for the AIF 'Trench' Team were playing for their country. This was the epitome of pure sporting spirit, according to Middleton, and he wasn't going to miss it.

On 18 January he caught the train down to Folkestone and the ferry across the English Channel to watch the 'Trench' team play the French Armed Service team in Paris. The weather was very chilly when the two teams met the next day. The AIF 'Trench' Team gave a good, hard, fast display of rugby and won 6–3, with the French giving it their best shot. It was a good start for the AIF.

Middleton made his way back to Le Havre the next day to catch the ferry. At this stage, many of the non-combatants were being demobilised and sent back home to England. This included many wounded and ill soldiers who were being sent back to England for better treatment and hospitalisation, and the British Red Cross base hospitals were being closed down. Le Havre was a busy port at the best of times and with troops piling onto transports, just about any available passage on a ferry back to England was at a premium. Middleton boarded the ferry with the crush of returning soldiers and a host of VADs (Voluntary Aid Detachment) – and there she was: the nurse who had treated him with such disdain and disinterest.

Marion Streatfeild had been just twenty-two years old when she joined the VAD in 1916. Her first words to Syd on the ferry might have been, 'Oh, I remember you. The Australian.' Whatever she said was enough for Syd to hang off every word she spoke from that moment on.

Marion lived in Wilbraham Place, in the swish inner London suburb of Sloane Square, and was the granddaughter of an Irish peer. She was possessed of a clear sense of duty. Once she had completed her nursing training, she was selected for 'special service' in September 1916 at Lady Murray's Hospital – where she had met Syd.

The VADs at British Red Cross hospitals initially had to pay their own way into nursing detachments, and many were, like Marion, from prominent and even titled families. These young women had to be multi-skilled. If a vehicle was required to transport patients to the railway station, the VAD jumped into the driver's seat. If an ambulance or motor needed a wheel changed, the VAD was up to the task.

By December 1918, Lady Murray's Hospital was decommissioned, and after final tidy-ups, signing of paperwork and perhaps a bit of sightseeing, Marion and her fellow VADs were on the Channel ferry heading back home, where, by some fortunate twist of fate, she ran straight into the smitten Syd Middleton.

Somewhere during this trip they found something special in common. Marion's confidence, resilience, independence and maturity were far beyond her twenty-four years. Middleton later wrote about their chance encounter: 'meeting you on the boat gave me fresh hope'.[2] He would write to her:

When I left that hospital, darling ... and I wanted Oh so badly
to kiss your pretty mouth and tell you that I loved you from first
seeing you but I wasn't game.[3]

A romance was kindled, and following his heart, and no longer just
his ambition and sense of duty, Middleton settled in London.

By 21 January, Middleton, energised by his meeting with Marion,
was setting a cracking pace. He was determined to ensure as many games
and sports were as well-organised, successful and popular as possible.
He was used to volunteering the copious amounts of time needed to
organise the countless details that made amateur sports organisations
run. Anyone who was a member of a rugby, cricket or rowing club knew
there was as much important work happening off the field as on it. The
one clear advantage the AIF already had was that amateur sport 'had
been so greatly fostered and encouraged throughout the AIF in France
that a solid foundation had been laid for the successful carrying out of
the programme'.[4]

Despite that, the logistical challenge was phenomenal.

The AIF Administrative Headquarters at Horseferry Road in
London was a rabbit warren of small, lightless offices filled with
the endless and onerous tasks of repatriation, all under the control
of General Sir John Monash, whose office of AIF Repatriation and
Demobilisation was based at 54 Victoria Street, SW1. Horseferry Road
was a vast operation and a hive of activity.

By mid-January, Middleton had drafted the terms and conditions
of the future workings of the 'Sports Section'. The AIF Sports Control
Board was then duly constituted on 31 January, with Brigadier-General
Thomas. H. Dodds as president. Immediately, Dodds sent orders, as
approved by the general officer commanding the AIF, to AIF depots in
the UK and Australian Corps Headquarters in France requesting

1. That first class athletes required by AIF Sports Control Board
about to be sent to France be held in England provided they
are willing.

2. That athletes in England and France awaiting return to
Australia for demobilisation be given the option of remaining
for international sport and forgo any claim to priority for
demobilisation ... and that necessary authority will be given for
the retention of those required.[5]

Another member of the Sports Control Board, who would be
the AIF contact in France, was the incredible war hero and Gallipoli
veteran, Scotch College and Melbourne University old boy, and all-
round athlete Lieutenant-Colonel Norman Marshall DSO, MC,
ably assisted by Lieutenant-Colonel C. V. Watson DSO and Major
R. J. Massie DSO.

The person who would be doing all the heavy lifting, as organising
secretary, was Major Syd Middleton DSO. Middleton immediately
continued the process of identifying talented sportsmen throughout the
AIF. The search incorporated a wide range of sports, particularly team
sports. Middleton knew many enlisted sportsmen personally but to be
sure he didn't miss any untapped potential, he drafted orders that could
be sent out to brigades asking them to report to him about any men
who had first-class sporting experience. He put the word out through
the AIF stationed in the UK, Europe and Middle East that 'sports
officers' should be appointed to identify any surviving sportsmen or
potential candidates in any sport. These sports officers worked at every
level, from company to battalion through to divisional or Corps HQ
command. Middleton's plan was to engage the diggers with as much
sport as he could muster and revive as many sports competitions as
possible, with the emphasis on team sports such as rugby, cricket,
Australian rules, soccer, shooting, tennis, athletics and, of course,
rowing. In effect, he was using the hierarchy of the armed forces for an
early form of sports talent scouting.

However, one resource the AIF Sports Control Board lacked was
a little thing called money. Almost all funding from the Australian
government was directed towards rehabilitation, training and
education, with the express intention of getting the AIF back to work
in a future peacetime economy. Of course, the AIF could still facilitate

many operational matters for the Sports Control Board. With a little imagination and the motivation of a man as driven as Middleton, the logistics of a vast army could be repurposed to build the infrastructure for the AIF Peace Games.

Everyday martial activities were maintained through AIF brigades and battalions – parade, drill and physical fitness training and exercise programs – so the men remained fairly fit. Motor lorries, staff cars, rail warrants, wagons and buses could move sports teams and equipment from venue to venue. The athletes or competitors who would eventually be selected for teams or events were still on the official payroll of the AIF so long as they trained in their 'sports sections', obeyed orders and followed instructions from superior officers.

However, the Sports Control Board still needed to supplement this vital military support with funds that would help, for example, to buy cricket bats, rugby balls, football boots, uniforms, jerseys, flannels, tennis racquets, training kit, blazers, tour accommodation, gratuities, oars and, of course, rowing boats. Telegrams were sent to Australia asking local racing clubs and state representative sporting associations for financial subscriptions and support.

Now that the Great War was over, the Australian Comforts Fund, which had kept the oft-deprived diggers in material comforts such as clothing, socks, cigarettes, Red Cross packages and foodstuffs throughout the four long years of war, was now approached for crucial financial assistance.

The Comforts Fund saw that the diggers still needed their support during the long repatriation process and offered the generous sum of £10,000 to assist with the Sports Control Board's expenses. Successful, wealthy and high-profile citizens, along with sports-minded philanthropists, were also approached. Many individual donors and wealthy philanthropists, both in England and Australia, also lent their support, either donating funds directly, or splashed out entertaining the Australians at elaborate English garden parties on their country estates or provided cheap accommodation.

One London-based expat Australian, William Sydney Robinson, or 'W.S.', had become one of Australia's first mining magnates when he made a vast fortune in a small western New South Wales town called Broken Hill. With his long-time associate William Lawrence Baillieu, from a wealthy Melbourne establishment family descended from squatter barons, he'd built a fortune supplying material to the dominion war machine, particularly zinc. By the end of the war, and for the next thirty years, W.S. would be confidant, advisor and lobbyist for the mining industry to prime ministers Hughes, Bruce, Scullin, and all the way to Curtin, Chifley and Menzies, not to mention having a personal hotline to American President Herbert Hoover.

Sometime during the Armistice, amidst frantic political posturing, foreign policy negotiations and consultations with Prime Minister Billy Hughes – who was in England, arguing for Australia's place at the postwar peace table – W.S. and Syd Middleton met and formed a close personal and professional relationship. W.S. would become a great supporter of Syd's campaign to meet the lofty goals of the AIF Sports Control Board. In particular, he was vital in establishing a competitive AIF rowing squad and getting a crew fit, relaxed and ready for the Henley Royal Regatta.

In November 1918, boxing tournaments were already underway throughout the AIF. Boxing had always had a place in the armed forces, and right from the get-go Middleton encouraged and expanded boxing tournaments to battalion, brigade and divisional levels. Middleton wanted to raise the profile of sports AIF-wide, and boxing would be the first step of this expansion. Pugilism was popular and easy to promote. All you needed to do was get the AIF Pioneers out to build a simple boxing ring inside a hall or tent. At a pinch, soldiers could stake out some open, even ground with ropes, which weren't in short supply.

It wasn't hard to find two men of correct weight who were keen to lay into each other. After four years of deadly hand-to-hand fighting in the lawlessness of total war, this kind of competitive ring fighting, under the strict Queensberry Rules, was appealing to veterans. A few rounds of getting belted in the ring was a walk in the park compared to the front – not to mention a good way to burn off aggression and lingering animosities built up over time. Inter-brigade boxing competitions in all weight divisions flourished and there was never a shortage of spectators.

Rowing, at the time, was a very popular sport and possessed a strong spectator following. With so many sportsmen in Europe, there was going to be no shortage of talented athletes, footballers, cricketers or oarsmen who could answer Middleton's call to arms – at least, there hadn't been, going into the war. The question was, how was he to find them, and what would the horrors of war have done to them?

8

The oarsmen of Pozières

If one of the outcomes of the end of a war is peace, then the other – often forgotten – is the plight of the survivors. These are the men and women who, at the going down of the sun, do grow old, whom age does weary and the years do condemn. Among them were oarsmen who had survived and who now found a unique opportunity, where they could, at the merest sniff of an invitation, get back into the boat.

By the time of the Armistice, all the oarsmen serving in the AIF who could still row or were keen to row were languishing in France or Belgium, keeping a fragile peace and waiting in line to return home. One infamous battle beyond Gallipoli united almost all these oarsmen – by some quirk of fate, many of the men destined to serve in Middleton's rowing squad had ended up in the slaughter of Pozières. Somehow, they had survived.

Tom McGill from Dulwich Hill, New South Wales, was one of the survivors. He served in the 20th Battalion and had been somewhat of a magnet for shrapnel and bullets. Three times he had been severely wounded in action. As a sergeant, McGill fought at Pozières and led digging parties under fire as they engaged the enemy. In May 1917, the then Second Lieutenant McGill was wounded at the 'blood tub' Second

Battle of Bullecourt, requiring an extended evacuation to hospital. Bullets had hit him in the arm and one had ripped through one cheek and exited the other. Fortunately, the bullet didn't hit his jaw. His son Barry McGill mused later in life that it was probably because he never stopped talking. It did blow out his teeth, though, and Tom wore dentures for the rest of his life.

At Ypres, in October 1917, Lieutenant Tom McGill received a serious gunshot wound to his left thigh and was again evacuated to Blighty, convalescing at the swish Prince of Wales Hospital (for Officers), Marylebone, London. As an oarsman and as a soldier, Tom was always determined to line up at the start and in January 1918 he was 'taken on strength' back to France with his beloved 20th Battalion, where he led night-time sorties into no-man's-land and again clashed with the enemy. Inevitably, on 8 April 1918, he was hit yet again, this time by artillery shrapnel. This time he spent months recovering in the AIF Le Havre Base Hospital before again returning to duty, pretty much resembling a human colander.

Arthur Valentine Scott, or 'Scotty', from Murray Bridge, South Australia had also survived. He had performed exemplary service in the 10th Field Artillery Brigade and was wounded in action at Pozières during the height of the fighting on 24 July 1916, then evacuated to the 1st District Base Hospital at Étaples.

Scotty had been promoted to lance corporal and then acting sergeant but then reverted back to corporal. He was considered a good soldier. Scotty had a penchant for the local mademoiselles and in early 1917 acquired a little trouble in the nether regions that kept him out of the line and in hospital for several extended periods. It was AIF policy that soldiers recuperating from venereal disease were docked pay for the time spent out of the line – they were hit where it most hurt, in the back pocket.

Scotty was transferred to the 11th Field Artillery Brigade in September 1917. In May 1918 at Agincourt, he refused to go up to the line when ordered, and stayed put. He was court-martialled but pleaded guilty, not bothering to fight it. The sentence was harsh. Scotty was reduced to the rank of gunner and sentenced to one year of hard labour in military prison, for showing a 'wilful display of defiance (to) a lawful command given personally by his superior officer in the execution of his office'.[1]

Archie Robb from Hobart, Tasmania had made it through too. He had served in the 12th Battery, 4th Field Artillery Brigade and, because he was mechanically handy, was soon promoted to fitter/sergeant. He had arrived in Alexandria just as Gallipoli was being evacuated and in March 1916 was shipped to Marseilles and the Western Front. Robb was transferred to the 2nd Divisional Artillery Column and worked for over a year with horse teams pulling artillery and ammunition limbers up to the firing lines.

One can imagine, as Robb pulled up to a line of active artillery in full fire and hitched guns to limbers to move to new positions, how deafening the noise would be, with the artillery dumping loads of 400 rounds of 18-pounder shells. Robb was then transferred back to the 4th Field Artillery Brigade and spent so much time around the 18-pounder guns that he ended up with severe concussion deafness. When the Armistice was signed, Archie was on leave immersing himself in the spectacular sights (but perhaps not the sounds) of Rome and its ancient wonders.

Fellow Tasmanian, good mate and stroke of the winning 1914 Interstate Championship Eight, Fred House from Sandy Bay, had also survived. He was an 'original' from Gallipoli, and had served with the big guns in the 3rd Field Artillery Brigade. At Pozières, the 3rd Field Artillery Brigade provided valuable assistance for the AIF 1st Division infantry, helping them to gain, hold and strengthen their objectives 'under cover of almost curtain fire by our artillery'.[2]

In Belgium during 1917, he had been gassed and evacuated to hospital and then returned to his unit. By mid-1918, Fred had been promoted from private to sergeant and in late 1918 was tapped on the shoulder for officer cadet school training, to receive a commission. While Archie was gallivanting in Rome, though, Fred spent his Armistice day flat out in a bed at Hampstead Military Hospital, diagnosed with renal colic.

A West Australian state representative oarsman, Gunner George William Mettam from Perth, survived. George Mettam volunteered on 8 May 1916, left Australia in September 1916, and was taken on strength in France on 21 July 1917 as an artilleryman in the 4th Field Artillery Brigade, then transferred to various heavy-duty siege batteries. Only a month after his arrival in France, he severely lacerated his hand and had to be transferred back to England for surgery. Mettam returned to France in November 1917, just in time for heavy artillery action around Steenwercke and Passchendaele.

Wily coxswain Albert 'Gig' Smedley, from New South Wales, had survived, too. As a teenager, Gig had coxswained plenty of rowing crews and knew how to get the best out of his club oarsmen. He served in the 22nd Field Artillery Brigade at Pozières and was mentioned in dispatches for 'good and gallant conduct in connection with the recent hard fighting round Pozières' and duly promoted, on 27 July 1916, to sergeant.[3] Gig's shooting skills were recognised, and he was sent to artillery school as an instructor at the Australian General Base Depot at Le Havre.

Syd Middleton's close friend and 19th Battalion comrade, Captain Keith Heritage, from Hobart, Tasmania – the 1912 Henley Royal Regatta Grand Challenge Cup winner, war hero, top bloke and champion oarsman – did not survive. Heritage had displayed great coolness and courage on the night of 25–26 June 1916 near Bois-Grenier. Helmetless, his face and hands blackened, he led an assault party accompanied by two raiding 'blocking parties', crawling across no-man's-land and into the enemy trenches, with the intention of collecting intelligence and taking prisoners. The raid went like clockwork and Heritage's force killed forty Germans and captured four prisoners. They would have had five prisoners but one irascible German 'caused trouble' and had to be summarily despatched.[4] Captain Heritage found a wounded digger when he returned to his line and singlehandedly carried him back to safety: 'Captain Heritage was the last man of the Raiding Party to leave the hostile trenches and he conducted the whole enterprise with coolness and such dash and was an excellent example to his men.'[5] Heritage was awarded the Military Cross for his actions and was mentioned in routine orders by the commander of the Anzac Corps, General William Birdwood.[6]

The 19th Battalion had only moved into Pozières on 24 July 1916. The ground all around Pozières was under constant gas attack and shell and machine gun fire, and had been churned into one flat, muddy morass of mulched blood and smashed infrastructure. On his rounds, Captain Heritage stumbled across two diggers who were totally exhausted and on the verge of falling asleep on guard duty. Heritage offered to keep watch for a couple of hours so they could sleep and handed them both some precious tins of rations. The soldiers ravenously scoffed the provisions, moved a few yards away and immediately fell asleep amidst the shrieking noise and shellfire. Heritage kept watch at his post until the inevitable happened: a high explosive artillery shell lobbed into his position and exploded, and a hot metal fragment struck him in the head, killing him almost instantly.[7]

Middleton was hit hard by his seemingly indestructible crewmate's death. Keith Heritage was one of a few distinguished diggers who served for Australia in the four separate theatres of the Great War: New Guinea, the Dardanelles, the Suez and the Western Front.

The effect that Pozières had on everyone, including all the oarsmen who experienced it, lived it and survived it, was deeply traumatic. The notion of the sanctity of human life had been stripped of all moral currency. One of the saddest orders issued from 1st Pioneer Battalion HQ during the action at Pozières read:

> The leaving of dead bodies in the trenches is an objectionable
> practice. Nearly every trench had numerous bodies or portions
> of bodies which from being walked in became covered with earth
> gradually they form an insecure footing and at all times lessen
> the cover available. Burial parties should patrol trenches and
> systematically remove such obstructions.[8]

The Pozières dead were reduced to mere 'obstructions', or farm fertiliser. Surviving Pozières with sanity intact was down to a blend of indomitable will and dumb luck – and if you survived, it wasn't necessarily lucky at all. The survivors of Pozières limped out of the war sporting battle scars and gas burns, full of lead, shrapnel and long-lasting psychological traumas that would manifest as 'shell shock', a condition not understood at the time as a form of post-traumatic stress disorder.

Within the ranks of these bent-but-not-broken, largely blue-collar soldiers, Middleton would find some of the AIF's finest rowing talent. But the last pieces of the puzzle would come from an even more unexpected quarter. As the men who would become Middleton's oarsmen were getting themselves shot, gassed, blown up or otherwise felled on the front lines, not far behind them another star oarsman was spending the war sewing soldiers back together.

9

Disher

Captain Harold Clive Disher, the youngest son of a wealthy grazier, was born in 1891 at Rosedale in Victoria and grew up on the family property. He attended Scotch College and rowed in the 1910 and 1911 Schoolboy Head of the River crews, then resided at Ormond College while he studied medicine at Melbourne University. He rowed for both Ormond College and the Melbourne University Intervarsity rowing eights. In 1914, Disher had represented Victoria at the Interstate Rowing Championships on the Yarra River.

Captain Disher volunteered for the AIF on 13 July 1917 and embarked from Melbourne on HMAT A32 *Themistocles* on 4 August 1917. After arriving at the Western Front on 16 October 1917, Disher's medical qualifications were in great demand and he was taken on strength with the 5th Field Ambulance on 1 November 1917 as a medical officer.[1]

Disher saw first-hand what the war could do to a man and saw more than his fair share of trauma as he treated and patched up the wounded. For a few weeks in February 1918, Disher was attached as regimental medical officer (RMO) to the 19th Battalion – a ship passing in the night with Major Syd Middleton, who had been posted to Aldershot, England to attend Officer Training School.

After taking some leave to England in March 1918, Disher was then attached to the 4th Field Artillery Brigade as RMO, where he saw out the rest of the war. During active service, the injury rate in artillery brigades was high. Even though artillerymen were very well drilled and trained, they did not experience the occupational health and safety standards that we have today. The work meant transporting artillery pieces and equipment that weighed several tonnes through deep mud – an extremely dangerous task in itself. Then there were horse-drawn limbers galloping at speed, hands caught in breech doors, dropped crates of ammunition – all enough to cause serious injury and precious time out of the line. And, of course, the artillery units always drew destructive return artillery fire from the enemy, which mangled and maimed men.

But Disher's work was not just about patching up battle injuries and wounds as they arrived from the casualty clearing station (CCS), though there was plenty of that. The RMO's primary role in an artillery brigade was looking after the health of the whole infantry brigade so that it remained fully functional, alert and highly effective. Preventative medicine was always better than cure. Thousands of twenty- to thirty-something men living crammed together usually meant a marked drop in personal hygiene. Throughout the war, disease and infection had been a massive problem for troops who slept in damp huts or in unsanitary front-line trenches – for example, 93 per cent of soldiers who survived a gut wound would later succumb to infection. Disease, viruses and infections could be as deadly as a high-explosive shell or bullet. All through 1918, Disher followed in the steps of Florence Nightingale, with monthly written reports on sanitation and hygiene.

When the wounded were dragged, stretchered, carried or hobbled out of the front line, the first place they would be taken was the regimental aid post (RAP), where they would be triaged as to whether they needed a quick patch-up and dressing (to remain on duty) or further medical intervention. By the time of the Great War, along with other scientific progress in medicine and surgery (such as antiseptics and anaesthetics), triage had developed into an essential and specialised emergency medical procedure for any mobilised army. RAPs were highly mobile medical units positioned close to the front line designed to handle a fast-flowing influx of wounded. From the RAP, the more seriously wounded were sent to the advanced dressing station (ADS), and from there they were sent on to the CCS, where the very seriously wounded were stabilised as far as possible and then carted further back to the relative safety of the rear lines by ambulance or motor lorry. Here Disher and teams of RMOs and nurses could medically intervene and perform surgery.

During 1918, gas warfare was very active, with gas shells often being fired at long range into the enemy. Apart from the obvious objective of incapacitating and killing, another aim was to keep the enemy wearing their gas masks, severely reduced their fighting capability. Many phosgene or mustard gas cases arrived at the 4th Field Artillery Brigade and Captain Disher had to make sure gassed blankets, contaminated with the residue of deadly phosgene particles, were regularly exchanged for clean ones. Apart from battle wounds, gassing and injuries, there were countless other outbreaks of sickness such as laryngitis, fever, trench foot and diarrhoea. In winter, there were many cases of frostbite and chilblains. There were also recurrent cases of rheumatism, venereal disease, and bronchitis and other respiratory ailments. There were pus-filled boils, scabies, and infections from lice or 'chats', which thrived in the stitching of coarse army uniforms, causing constant scratching that impacted on the efficacy of an army in the front line.

Fresh water was vital to keeping a brigade healthy. Disher's medical supervision included ensuring that all supply carts of fresh water delivered to the front line were boiled and chlorinated. Nothing was left to chance. Fly screens were secured on cookhouses and latrines, with the pits dug as deep as possible; camp drainage had to be in order; and even the horse manure dumps from the artillery stables were removed, as in hot weather 'they were a breeding ground for flies and disease'.[2]

By the middle of 1918, Captain Disher's efforts in raising the sanitation and hygiene standards of the 4th Field Artillery Brigade, combined with regular exercise and sporting competition, were having a positive effect on the health and fighting efficacy of the diggers. Disher reported:

There has been every facility for cricket, football and swimming
and the advantage of each of these has been made of good use
by the personnel ... There is a much better appreciation of the
importance of the A.A.M.C. [Australian Army Medical Corps]
work etc in the Brigade than there was at the end of last month
and I think a good relationship between the different branches of
the service has been properly established.[3]

By the Armistice, after almost a year spent patching up injuries and
tending the wounded in the rear lines, Captain Clive Disher couldn't
really tell the difference between war and peace anymore. He wrote
home describing his feelings about the Armistice:

It was all very quiet here things seemed to go on just the same.
I was on the boat crossing over when we heard + when the sirens
etc greeted us on our arrival there was not much excitement and
the armistice was hardly referred to in conversation. What feeling
there was one of thankfulness, but I doubt if we have quite
realized it yet for army life is much the same peace or war when
you are out of the line.[4]

In late 1918 and early 1919, the AIF troops were getting bored with
the confusion of repatriation and the long wait to go home, and the
rising incidence of pilfering from supply trains and the illegal shooting
of game in local forests was met with stern threats of court-martial.
The different AIF sports committees at inter-battalion and inter-
brigade levels attempted to distract, occupy and calm the diggers 'and
the amusements for the men [were] in good swing'.[5]

Meanwhile, as early as January 1919, the Americans, now firmly
ensconced in Paris for the Paris Peace Conference, were also calling
for entries for their Olympic-sized Inter-Allied Games, scheduled for
22 June – 6 July 1919. Already schedules and plans had been drawn up
for athletic events and the Americans began construction, within the
edge of the Bois de Vincennes, of a huge concrete stadium – Pershing
Stadium, named after US Army commander General John J. 'Black Jack'

Pershing – designed to hold an impressive 70,000 spectators. This was the American's gift to the French people, perhaps in return for an impressive copper sculpture that adorned New York Harbour, greeting Europe's poor, tired, and huddled masses, a gift from the French people in 1886.

Another Australian champion oarsman stranded in the middle of Europe by the Armistice could be found in the small village of Anseremme, Belgium. Lieutenant Harry Ross-Soden was a 1912 Olympic Games oarsman and one of the four Henley Royal Regatta Grand Challenge Cup winners to volunteer to fight for King and Country. Harry, a solicitor in civilian life, had joined on 21 September 1916 and embarked as a private from Melbourne aboard the HMAT *Ballarat* on 19 February 1917. He arrived in England on 26 April 1917 and spent almost all of the rest of 1917 training for the machine gun battalion and gaining his commission in Grantham, England. Second Lieutenant Ross-Soden arrived in France on 23 April 1918.

Just a month after his arrival at Camiers in France, Ross-Soden, who was attached to the 4th Machine Gun Battalion, fell ill and spent frequent intervals in and out of hospitals till the end of the war. No sooner was he declared fit than a few weeks later he would be readmitted to hospital without his painful condition ever being diagnosed.

Only after being transferred from the 1st Red Cross Hospital, Le Touquet to Wandsworth Hospital in England on 10 July 1918 was Harry diagnosed with a 'stone in Bladder'.[6] For the remainder of 1918, Harry was posted to depots at Tidworth and Sutton Veny. When he was finally fit enough, Harry Ross-Soden found himself in Belgium from January 1919 onwards sitting on various court-martial panels, trying to enforce military law and also acting as prosecutor.

> Life in this place is monotonous enough but very busy since I became Batt Q.M. as I have had extra jobs thrown on me ever since. That's the worst of being a success. I have been very busy with returning equipment of the unit … and have had to do the court martial work as well as there is no one else a solicitor or anyone with my Court Martial experience. I have also to prosecute in the trials.[7]

Already, there was a pervading sense that the Belgians and French were irritated about the British occupying their homelands. Many of the farming and working-class locals were concerned about rebuilding their communities, finding jobs and earning a decent living in a postwar world. They were also drawn to a new working-class ideology called Bolshevism, which was spreading west from its home in Russia faster than the Spanish influenza had been able to spread east. Writing to his brother Alf, who ran a sprawling rural family property, 'New Park', near Morundah in New South Wales, Ross-Soden highlighted his concerns:

> There are some latent Bolshevists round here who have been
> stealing & surreptitiously destroying property, and then blaming
> the Diggers. On top of this they have requested the authorities
> to have us removed, to leave the coast free for them to rise and
> 'Bolsh' but we are now to stay here for 5 or 6 weeks.[8]

The Australians were beginning to feel they had outstayed their welcome, and many among the AIF ranks were growing restless themselves. By mid-February 1919, there had been much movement at Horseferry Road and word spread around France and Belgium of the ambitious sports competitions the Sports Control Board had planned in England, pricking the ears of bored, energetic sportsmen. There was talk of inter-Allied rugby matches at Twickenham; cricket tests at Lords; a lawn tennis tournament at Wimbledon; and – music to the ears of any ambitious young oarsman – a rowing regatta at Henley.

With the Americans throwing their huge financial resources and manpower at staging their Inter-Allied Games, Syd Middleton recognised that he needed to ramp things up regarding the British games and, in particular, his passion for rowing.

As early as 1918, American leadership had begun to plan for the eventuality of battalions of well-armed, adventure-hungry Americans sitting idly in the middle of Europe, postwar. From Paris, the director of athletics, American Expeditionary Force (AEF), Elwood S. Brown wrote on 15 October 1918 to the general staff, GHQ, AEF:

Fundamentally our Army is a physical machine. Physical vitality
is the chief element, the most important asset. Two million men
are now engaged in the strenuous game of beating the Hun. They
are in hard daily labor, intensive military training or engaged in
actual fighting – physical expression, nearly all of it. When this is
suddenly taken away no mental moral or social program however
extensive will meet the need. Physical action will be the call;
games and play, informal and competitive, will be the answer.[9]

Not unusually for Americans, they were going to think big – really
big. It was going to be epic. Item number 4 in Elwood S. Brown's
proposal read:

A Military 'Olympic' would bring together the best athletes in
every sport from all the Allied Armies and would undoubtedly be
the greatest gathering of athletes ever seen.[10]

With the war still in progress, the Americans initially filed Brown's
proposal away, but kept it handy for when circumstances changed –
which they ultimately did.

The Americans lost no time inviting Allied countries to participate
in the games. They had been stoking interest with European and Middle
Eastern Allies since early January 1919.

One quarter of the 'Big Four' at the Paris Peace Conference, the
Italians, were exceptionally keen to rub shoulders with the Americans
and join the party. The Italian supreme commander, General Armando
Diaz, still basking in Italy's defeat of the Habsburg Army, eagerly
responded to General Pershing's personal invitation to participate in the
Inter-Allied Games:

It is also my opinion that to gather together in a friendly contest
the representatives of the courageous armies which contested
fraternally on the battlefield in a spirit of sacrifice and of military
virtue, would contribute to uphold and increase those bonds
of comradeship.[11]

The French had also caught the sports bug and announced plans to hold an inter-Allied rowing regatta on 27 April 1919, on the River Seine in the heart of Paris. Perhaps the Seine wasn't the ideal venue for a battle of top-class oarsmen, with its fast, meandering course and numerous stone bridges, but no one could deny it would be a spectacular venue. For the French, who had just had their backyard trashed by four years of war, it was the perfect opportunity to showcase Paris and, perhaps, show the world that what everyone had been dying and fighting for had indeed been worth saving.

10

Getting back into the boat

Middleton was knee-deep in organising the best international military competitions possible, but he quickly realised he couldn't do this on his own. He also recognised he was losing, at a very alarming rate, many good potential athletes and oarsmen on the transports heading back home. The make-up of the Sports Control Board panels was also often changing, with a revolving door of selectors, officials and administrators. A master tactician as always, Middleton decided he needed two things above all else: the right people to delegate responsibility to, and sporting events that would capture the hearts and minds of Australians everywhere. With that in mind, Syd was keen to promote team sports within the AIF. The British and dominion sports control boards were already determined to emphasise the 'amateur' spirit, and team sports that were a tradition in the British and dominion countries.

While the Americans were building their grand stadium in Paris, the British recognised they already possessed first-class sports venues, with a rugby stadium at Twickenham, rolled cricket pitches at Lord's, manicured lawn tennis courts at Wimbledon and a nice straight stretch of river ready to be rowed over at Henley.

Henley-on-Thames is a small town on the River Thames, nestled in a narrow valley that is rich, green and chocolate-box beautiful. Situated almost on the junction of the wealthy Buckinghamshire, Oxfordshire and Berkshire parishes, Henley-on-Thames is distinguished by the twin towers of religion and commerce: the church tower of St Mary the Virgin and the chimney stack of the local W. H. Brakspear & Sons brewery.

Grand, picturesque country estates such as Fawley Court or Phyllis Court dot one side of the riverbank and the town has a strong agricultural connection with the surrounding fertile, green fields. After the opening of the Great Western Railway rail link to Henley in 1857 and the burgeoning success of the regatta, the town expanded and by the time of the Great War it had become a fashionable riverside resort, and a desirable residence for the prosperous middle classes and professionals of London. By the end of the war, Henley – a haunt of the British elite – remained untouched by the deprivation and horror of war.

The contrast between the mud, blood and industrialised carnage of the fields and villages of the Western Front and the beautiful rolling manicured lawns, clean tarmac roads, well-kept manors and bucolic greenery of Henley could not be more pronounced. If the dead British and dominion oarsmen of the Great War had been promised a seat in a boat at the Valhalla for rowing, Henley-on-Thames would be the place. In summer, the flow of the River Thames is at its most gentle; sometimes it seems not to flow at all. The rhythm and mood of Henley town, just like the water, is slow-moving and mellow.

The Thames riverbanks around Henley, and the nearby towns of Marlow and Cookham, were reputedly the inspiration for Kenneth Grahame's much-loved characters of Ratty, Mole, Badger and Toad in *Wind in the Willows*, first published in 1908. Fawley Court, situated on the Henley Reach, was allegedly the inspiration for Toad Hall. As Ratty dreamily rhapsodised to Mole when he took Mole on his first boat ride, 'there is nothing – absolutely nothing – half so much worth doing as simply messing about in boats'.[1] Henley Reach is one of the few long – at one mile and a quarter – almost perfectly straight stretches of the River Thames: an ideal and natural home to the sport of rowing.

The very first 'Boat Race' between Oxford and Cambridge universities was held on Henley Reach in 1829 but only once, after Cambridge complained that it was too long a distance and that a more suitable 'middle ground' should be raced on the River Thames between Putney and Mortlake in London.

At the downstream end of the Henley Reach, at the start of the Henley Royal Regatta rowing course, is Temple Island. This island emerges from the river with its tall, luscious trees and garden surrounding an ornamental white 18th-century neo-romantic folly topped by a Romanesque cupola. In the 19th and early 20th century, the near Berkshire riverbank side of Temple Island was difficult to navigate – narrow, shallow and overgrown with reeds. On this Berkshire bank is the fecund flood plain of Temple Island Meadow, a large expanse of grassland perfect for Berkshire aristocrats to graze their dozy and fatted livestock. The steady downstream flow of the River Thames to London has naturally shaped – with a little human assistance – the leading point of Temple Island into a thin 'bow' which pushes against the flow and gives the impression that the island is slowly cruising upstream. For oarsmen, Temple Island splits the river into a secret playbook of complicating eddies and fast-flowing channels.

At the upstream end of the Henley Reach is the finish of the Henley Royal Regatta course. Here, sitting on the very edge of the river, is the red brick and slate-roofed township of Henley. The finish is 200 yards short of the 200-year-old, five-arched stone bridge which joins the well-to-do and genteel parishes of Buckinghamshire and Berkshire. Carved on the keystones, glowering over the stream from opposing sides of the bridge, are the stern faces of the river gods Isis and Tamesis, originating from Julius Caesar's expeditions to Britain in 54 BC, Egyptian and Greek antiquity all liberally mixed with doses of Anglo-Celtic folklore.

Located between the Henley Bridge and the finish line on the Berkshire side of the River Thames is what could be described as the grand boat-palace of rowing, the cossetted Leander Club. The Leander Club was first established on the Tideway, London in 1818 but then a clubhouse was built at Putney in 1866, and a newer, grander one on the Thames at Henley in 1897.

The dominance of the Leander Club on sport – any sport, but particularly rowing – cannot be overstated. Its pedigree and victories at the highest levels of rowing in international and Olympic competition are unsurpassed. As a single club, Leander has been more successful than whole countries. Just as the Marylebone Cricket Club cast a shadow over cricket, or the All England Lawn Tennis and Croquet Club ruled with conviction at Wimbledon, the Leander Club ruled the sport of rowing. Like its future mascot, the cerise hippo, the Leander Club was indisputably 'the king of the river'.

The idea of an annual rowing regatta on Henley Reach was first proposed by Mr W. P. Williams-Freeman and seconded by Captain Edmund Gardiner of Remenham Lodge at a public meeting attended by the good burghers of Henley on 26 March 1839 at the Henley Town Hall.[2] From the beginning, the regatta was both financially and socially driven. It would bring much-needed income into the local economy and provide the town with a 'source of amusement and gratification to the neighbourhood, and the public in general'. Because of the Reach and the gentle flow of the Thames during summer, Henley quickly found favour among oarsmen as a place to train and race, and spectators were drawn to the green beauty of Henley and also its convenient location, a mere 33 miles by road or rail from London.

The following year, the regatta was expanded to two days to accommodate more events, making it a nice little weekend escape to the country for London-based oarsmen and regatta spectators. The Henley Regatta continued to be a very well-attended event – these days often hosting up to 200,000 spectators over at least five race days – and firmly established itself as an integral part of the English summer sports calendar, along with Royal Ascot, Lord's and Wimbledon.

The regatta itself was organised and run by a small clique of rowing illuminati, the 'Henley Stewards', who worked with the local council to maximise attendance and manage the increasing scale of the event. Its fame was further increased when the Henley Regatta received royal patronage in 1851, after Queen Victoria's consort, Prince Albert, attended the regatta and agreed to become the royal patron. From then on, every reigning English monarch has also offered patronage, and with the exclusive 'Royal' inserted the regatta at Henley was transformed into the prestigious Henley Royal Regatta (HRR).

Over the years, interest in the regatta had increased and it had expanded from two to three and then four days of racing, with the workload of running the regatta ever-increasing. In 1881, the Henley Royal Regatta elected its first 'committee of management', consisting of twelve elected stewards. This original committee balanced well the virtues of church, state and industry with the election of Reverend E. Warre and Reverend R. W. Risley for the church, the Henley mayor for the state, and Mr W. H. Brakspear, owner of the local beer brewery, for business.

Since then, a committee of twelve powerbrokers had steered and shaped the Henley Regatta. For over 180 years, this committee has continued to instil the principles of fervent amateurism, upholding the rules of rowing racing and established durable, if opaque, appeal processes, dress regulations and regatta protocols. These rules have stood the test of time and have allowed the Henley Royal Regatta to prosper as a top-class rowing competition that combines elite oarsmen and -women with journeyman club oarsmen and -women, as well as university and school-level rowers. The close proximity of the boomed course, which at one point brushes the Berkshire riverbank, provides one of competitive rowing's closest viewing platforms for keen spectators.

During the Great War, nothing much to do with rowing happened in Henley. The River Thames had been requisitioned, and from a place of gentle aquatic recreation that ladies and gentlemen swanned across in punts it became a flowing artery of wartime economy and military-industrial river traffic. The long-running regatta fell fallow.

After the Armistice, the weight of war was lifted from the shoulders of a ravaged and grief-stricken England and its Allies. The thoughts of many British oarsmen turned to the question of what they could do next to move on from the grim red stain of the past and resuscitate the sport of rowing. The Leander Club, parked on the riverbank of the Thames at Henley, had wistfully watched the river, denuded of leisure boats, slip past its grand clubhouse for four long years.

Within twelve days of the signing of the Armistice, a letter appeared in country lifestyle magazine *The Field* urging the revival of Henley Regatta. The editor of the magazine, Sir Theodore Cook, also a Henley steward, wrote under the letter, 'We have received several communications on this subject, and shall have something definite to say about it shortly.'[3]

The Leander Club decided to 'summon a Meeting of the Officials of all Clubs affiliated to the Amateur Rowing Association and Regatta representatives', asking them to assemble in Henley on 22 January 1919. After the rowing club delegates stepped from their launches onto the hallowed turf of Temple Island and filed inside, the calls for the resurrection of the regatta began. Lieutenant-Colonel William 'Flea' Fletcher DSO moved the following resolution:

> That in the opinion of this Meeting, although it is not desirable
> that Henley Royal Regatta be held in 1919, an interim Regatta
> should be held at Henley in June or July, and that the Stewards of
> Henley Royal Regatta be requested to undertake the management
> of such Regatta.[4]

Very few of the stewards, if any, actually lived in Henley, so on 10 February 1919 the annual meeting of the stewards of the Henley Royal Regatta convened in London, with Colonel Frank Willan from Oxford University presiding, to appoint the 1919 committee of management who would consider Lieutenant-Colonel Fletcher's January motion: that the Henley Royal Regatta should be staged in July but in a reduced or 'interim' regatta format.

Perhaps with the devasting toll of dead oarsmen foremost in their minds, they also decided that in the proposed, modified Henley Regatta the Grand Challenge Cup for eights should not be contested.

However, the stewards were under instructions, likely from government or British Army authorities, to include races 'for crews composed of men who have served in the Home, Overseas, or Allies' Forces. The property and funds of the Stewards are to be used for this regatta.'[5] This posed an immediate problem: how were the stewards, after four years of no competition or generated income, to fund a major regatta for Allied crews without recent income, and with increasing expenses and inflation, without going into massive debt?

At their 10 February meeting, the Henley stewards duly elected to the Regatta committee of management the established rowing illuminati of Lord Desborough, Colonel the Viscount Hambleden, Colonel the Lord Ampthill, Mr F. I. Pitman, Mr R. C. Lehmann, Lieutenant-Colonel 'Flea' Fletcher DSO, Mr W. H. Eyre, Mr C. Gurdon, Mr W. D. Mackenzie, Captain C. T. Steward and Colonel H. G. 'Tarka' Gold OBE, with Colonel Frank Willan presiding.

The after-effects of the Great War, combined with a second wave of the Spanish flu, took a personal toll on the Henley stewards. During 1917, Captain W. F. C. Holland, a member of the Henley committee of management and 1891 Leander R.C. Grand Challenge winner, had died from a toe infection, the result of frostbite in the trenches. And four days after the 10 February meeting, Lieutenant-Colonel Fletcher DSO – a veteran winner of the 1891–93 boat races, rowing for Oxford University; 1891 Grand Challenge Cup winning crewmate of Captain Holland; explorer; big game hunter; and noted rowing coach – died, just six months short of his 50th birthday.

In early 1917, Fletcher had been commanding his battalion at Armentières when he was severely gassed. It was the second time deadly mustard gas had ever been deployed by the Germans. Fletcher was evacuated to hospital along with 456 men of his regiment. By mid-1918, Fletcher had resigned his own commission from the British Army and returned in July to England 'broken in health'.[6] As Spanish influenza swept through England and Europe again in 1919, 'Flea', with his weakened lungs, was one of many thousands of victims who sadly succumbed to the pandemic. Sir Theodore Cook wrote:

> he gave his life for his country no less surely, though more tardily, than if he had fallen on the field. It is no exaggeration to say his loss to the Henley Stewards and to the whole world of Rowing was irreparable.[7]

But death could not stop the wheels of the regatta turning and Mr G. D. Rowe was elected to replace Fletcher on the committee.[8] Exactly what shape or form this new 1919 Henley regatta would take would require further careful planning and fortnightly meetings, but the important thing was that the regatta was now officially on.

Middleton understood that for an AIF crew to row the Henley Regatta in peacetime would be a victory for morale like no other. He pulled in Major Eric Tulloch, a Victorian representative oarsman perhaps a few years past his prime, to take charge of the rowing eight selection. Tulloch trawled through potential AIF rowing candidates and sent out telegrams advising them that they were up for consideration. West Australian state representative oarsman Gunner George Mettam received a cable from Administrative HQ at Horseferry Road: 'You will be interested to know that a start should be made very shortly and we will probably be asking you to come to Headquarters for trial and training purposes.'[9]

This would have been an irresistible offer for any oarsmen worth his salt. It was also said that King George V himself was going to be presenting specially commissioned gold trophies to the winners. Already the idea of 'international' sport competitions among the best athletes the AIF possessed was taking hold and piquing interest. But getting reliable information in a premodern media world was extremely difficult. Like many diggers in Europe, Harry Ross-Soden had to rely on the hollow words of those in charge and hope there was some truth to what they were being told about their increasingly uncertain future.

> I have not heard any more about the crews that the AIF were
> intending to enter for Henley in June next ... if the crews turn
> out to be good enough, they may be kept together as crews and
> brought home via Canada and USA competing against local and
> international crews in each country. Of course, it's only a very
> base chance – but still 'hope rises eternal etc.'[10]

On 28 February, Brigadier-General Dodds, the first president of the Sports Control Board, took early repatriation and was replaced by Brigadier-General T. H. Griffiths, who took command of the AIF

Administrative Headquarters. Even though it was, at times, difficult for Middleton to maintain continuity while implementing his sports program, he now had a direct ear at the highest levels of command. He capitalised on this and started to pull strings in order to get the men he needed for his competitions to work. He immediately set about wiring direct his vast personal network of sportsmen scattered throughout the AIF in France, Belgium, Egypt and the Middle East. Getting into contact with all his old rowing mates, such as Harry Ross-Soden from the 1912 Grand Challenge and Olympic Games, was a top priority.

After quite a deal of sleuthing, Syd Middleton eventually tracked Ross-Soden down.

> A few days ago, I received a wire from Sid [sic] Middleton asking
> if I were available to organise crews for Henley 1919 under the
> AIF Sports Control Board in London. I got the CO's consent to
> answer 'yes' and am now awaiting a call to London any day.[11]

He was given a transfer as 'selector of Rowing teams' on 28 February and caught up with his old crewmate Syd at Horseferry Road on 5 March 1919.[12]

By early March 1919, Middleton's selection plans and rounding up of athletes was drawing in good numbers of men from throughout the AIF. With the support of General Monash and many other top-brass officers, Middleton was pulling rank far above his status and possibly at times putting noses out of joint – but things were moving. Back in Australia, the *Referee* noted:

> To judge by the cable messages coming through from London,
> the efforts made by the AIF controllers of sport to arrange a
> series of contests in all branches of sport for the men awaiting
> embarkation for Australia is meeting with success. In this matter
> the military authorities disclose a shrewd idea of what is best to
> keep the men occupied mentally and physically, so that neither
> stagnation nor discontent shall manifest itself during the irksome
> waiting period.[13]

Athletes from all fields of competition were submitting their sporting credentials to the Sports Control Board and then, after a paper selection, were ordered to catch the ferry and transports from Le Havre and report for 'duty' at the Sports Section at 130 Horseferry Road. Over 200 diggers applied just to the Rowing Section. There, the authority would fact-check a sportsman's credentials. If, after being tried out, it was found a digger wasn't up to scratch, 'he was marched out to one of the camps for repatriation.'[14]

Also languishing in Europe in early March 1919, in the small Belgian town of Thuin, was Captain Disher. He was extremely frustrated with the work of endless medical assessments and writing medical reports for the men on the draft home. What had been 'home' to the men for the last three years – the 4th Field Artillery Brigade – was now feeling less and less so.

Brigades and units were halving and halving again, folding into fewer and fewer holding units. The frequent farewells at the railhead station to departing AIF members were becoming increasingly fraught and emotional as friendships disappeared into the long, complicated journeys home. Doubts and uncertainties continued about the ambitious demobilisation plans. The weather was cold, miserable and often snowing. The flu was claiming many lives. There was the persistent allure of Australia – but not at the expense of languishing in cold and cramped AIF base depots in England. Disher wrote:

> Some weeks ago, the authorities asked for particulars of sporting
> records of members of the AIF ... A few days ago, a wire
> came through asking if I was available to go to England for
> International rowing. I replied that I was desirous of going ...
> but I don't want to go over and not get in to the crew and then
> be sent to some camp in England. I should muchly prefer to stay
> over here if that is the case.[15]

11

Putney

By January 1919, the conditions on the streets of England weren't pretty. The winter was one of the coldest on record and the Spanish flu was back with a vengeance. Miners, dockers, seamen and even the police were striking for higher wages, and the effects were also evident in the British Army. The mutinies and growing dissatisfaction of British soldiers who had not yet been demobilised were spreading to seaports at Folkestone and Dover as early as 3 January 1919. At the port of Southampton, 5000 British soldiers took over the docks and refused to board a transport bound for France to enforce the Armistice and man the Army of the Rhine. Fortunately, the mutiny was resolved bloodlessly but the agitation of the frustrated British troops – agitation that could boil over to outright violence – did force Winston Churchill, newly appointed Secretary of State for War, to introduce his own 'first in, first out' demobilisation plan.[1]

Finding jobs for the 3.5 million men was always going to be a tall order. The women who had filled in for the lack of 'manpower' in factories, business and industry were now being squeezed out and back into domestic roles to make way for the millions of demobilised British soldiers. As Winston Churchill said:

The victory will be absolutely barren if we are not able to bring
our soldiers quickly home to active conditions of industry and
employment; if we are not able to place British industry on the
peace field with every advantage to resume its productive energies;
if we are not able to deal fairly and reasonably and in such a
manner as to leave no legitimate feeling for soreness and resentment
behind with that great mass of men and women, particularly
women, upon whose faithful endeavors munitions for the British
armies has been based. We owe it to our soldiers to make good
arrangements which will secure their position on their return.[2]

The switch to a peacetime economy was always going to be difficult.
The wartime economy had been geared to mass-produce tanks, guns,
warships, munitions and weapons. Now industry needed to refit and
recalibrate its industrial machinery and engineering to produce less
lethal domestic products.

There were food shortages and long queues of people waiting on
the cobblestone streets of London hoping for rations of butter, which
remained rationed until 1920. Many people were eking out a meagre
living on the mean streets of London and a sense of civilian unrest was
steadily growing. The British government was perceived to be overly
focused on international treaties and securing their place in the new
world order. Churchill continued:

Our only wish is to help industry and labor to cross from one
side of the road to other – from the war side to the peace side –
with a minimum of disturbance and anxiety.[3]

The oarsmen, returning from a hellscape of mud and death to the
manicured gardens of England, must have wished for the same thing.

The temporary billets for the first oarsmen reporting for duty at the
Sports Section were situated in the central district of Warwick Square,

101

not far from the AIF Headquarters in Horseferry Road but some distance from the established and more genteel rowing community of Putney. Throughout the war the district around Warwick Square and Horseferry Road had gained a reputation of ill-repute, as 'a hot bed of immorality, undisguised and unchecked ... Prostitutes of all types and ages ... parade the streets and loiter [on] the corners',[4] ready to solicit the Australian diggers. Middleton likely thought the sooner he could find accommodation at Putney, the sooner the Rowing Section could focus solely on their rowing.

The stretch of the River Thames between Putney and Richmond was the home of rowing for many of the big, established rowing clubs of London, but it didn't always provide good water. The Thames at Putney was affected tidally by the North Sea and could rise and drop 23 feet twice a day. In parts it could get quite rough, thanks to notorious fast-running streams or channels. Perhaps without having toughened his hands yet, Major Alan Audsley, who had recently arrived at Putney, wrote, 'Rowing against the tide on the Thames is rather strenuous as she comes in and out at a rate of knots.'[5] An English oarsman with local River Thames knowledge always paid attention to the direction of the stream as they headed out to row – unless he was a glutton for punishment. If he set out in the wrong direction, he would face a tough row back against a steady tidal flow.

Towards the Richmond end, the Thames is sectioned by a series of locks that help mediate the more dramatic tidal rises and ebb tides. This part of the Thames makes conditions for rowing slightly more genteel and leisurely.

The travel between Warwick Square and Putney Embankment, where the squad would train, was logistically awkward as it required either busing the squad back and forth or a thirty-minute trip on the London Underground. Even though uniformed AIF men could be issued rail warrants for free travel, the prospect of them dribbling into the rowing shed in ones and twos and threes meant precious time lost on the water.

Middleton came up with the idea of conveying the whole squad to Putney for training by motor launch.[6] But any daily commute was not ideal. As every good rowing coach knows, 'miles make champions', and every ten minutes lost getting to or from training meant a mile on the water. The best option was to have the Rowing Section live together, train together and bond together as a national AIF crew.

Finding suitable accommodation around Putney was another major problem for Middleton, on account of the entire Welsh Guards regiment being billeted in the Putney district. Food shortages and expenses ballooned by inflation also compounded the issue.

It was just one more problem in a never-ending barrage for Middleton. He was working himself into the ground to get all the rugby, cricket, rifle shooting, golf, tennis, athletics, boxing and rowing events up and running. The pressure to organise and convene all the AIF sports once again took a toll on his health, and he was soon burnt out again.

On 3 February, Middleton was admitted to the Third London General Hospital in Wandsworth. His condition was listed as 'NYD': 'not yet diagnosed'. Middleton was suffering from acute bouts of depression and psychological trauma stemming from the Great War. The medical authorities still did not know much about the traumatic effects of industrialised war, but the term 'shell shock' had been in use from the early days of the war; the trauma so many men were experiecing was thought to be caused by the actual concussive effects of nearby explosions that caused a 'commotion' in the brain, which was literally 'shocked' by the exploding shell. What was worse for Middleton was that he considered his debilitating stress-related illness and fragile mental health a sign of personal weakness.

The last thing he wanted was for Marion to see him in such a state. Perhaps he recalled her initial dismissive treatment of him as a patient at Le Tréport. He forbade her to visit as he wallowed in self-pity and obsessed about neglecting his duty to his AIF athletes and rowing squad. He later wrote, '... and when I was damned ill at Wandsworth I thought it my duty not to let you come to me as I wanted you so very badly to do.'[7] Bouts of post-traumatic depression were to dog Middleton for many years. He stayed in Wandsworth Hospital for almost three weeks. When he was released and returned to the Sports Section on 25 February, he found the rowing program barely functioning.

The Sports Control Board had missed Middleton's drive and hard-nosed, take-no-prisoners attitude. And conditions for the oarsmen at this point were not ideal: some of them 'are rationed and living with the football team, eight are living on subsistence allowance, and seven are able to remain on duty and row as required by coaches during the afternoon'.[8] Warwick Square did have its benefits, being close to the bustling London West End social scene and entertainment, but the oarsmen were here to row and not to gad about. They were in desperate need of accommodation close to Putney so that training could be more efficient and the oarsmen more accessible.

Major Middleton had already approached the prestigious London Rowing Club (London R.C.) – situated on Putney Embankment on a boulevard crowded with established rowing clubs, boat builders and waterside workers – about using their facilities as the training base for the AIF rowing squad. The London R.C. 'shed' was (and still is), despite the name, an impressive, three-storey red-brick building. The clubhouse balcony overlooks the Thames, which is literally a stone's throw away – a little further at low tide. London R.C. was home to many graduates of Oxford and Cambridge universities, including its president, and Henley steward, Lord Ampthill, and its membership included many alumni businessmen and professionals such as lawyers, bankers and other captains of industry and commerce.

The committee of the London R.C., still reeling from the culling of their active rowing membership as a result of the war, had no objection. These London rowing clubs were experiencing the same high inflation and rising costs as the Australians. *The Times* wrote:

> the increased cost of everything caused by five years of war
> applies equally to rowing. To purchase, hire, and upkeep boats
> of all kinds has always been a considerable item on the books
> of clubs ... It is essential if we are to maintain the undoubted
> advantages of English national games, that all forms of
> sport should be within the reach of everyone, and of all the
> English games in which teams are engaged rowing is one of
> the most expensive.[9]

The New Zealand and Canadian rowing squads were also training from Putney Embankment and the international flavour along the boatsheds was generating quite a lot of interest from the locals, who frequently gathered on the bank to watch the oarsmen row. The London R.C. building had multiple boat bays, a grand boardroom, on-site accommodation – already booked by the smaller Canadian squad of oarsmen – and they had centre-seated training boats and oars.

Thus began a period of British and dominion détente, in which Putney became quite cosmopolitan. The English rowing clubs extended much assistance to the foreigners, but always with an eye to getting their accounts back into the black.

The New Zealanders had hired the Thames Rowing Club facilities a few doors down from London R.C., where, it could be argued, the squads could keep a close eye on each other. The AIF rowing squad was also making good use of the Thames Rowing Club's indoor rowing tank to assist 'in the blending of styles'.[10] As far as the Putney rowing clubs were concerned, it was good to receive some much-needed income from the hiring out of their boats, accommodation and facilities to the dominion crews, as well as to see their rowing boats back out on the Thames tideway where they belonged.

12

Gathering the oarsmen

From early March 1919, Middleton's old 1912 Olympic crewmates were arriving to take their place as rowing squad selectors, stand-by coaches, administrators and managers.

Harry Ross-Soden had arrived in early March to assist and take an active role in the administration but he was also keen to step back into the boat as an oarsman. In the spirit of Australian interstate détente, Middleton appointed Major Eric W. Tulloch, a Victorian ex-representative oarsman, as officer commanding of the Rowing Section, and he assumed the role of stand-in coach and manager. In the early stages of coaching, Major Tulloch was able to take a lot of the work off Middleton's shoulders. Assisting Major Tulloch on a rowing subcommittee were Lieutenants Oswald J. 'Ossie' Wood, the prewar secretary of the New South Wales Rowing Association, and the ever-dependable Harry Ross-Soden.

For this subcommittee, 'the chief difficulty at the beginning was to keep the best men in England. They had been away from their homes for long periods, and were, naturally, anxious to return. This, of course, was a difficulty not peculiar to the AIF.'[1]

Lieutenant Harry Hauenstein had also arrived at Horseferry Road in early March and immediately made his dogged presence felt at the

AIF Sports Section. Harry had also brought his brother Lieutenant Dennis 'Paddy' Hauenstein along to try out.

Paddy was a competent oarsman but a much better rugby player, and lived in his brother's distinctive shadow. When Harry started rowing at Leichhardt R.C., Paddy also joined. Harry joined the NSW police, and Paddy did too, and was made a probationary constable on 23 April 1908. But Paddy didn't seem suited to policing – he was newly married and with a growing family, and perhaps found the work too taxing – and he resigned on 11 March 1910.[2] After that he was forever in search of labouring work to support his wife Grace and three children.

Syd Middleton knew that if the AIF were to have any chance of success at Henley, Harry Hauenstein – who had a reputation for being outspoken and headstrong – was a necessity. His expertise was needed for crew selection. Ideally, he would row in the boat. If that meant Paddy would tag along, then so be it.

Hauenstein's arrival meant some potential conflict of ego between him and Middleton. The two big men from the 1912 Henley Grand Challenge weren't shrinking violets and there was arguably some bad blood between them, connected to a controversy involving the Australian Olympic rowing team at Stockholm. A crucial decision about the final selection of the Stockholm Olympic crew had been unilaterally made by Syd's older brother, Bill Middleton, as Australian crew coach. The crew suffered a surprising defeat in the Olympic rowing event, losing to Great Britain, and this led to much press speculation, private recriminations and a degree of simmering personal grievance among members of the Australian crew. But a war had happened since then, and Middleton probably thought that ill-feeling and long-held grudges would dissipate in a world eager to forgive and forget and make peace.

There was a steady stream of AIF oarsmen reporting for rowing duty and there was certainly a great sense of excitement and anticipation in the air, peppered with doubts about rowing ability and whether this confluence of oarsmen would get on, and work together.

During February and March, many oarsmen, all with state representative experience, were trialled: Captains G. E. Gill,

W. G. Gordon and Lieutenants H. K. Goyen, G. M. Muirhead, M. F. Willey, Warrant Officer R. J. Clarke, Sergeant A. A. Pitt, Mr G. A. Rogers, Trooper J. A. Jonsson and Corporal Coghill. Major Tulloch soon had the oarsmen out training on the Thames for at least two sessions a day. The aim was to select a rowing squad of two crews of eights (plus coxswains); a four-man boat, sans coxswain; a pair-oar boat; a single sculler; and some 'emergencies' to fill in or replace any injured crewman.

All up, the final racing squad would consist of between twenty-four to thirty oarsmen – a lot of musclebound men, and few resources to feed them with. Initially, the squad had at their disposal one eight-man clinker training boat, on loan from London R.C., so the crews switched and swapped in various seating combinations during the many morning and afternoon shifts on the water. Though Tulloch's representative rowing days were well and truly behind him, he ran a fairly tight program and jumped into the boat when required.

If the electric coaching launch, affectionately dubbed 'Thelma', was unavailable, Tulloch could often be seen pedalling furiously on a bicycle along the Putney Embankment towpath, following his crew, steering with one hand and yelling through a loudhailer held in the other. This type of training proved exhausting and dangerous for both coach and oarsmen, and the parade of trialling oarsmen sent out onto the water, hoping to make the cut, but sent back to their units at times resembled a fast-revolving door.

Middleton was missing one other vital ingredient for success at Henley: the right man to fill the 'stroke' seat of the AIF No. 1 eight-man crew. In rowing, the stroke seat is often regarded as the prime seat in the boat – the most glamorous even, if there could ever be a glamorous seat in a rowing boat. If anyone is to lead a crew, it is more often than not the stroke man, and they do so from the rear. From their position in the stern, the stroke sets the rhythm and pace of the rowing stroke for the crew. Everyone else in the boat must observe and follow.

A curiosity of the stroke seat is that the occupant can see no one else in the boat bar the coxswain sitting in the cockpit opposite, face encased by the helmeted loudhailer. At times, the eye contact between a stroke and a coxswain is meaningful enough that it can make the difference between winning and losing a race. It can be incredibly intimate – but more often just downright uncomfortable. Each attempts to look elsewhere if at all possible. In between breaths and with gritted teeth, the stroke grunts orders to the coxswain, who relays those orders (with his or her own intuitive reinterpretation) to the rest of the crew.

The stroke, with their natural confidence in their own physical ability, tactile sensitivity, incredible insight into rowing nuances and innate power to 'use the force' within the boat, can usually identify every single instance of bad technique, bad posture, bad timing and 'trouble' behind them. A good stroke can sense a problem somewhere among the crew without having to actually observe it. To sit in, to ease into, to possess, to 'own' the stroke seat requires a special talent akin to a sixth sense.

Middleton had a particular stroke in mind, someone with the talent to bring the ragged, disparate parts of the rowing crew together into one cohesive engine. Word had reached him of Captain Clive Disher, the young interstate representative oarsman from Victoria and Melbourne University stroke man.

When Clive Disher had rowed for Victoria at the 1914 Interstate Eight-oared Rowing Championships on the Yarra River, Victoria he was in the number 6 seat, and the crew came a disappointing fourth place to the able Tasmanian crew with the talented Fred House on stroke, with his 'wing man' Archie Robb backing him up in the number 7 seat. Maybe Disher felt that his not being stroke was the reason the crew didn't perform as well as they could.

Middleton had made numerous approaches through all the official channels open to him to have Disher released from his important medical duties in France for more important rowing duties in London. He expressed his disappointment to the Sports Control Board members:

There is an absence of candidates for the stroke seat and this might prove a very serious difficulty. Disher cannot be spared from France and from what is known of his record in Australia he is the most likely man to fill the vacancy.[3]

But Middleton wasn't going to give up easily, even if it meant going all the way up to Disher's fellow Scotch College alumnus General Sir John Monash.

13

Making the cut

At the same time, in early March 1919, a hopeful and wide-eyed oarsman from South Australia, Gideon Maurice Penny, who had responded to Middleton's call for oarsmen to trial, arrived at the Sports Control Board HQ and bumped into old railway workmate and fellow Murray Bridge club oarsman Arthur Scott. Scotty, always streetwise and a fast learner, quickly took Penny in hand and, keen to get a fellow Murray Bridge oarsman into the mix, wasted no time introducing him to the formidable AIF Rowing Section selectors:

> Scotty had only arrived a few days earlier, but had been on a
> couple of trial rows, he knew a couple of the administrators
> who had rowed interstate at home and to whom I had to report.
> Scotty took me along, but I learned that these four high ranking
> officers were members of the first Australian Crew in 1912
> to compete, and winners of the Challenge Eights, Henley on
> Thames, and later runners up in Olympics at Stockholm. After
> this I was beginning to think I would be out of my depth, when it
> came to oarsmanship with only my maiden performance at home
> and only one season in competitive rowing.[1]

Middleton thought he pretty much knew the location of all the oarsmen in the AIF who had the requisite experience and first-class form. He was personally wiring oarsmen and putting together the official transfer paperwork. Many athletes were split between the emotional pull of family, wives and girlfriends and the attraction of world-class competition. To stay was to enjoy a once-in-a-lifetime opportunity: to have the resources, facilities and high level of competition, without having to spend eight weeks travelling by sea to compete. The lure of international competition was especially compelling for those who were not married, had no dependants or were undecided about their future career. It wasn't a given, though, and Middleton missed out on many of his hopefuls. Through choice or clerical error, some top-class Interstate Championship representative oarsmen returned home as soon as possible. For many the call of home was too strong to resist.

To fill the gaps, Middleton was still scoping the AIF for potential oarsmen. He tracked down a current member of the Sydney Rowing Club, the recently promoted Major William 'Alan' Audsley, who had represented New South Wales in the 1913 Interstate Eight-oared Rowing Championships and backed up as an 'emergency' for the 1914 NSW crew. Major Audsley was well connected and on his way up in military circles. The young major, aged twenty-six, thought his time in London the perfect opportunity to socialise, enjoy his new rank, attend the theatre, reacquaint himself with extended family and further his army career. Single, and relishing his new-found status as a major, he was intrigued by the idea of rowing at Henley.

> On the 10th a cable came to HQ to ask if I could be made available to row in the Australian crew for Henley and of course they wired back to say yes ... I left Lobbes on Saturday and arrived in London on Sunday afternoon, reported on Monday morning and had my first row on Monday afternoon. They have some jolly fine oarsmen here and the eight is going to take some getting into ... It will be a grand experience because it will be the biggest Henley regatta held so far and the race is open to all the Allies.[2]

Middleton continued to search for suitable digs in Putney so that more time could be spent on the water rather than commuting back and forth from the possible salacious distractions of Warwick Square and Westminster. The sport of rowing demands close-knit teamwork and strict discipline to maintain and rig a boat, get the boat onto the water and then work hard in any conditions and for hours on end in stressful conditions. If the rowing squad was going to work and improve together, Middleton felt they would need to get to know each other and develop a deep sense of camaraderie. Consider as well that these men had just stepped out of the deadliest war the world had ever seen. Middleton likely foresaw that the best support for these oarsmen, these survivors, would be found in each other.

The approach of a sports 'camp' is how many elite sports squads today also train. Rowing camps held upon accessible and exotic stretches of water have been an essential part of rowing training for years. The water at Putney wasn't exactly exotic, though. The weather was unpredictable, as a freezing winter refused to turn into a beautiful spring. However, nothing was going to stop training, not even snow squalls. In a letter to family, Audsley wrote:

Had about a 10-inch fall of snow here the night before last, rather unusual for London and yesterday we rowed in a bit of a snow storm. Ugh! It was cold.[3]

Towards late March, Middleton eventually found what he was looking for in Oak House, a freestanding mansion situated on Putney Hill and large enough to accommodate his rapidly growing AIF rowing squad. The fact that the oarsmen would be piling into a large share household created a fair degree of excitement and expectation among the selected oarsmen. The prospect of not living in stuffy officer clubs, basic barracks or tented camps was also a definite bonus. The mood among the oarsmen was convivial and joyous. Finally, they had something to be happy about. Audsley informed his mum and dad:

It is a bonza old place with about 20 rooms in it, and a decent garden belongs to Sir – somebody or other … it is in a good situation on the top of Putney Hill and about 10 minute's [sic] walk to the boatsheds and we all should be a happy family and comfortable here.[4]

By now, many diggers felt a kind of affinity for England. The AIF survivors had been fighting in France and Belgium for four long years; they had taken frequent leave to England, met mates at the Anzac Buffet in London, attended the theatre in Soho, trained in its officer cadet schools based in Oxford, Cambridge or Aldershot, and visited, like excited schoolboy tourists, the famous sites of Big Ben, Trafalgar Square, Richmond Common, the British Museum, Buckingham Palace, Windsor Castle and Westminster Abbey, to name a few. Of course, there were those unlucky diggers who'd spent miserable months in training depots and bleak, wet and windy camps at Sutton Veny on the Salisbury Plains, but for many, England was the Mother Country and a place they felt they knew. The imperial causes of the King and 'Mother England' were also at the heart of the reason they were there fighting in the first place.

By the beginning of April 1919, most of the oarsmen had now reported for duty and been trialled, and those selected for the squad were now encamped in Oak House. There was a great sense of anticipation; they were free of rigid parades and drills and dull military routine. When Gig Smedley arrived at Oak House, he proudly showed off his newly tailored suit, tie, vest, hat and patent leather shoes. A South Australian oarsman, Gunner William 'John' Begg, had arrived kitted out in an equally dapper three-piece suit – perhaps a more familiar form of dress from his prewar occupation as an accountant. Together, Gig and Begg posed like silent movie stars on the steps of Oak House, smiling with relief that they had made the cut. Other oarsmen also clowned around for photographs on the Oak House steps, forming an amusing gymnastic tower of faces, dressed in their army uniforms, with mischievous Gig perched high on top. Tom McGill, Scotty, George Mettam, Archie Robb and Fred House had also settled in and were to add some much-needed, long-term backbone to the squad.

As a group, the oarsmen delighted in strolling on the thick lawn of a peaceful suburban London backyard, surrounded by garden and vegetable plots. The stark difference between living in a dugout at the Front and their new digs at Putney couldn't have been more chalk and cheese. The AIF Sports Control Board even supplied an army cook and a steady stream of groceries and fresh garden vegetables.

In this brave new world of peace, there would be no need for rank or military hierarchy. What would determine one's worth and earn respect from among the oarsmen was going to happen on the water.

The Australian style

Captain Clive Disher had initially welcomed the idea of rowing with the AIF but after several delays in getting a response from the Sports Control Board in London, the medical authorities thought he was better kept in Belgium fulfilling his medical duties, and refused permission. Frustrated, Disher began to lose interest in rowing, fearing that his late arrival in the squad would cruel his chances of making the cut. He wrote:

> the SSMS Corps (the head medical man over here) refused to let me go. Can't say I like the gentleman. The Sports people have wired over to London now and I will probably go along presently but with a crew it is so difficult to break in to it when they have once started ... However, if they want me, I am here and quite willing to go tomorrow.[1]

On 26 March, Captain Disher was finally granted leave from his brigade to undertake what he believed to be further medical training and departed Thuin for London. He left with instructions to make his way to Le Havre for the channel ferry, and to report to AIF

Administrative HQ at 130 Horseferry Road when he arrived in London. After a dreadfully rough ferry ride across the English Channel – Disher thought he would die from seasickness – he recovered enough overnight to report for duty the next day.

Having by now given up on any idea of rowing, Disher presented himself to the Medical Section, hoping to further his medical career with either an attachment to a top-class London hospital or postgraduate medical study.

The Medical Section must have scratched their heads when Disher lobbed into their office asking for orders. The medico adjutants ruefully informed him that, by their records, he wasn't required for duty here at all, but rather down the hall and around the corner at the Sports Section. Disher wasn't happy and he told them so. Nothing much they could do, they replied, and pointed him down the hall. Fuming, Disher strode down to the Sports Section, and into room 38, where Middleton worked. Major Middleton, sitting behind his desk, silenced Disher mid-sentence and airily dismissed his concerns. As Disher described it:

> Well I have landed myself in the soup this time. I went down to
> Headquarters on the 27 (March) and saw the Medical Authorities
> who though I told them I had come over to do some work told
> me they thought the rowing people wanted me. I wasn't very keen
> about it, but I went around to see them and was almost clasped
> around the neck and was carted off that afternoon to Putney to
> row stroking the crew.[2]

Although Middleton wasn't going to row himself, exhausted as he was by his workload, it was clear he was going to take special interest in who was in the squad and how the squad was run. With his hands finally on the fabled Victorian rowing prodigy, Middleton immediately shanghaied Disher into the Rowing Section and Disher reluctantly went along, unable to talk himself out of his predicament. It's likely Middleton, who had a staff car at his disposal, drove Disher straight to London R.C. that afternoon, briefly introduced him to the rest of the squad and immediately stuck him in the boat as stroke. Fred

House, the stroke of the victorious 1914 Interstate Tasmanian eight, who had up until this time been stroking the Rowing section's No. 1 boat, was bumped – possibly without too much fuss but with some guarded suspicion – into the number 3 seat to make way.

House probably wanted to size up the upstart, who hadn't even introduced himself, and make his own assessment as to what he was like as an oarsman. Middleton would have thought the whopping £2 to hire the coach's launch definitely worth it to see how the new boy – who had likely talked himself up – would perform in his first hit out.

When he settled into the stroke seat, he probably thought he had it in the bag. He had always excelled at rowing and made the cut for every crew he tried out for. But Disher's first row as stroke was a disaster.

To say that Middleton was disappointed and deflated would be putting it mildly. After Disher and the crew returned to the Putney Embankment and put away the boat, Disher was immediately told in no uncertain terms by Middleton – and also in all likelihood by Harry Hauenstein, who had been rowing in the number 5 seat – that his interloping Victorian style just wasn't going to cut it. Middleton had already made it clear to the rowing squad that the 'Australian' style was the method the new squad would use. It had been pioneered by Sydney Rowing Club and former NSW state representative stroke man Roger Fitzhardinge, as well as by Syd's older brother and former Australian rowing coach Bill Middleton, and championed by the 1912 Grand Challenge crew. Disher lamented:

> I think I rather disappointed them as the coach told me that my style was the very latest Victorian Style but was not suitable for stroking this crew as they came from almost every state + the New South Wales Style being about the medium of the styles they would have to adopt it. So, I am put back to 6 to learn the NSW Style ... but can't say I am taking much interest in it. Getting too old for rowing though nothing would please me better than to stroke the AIF crew at Henley on Thames or a seat in it should be quite an honour. It remains to be seen whether I can change my style quickly enough for me to be of use for them as stroke.[3]

By early April, the Rowing Section at Putney had culled its numbers and settled on a core group of roughly twenty-five to thirty oarsmen, including hangers-on and managers, out of more than 200 who had stepped forward. This core group was from all over Australia (barring Queensland), demonstrating Middleton's policy of searching far and wide to gather the best athletes possible. Beside Captain Harold 'Clive' Disher, Victorians were well-represented, with Major Eric Tulloch MC, Lieutenants Lyndsey 'Lyn' Davis, Harold 'Nip' Newell, L. Armstrong, J. 'Chung' Howieson and H. Soward, and Trooper J. Jonsson making the cut. From New South Wales were Major Alan Audsley, Lieutenants Harry Hauenstein MM, Tom McGill, Dennis 'Paddy' Hauenstein and Oswald 'Ossie' Wood, Sergeants Eric J. Harrison and Albert 'Gig' Smedley, Driver Alma Cox and Corporal J. K. 'Googly' Cogle. The Tasmanians included were Lieutenants Fred House and Harry K. Goyen, Warrant Officer Roy J. Clark and Sergeant Archie 'Blond' Robb. South Australia was represented by Sergeants Gideon 'Blue' Penny and W. 'John' A. Begg and Gunner Arthur 'Scotty' Scott. And from West Australia there were H. A. 'Brum' White and Gunner George Mettam.

The oarsmen considered for the single scull were Major H. E. Stevens and Lieutenant Alma Cox. Also joining the squad was Alf Felton, a top-class professional sculler who acted as a training sculling partner for Cox. The oarsmen chosen were primarily state representatives but there were varied levels of experience, physique, conditioning and talent. Many years later, Fred House amusingly recalled the variety of shapes and sizes of the initial rowing squad members, and how 'they included baby elephants and midgets.'[4]

It became increasingly clear to the oarsmen that they had a style problem. The vast continent of Australia, with its state-based allegiances, had resulted in the evolution of isolated rowing techniques. These technical variations made for subtle but vital difficulties such as, for example, hands moving too slowly away from the body, early leg drive, seats rushing too fast up the slide and oars slammed into the water at the catch by the shoulders. It was obvious to the trained rowing eye (read 'Middleton') that the infinitesimal variations and subtle internal timing sequences of the rowing strokes needed to be unified into one true Australian rowing style.

There was some precedent for this. Middleton and Hauenstein had already pioneered an egalitarian, blended 'Australian' style, based on the dominant NSW rowing style, winning them their stunning Grand Challenge victory at Henley in 1912. If there was one thing Syd and Harry – literal and figurative giants of Australian rowing – could agree on, it was technique. They were both dogmatic about using the 'Australian' style and weren't going to be persuaded otherwise. There was no trouble with Harry Ross-Soden, a Victorian, because he had already had his rowing 'road to Damascus' moment, having been inculcated into the 'Australian' style during his time with the 1912 Olympic and HRR Grand Challenge Cup crew.

The squabble that arose over rowing styles highlighted a major problem for Middleton, Hauenstein, Tulloch and Ross-Soden, who formed an ad hoc coaching committee. Who was going to be coach? The oarsmen desperately needed someone who could be the eyes for Middleton and constantly bend the 'bad' technique of interstate oarsmen into one coherent and unified whole.

Tulloch was inculcated in the Victorian style and wasn't seriously considered as a head coach. Even Disher was a bit disparaging about his rowing acumen: 'Tulloch is a very good chap – bores me, thinks with his tongue and lacks brains.'[5] Getting an English coach – such as the outspoken and highly successful Oxford University Boat Race veteran, 1908 Olympic gold medal winner and coach of Yale University from 1913 to 1916 Guy 'Gully' Nickalls or the Oxford zoology professor Gilbert Bourne – was absolutely out of the question. The last thing Middleton wanted was a didactic English rowing coach trying to impress upon his charges the very neat, ordered and prim-looking 'Orthodox' English rowing style. Cables were sent to Australia asking if the NSW super-stroke Roger Fitzhardinge was available to coach, but the response was negative.

Middleton then seriously considered wiring the very successful Wesley College, Melbourne, rowing coach Charlie Donald (lo and behold, a Victorian) to make the voyage to England. However, the

Mother Country was in the throes of extreme inflation and costs for just about everything were through the roof. The Rowing Section was still looking to hire a top-class racing boat for training, as well as ordering new training and racing oars made to Australian specifications, and the initial quotes for these oars were off the scale. Compared to prewar Australian prices, the cost of handcrafted oars had 'jumped enormously, oars being £3.5.0d each against £1.10.0d in Australia'.[6] As well as the added cost of an eight-week voyage to England, the subsequent delay meant that Australian coaches such as Charlie Donald would only arrive by late May at the earliest. It simply did not stack up. Most of the crew selection, technical rowing re-education (for the non-NSW oarsmen) and stamina work would need to be well and truly completed by then, under expert guidance.

After a few more rowing sessions, Disher wasn't a happy man, having been unceremoniously bumped from the stroke seat of the No. 1 crew:

> I stroked the first eight that night but didn't prove satisfactory ... got put back to 'B', then after a couple of days, 2 in the second eight and then 2 in the four after a few nights, so you see I was rowing perfectly? Wasn't enjoying myself much, kept worrying about work I felt I ought to be doing so decided I would chuck it the next week by that time I was rowing 'B' in the 2nd eight.[7]

The Rowing Section was now hamstrung, being coached by an ad hoc committee of experts from the 1912 Australian crew. Depending on his own rowing commitments inside the boat, Harry Ross-Soden sometimes coached the morning or afternoon session. Other times, Middleton drove from Horseferry Road to coach in between his busy schedule organising all the other sports events.

Harry Hauenstein, rowing in the middle of the boat and sitting in the number 5 seat, no doubt, coached from inside the boat. Hauenstein was a force to be reckoned with and knew a lot about the technical side of rowing. But diplomacy was not his forte, and his interjections began to fray tempers within the boat.

It wasn't an ideal situation, and Middleton knew it. Not having a full-time rowing coach, only exacerbated Disher's feeling that rowing was a waste of his time when he could be undertaking important medical training with an esteemed London hospital or with a prestigious royal medical college.

I am not taking much interest in the rowing. The thing is not being run too well at present and it rather bores me. I expect as time goes on it would improve but there are no proper coaches and it is not worth while going out without a coach as you have to most times. The housing arrangements are very good but after all coaching is the more important thing. It is a pity as there are quite a number of good oarsmen available.[8]

Feeling hung out to dry, Disher finally took the matter into his own hands and boldly marched into Horseferry Road and demanded to see the assistant director of medical services about potential medical work or training. Once again, the Medical Section scratched their heads and gravely pointed Disher back down the winding corridor to the Rowing Section.

Disher knew exactly where to go and asked to see Middleton in his office immediately. It was not a pretty confrontation. Middleton was often dour at best and didn't suffer fools gladly, especially if they were being petulant. Disher felt the full force of Middleton's displeasure, and noted he 'were rather wrath about it':[9]

... was told they had gone to a lot of trouble to get me over ... So I told him I had done none of the asking and where upon he cooled down and asked me to let things stand for a few days. I told him I wanted to do work as I had originally intended to do as I wasn't wanted at the river evidently, it was no use wasting my time down there. However, I was persuaded to stay for a few days.[10]

Deep down, Middleton knew he needed a competent stroke man and, as difficult as this confrontation had been, he had to be conciliatory, even against his more naturally fiery inclinations. Perhaps he was also impressed by Disher's preparedness for a full-on stoush. Regardless, Middleton had gone to a lot of effort to expedite him to London, and still thought Clive Disher had something to offer as an oarsman and wanted him to remain in the squad. He even offered Disher a position on the rowing selection committee to entice him back into the fold. Disher wrote to his old coach Charlie Donald about his mixed feelings:

> I hope you understand my attitude about their rowing. If I am
> not wanted I want to start work as it is important I should learn
> something again and yet I feel it isn't the right thing to do to
> leave a show because I am not wanted for the first lot. However,
> I hope I want not to be wasted.[11]

Now with his tail between his legs, Disher took a few days off and then skulked back to Putney. It was only then that he realised that the stroke he had bumped from the No. 1 crew was none other than the mighty Fred House, who had stroked the Tasmanians who had whipped Disher's hapless Victorian crew on their home waters of the Yarra River in 1914. That made him feel better. Disher knew then that if he was going to be stroke of the No. 1 crew, he had to earn the right to sit in the seat. Just in time, too, as the stakes were about to be raised tremendously.

By the end of March, the Henley committee of management were authorised to announce that His Majesty King George V had 'graciously promised to present a Cup to the winners of the Eight-oared Race for crews representing the Allied Forces'.[12] As was traditional at Henley, the name of the Allied eight-oared event reflected the name of the prize: the King's Cup.

Middleton now had to decide whether or not to send a crew to Paris to compete at their regatta on the River Seine on 27 April 1919. Despite his frequent requests, he was receiving next to no information from the French regatta officials. Rowing in France was considered by the Australians to be in its infancy, and there were doubts as to whether the French could organise an international-level regatta and whether the Australians should even compete.

New Zealand had already expressed their intention to row in Paris and that weighed heavily on Middleton's mind. He knew from his rugby days, playing the Test series against the New Zealand All Blacks, that the New Zealanders were up for stiff competition whenever and wherever they could get it. In fact, they thrived on it. If their trans-Tasman Anzac comrades were willing to race, they might get the jump on the Australians and head into Henley buoyed by a victory. Middleton was an extremely astute sportsman; he intimately understood the winning-edge psychology of sport and was concerned about the effect racing in Paris might have on the oarsmen whose first priority was to win the King's Cup at Henley.

Middleton and Ross-Soden decided to make a flying visit to Paris to inspect the course, the boats and the general arrangements. They discovered the River Seine rowing course was 2500 metres in length, would squeeze five lanes of crews across in the final and involved rowing under six arched bridges on a fast-flowing stream that would give certain crews an advantage over others.

Middleton already had an acute disdain for racing on rowing courses where arched bridges were involved, which had its origins in Stockholm. On further inspection, Middleton and Ross-Soden discovered the French were providing heavy clinker-style rowing boats or eight-man 'tubs' for the crews, with fixed bench seats and no outrigger.

Notwithstanding the substandard course, inferior boats and inadequate regatta practicalities, competition was still competition. In his weekly report of 7 April to Lieutenant-Colonel Massie, outlining his assessment of the Paris regatta, Syd Middleton wrote:

> The real point is this, we might send a good crew across,
> have a bad boat allotted to them or draw a bad one, and still
> be beaten by a much inferior crew. Being young oarsmen, it
> would break their spirit for the big race later on. On the other
> hand, all conditions being equal, a win in Paris would be a
> great incentive.[13]

But conditions weren't going to be 'equal' in Paris. For Middleton, that was the end of the matter. The formidable New Zealanders could have it. The AIF Rowing Section would now focus their efforts on winning the King's Cup at the Henley Regatta. But first, they had to find a top racing boat to train in, and a coach. The answers to these problems would turn out to be right under Middleton's nose.

15

The boat

Only a handful of people in the world could, guided by instinct and touch, delicately hand-plane and steam wood into the smooth, malleable, streamlined curves of a 60-foot racing eight. In fact, it all came down to 'the Three Georges'.

In Seattle, in upstate Washington in the United States, was the legendary Doggett's Coat and Badge winner, rowing philosopher and sculler George Yeoman Pocock and his brother Dick. George and Dick Pocock had emigrated from England and in 1911 started a boatbuilding business which prospered until the outbreak of war put boat orders on hold.

During the Great War, the Pocock brothers were commissioned to build floating pontoons for a wooden seaplane factory called Pacific Aero Products on the Duwamish River in Seattle. This company had been started by an upstart pioneer of aviation, William E. Boeing, who had secured a lucrative contract to build seaplanes for the US Navy. After the war, seaplane orders dwindled and the Pocock brothers were back in the racing boat building business.

They were soon commissioned to supply racing eights for the University of Washington's 'Huskies' rowing squad and started Pocock

Racing Shells, situated in a now unused waterside aircraft hangar on the University of Washington campus. The Pococks came of a long line of boatmen. Their father, Aaron Pocock, had been the revered 'boatman' for Eton College, England; rowing and boatbuilding were in their blood. George Pocock was the source of many great homespun quotes and philosophies that characterised oarsmen and the art of rowing.

After the war, George became renowned as the master racing eight boatbuilder with his now world famous eight-man racing shell *Husky Clipper*, in which the American men's Olympic eight won gold at the 1936 Berlin Olympics. This masterpiece of wood designed for water still floats from the rafters of the University of Washington's Conibear Shellhouse like a wooden angel, overseeing generations of Husky oarsmen and -women to this day.

In England, among the many family boatbuilding dynasties, there was another George: George Sims of the Sims & Sons boatbuilding company based at Putney. Sims & Sons had started in 1899, when George Sims built the Cambridge University racing boat which stopped the Oxford Dark Blue run of nine wins in the Boat Race. George designed boats that were a cocktail of Empire woods: British Honduras cedar for the skin, English sycamore for the ribs, and Canadian silver spruce for the keel. Sir Theodore Cook, art critic and former captain of Oxford's Wadham College rowing club, compared the craftmanship of George Sims with artist Joseph Turner's romantic paintings when he wrote:

> As he did it, the thing savoured of Turner's notion of perspective, a realisation of what should be, without any knowledge of what must be. There was that strange sympathy in the boat builder which ... is outside of all calculation.[1]

The third George was in Australia. George Towns was a former professional world sculling champion who had established a highly successful boatbuilding business on the Parramatta River at Gladesville. Towns had been born at Hinton, near Maitland, New South Wales, and he, too, was the son of a boatbuilder. He was an exceptional oarsman and his talent was quickly noticed in Australian rowing circles.

After travelling to England in 1897 to compete as a professional oarsman, George spent several years in England and Canada rowing professionally and taking on sculling challengers for prize money. These rowing events were comparable to modern boxing bouts, with big prize money and bigger personalities – one-on-one contests which attracted spectators in their tens of thousands, decked out in their finery. It was a festive occasion, and both love of sport and sly side bets abounded.

In 1901, George defeated the Canadian Jake Gaudaur, Snr for the World Sculling title. After his much-heralded return to Australia in 1902, he defended his title on the Parramatta River in 1904 and continued rowing for a while before making the natural progression into boatbuilding. George established his riverside boatyard where the present-day Sydney Grammar School boat shed now stands.

George Towns produced beautifully crafted boats made out of Australian red cedar (*Toona ciliata*), or 'red gold', which grew all along the east coast of Australia. Australian red cedar was harvested to the point of commercial extinction by the early 20th century. Nonetheless, these beautifully crafted racing boats lasted for years on the water when properly looked after, and in the right hands.

One of George's prized handcrafted Australian red cedar racing eights was the specially commissioned *Q.L. Deloitte*, named after the 'father of rowing' and driving force of New South Wales rowing, Quarton Levitt Deloitte ('Q.L.' to the fans) – the general manager of the Colonial Sugar Refinery. The boat had been commissioned in 1909 and raced at several Interstate Championships before being shipped to England for the 1912 Grand Challenge and Stockholm Olympics.

Raced by the 1912 Australian rowing crew, competing under the sky-blue colours of Sydney Rowing Club, the *Q.L. Deloitte* was the winning boat at the 1912 Grand Challenge Cup, at the ancestral home of rowing, Henley-on-Thames. Q.L. himself had travelled with the Australian rowing squad to watch his boat and boys win from aboard the umpire's launch – sitting alongside His Majesty King George V, Her Majesty Queen Mary and Princess Mary.

Among the winning crew members who would later volunteer for the Great War, which of course included Syd Middleton, Harry Hauenstein and Harry Ross-Soden, were Keith Heritage and Sydney Rowing Club stalwart and superb horseman, John 'Jack' A. G. Ryrie.

Middleton wanted both his eights to train in the boat that they would actually race in and not splash around in 'training' clinkers or antiquated boats dug out from the dusty back reaches of a London rowing shed. Luckily for him, just along the Putney embankment from the London R.C., having been housed at the Thames Rowing Club for the past seven years, was the *Q.L. Deloitte*.

Middleton, Hauenstein and Ross-Soden knew the boat intimately and eagerly vouched for its quality and craftsmanship. The only sticking point was money. When the *Q.L.* was commissioned from George Towns in Australia, it cost a tidy £60 to build. After the Australians won the Grand Challenge in 1912, they didn't ferry the boat to the Stockholm Olympics as it was considered too costly to transport. Instead, they sold a pretty much brand-new cedar boat to the Thames Rowing Club for a 'mates' rate' of £20.

Now, with London rowing clubs struggling to bolster memberships, reeling from inflation and the costs of upgrading their own fleets, the Thames R.C. were brutal with their asking hire price, a whopping £50 – provided they didn't actually want her at the time. So much for mates' rates. Middleton wrestled with the high price, but having some precious Australian red cedar back on the River Thames with an Australian crew in it would bolster spirits. He knew he had to have the *Q.L.*

As a new boat costs £120 and a hired one would be side seated and cost say £40 to alter, we are between the devil and the 'deep blue', also the men will have confidence in the Australian boat.[2]

Besides, the New Zealanders had already taken the plunge and ordered a brand-new eight from George Sims. They only required one eight to put to water and so could afford to splash out. When it came to building boats, Sims could work wonders and it has been said the New Zealand boat was built in a miraculous two days – though one might suspect that George had an eight he had prepared earlier and quietly grabbed off the rack.

When the Australians took possession of the *Q.L. Deloitte* from the Thames R.C., they were impressed by its condition.

> last Saturday we got into our racing boat, the old Q.L. Deloitte
> for the first time and there is not the slightest doubt that she is a
> beauty, we had very little trouble sitting her [up] and considering
> it was our first row in a racing boat, she went very well indeed.[3]

The funds from the Australian Comforts Fund and generous individual benefactors such as W. S. Robinson would have to stretch to cover the cost of the AIF Rowing Section hiring not just one but two eights, one coxswain-less four and two single sculls, plus a new set of eight oars from Norris & Co. Middleton also put in an order with Aylings oarmakers for an additional set of oars that would match those the 1912 crew had used at Henley. Everything had to be planned down to the minutest detail, and nothing left to chance, in Middleton's ambitious campaign to win the newly announced King's Cup.

16

Fairbairn

On almost any given day during April, the Putney Embankment was
teeming with curious locals fascinated to see the New Zealanders,
Canadians and Australians hard at rowing training. These three
dominion Allies had earned a reputation as fighters during the war and
here was an opportunity for the London set to see them in action as
athletes and appreciate their renowned fighting spirit. The Americans
were still in France, training on the River Seine with, of course, the
French. The English were the only ones missing in action. Many London
rowing clubs were still in disarray and reeling from the loss of active
members. There was talk of Leander R.C., Thames R.C., the combined
British armed services or the newly established flyboys of the RAF
fielding crews for the King's Cup, but so far they hadn't materialised.

London society flocked to the Embankment and promenade to
observe the boats being launched and the crews setting off. Rowing
was very much a sport where punters and spectators followed the form
of crews and oarsmen. Pundits scrutinised form and rowing style as
crews set off towards Hammersmith Bridge and beyond; when they
returned, the oarsmen were aware of the stickybeak attention along the
Thames Path. It's likely these cocky foreign military eights would have

put on short practise 'sprints' that would enthral the locals strolling between Hammersmith Bridge and Putney Bridge.

The New Zealanders were attracting the same adoring attention as the Aussies. Their rustic charm was a great hit with the mesmerised locals. All the soldier oarsmen possessed almost Adonis-like physique: tall, powerful, muscular, and grinning as they stepped out of their boats. Major Audsley commented on how the Australians had

> caused quite a lot of excitement amongst the holiday crowd at
> Putney on the embankment who appeared to be very interested
> in the Australian crews. Small boys are a jolly nuisance and
> persist in getting in the way clamouring to be allowed to carry
> our oars in.[1]

Watching with great interest from amidst the throng was a moustachioed gentleman in his early fifties, dressed immaculately in an overcoat, hat, scarf and tie and leaning on a walking stick. He no doubt noted details of oarsmanship and finesse that the genteel classes missed.

As the Australians rowed by, he raised an eyebrow as he watched from the riverbank. Perhaps he recognised some of the crew from the 1912 Henley Australian campaign. He most certainly winced at their current mash of rowing styles. The word was that the Australians were looking for assistance, and perhaps he was the man to help coach this motley Antipodean crew. They needed to get back to basics, back to fundamentals, and relearn from the water up. Middleton received word that the controversial icon of British rowing and successful Jesus College, Cambridge rowing coach Steve Fairbairn would like to offer his services.

For Middleton, Steve Fairbairn's offer was like a gift from God. For a start, Fairbairn was an Australian – though if you were Australian you might not have thought so, at least not on first impressions.

When Fairbairn arrived in England in the summer of 1881 as a wide-eyed young Antipodean, he accepted a £1 wager from a cheeky Englishman to paddle a canoe from London to Henley in less than twenty-four hours. He had no idea how far it was but accepted the wager, set off at midnight and 'covered the sixty odd miles in twenty-three hours'.[2]

He never received his prize, but the wager wasn't important to Fairbairn: for him, it was all about the journey. He was also an inveterate 'tramper', who had tramped from one end of Tasmania to the other, and in England walked with his cousin from London to Inverness, Scotland. When faced with a task – or, more rightly a destination – Steve Fairbairn put his head down and put in the hard miles. His famous mantra, which inspired many future generations of oarsmen and rowing coaches, was 'Miles make champions'. At Cambridge University and Jesus College, Cambridge, Fairbairn had assumed very high status as a coach, to the extent that he 'shared the distinction of being chiefly known by his Christian name'.[3] He had become one of a Holy Trinity of entities known exclusively by their first names: Jesus, the son of God; George, the reigning monarch of England; and a private-school-educated Australian expat oarsman and rowing coach from rural Victoria, Steve.

As an oarsman, Fairbairn's career was solid if not stellar. As a young student at Geelong Grammar from 1874–80, Fairbairn was pretty much a Renaissance man. He was an exceptional sportsman who took part in cricket, swimming, athletics and Australian Rules, as well as rowing in the school senior eights. He also found time to top the school in mathematics and be a school senior prefect.

He maintained that in his last year at Geelong Grammar, he coached the eight from the stroke seat.[4] There was nothing much Fairbairn wouldn't take on as a challenge, or an opportunity to physically test himself. Upon matriculation, his wealthy Victorian grazing family could easily afford to send him, the fifth Fairbairn of six brothers, straight to England, where he read law at Jesus College, Cambridge.

Cambridge University was already a familiar destination for the Fairbairn brothers and their cousins. Steve's five brothers and the extended Fairbairn family were 'a striking example of heredity in rowing, no less than twelve of them having rowed in a Jesus first boat'.[5] These Fairbairn family members could be called the twelve rowing apostles of Jesus. Fairbairn was obviously in his element. He immersed himself in everything English and became a devoted 'wet bob' (rower) for Cambridge University.

Rowing was his passion; he loved everything about it. He rowed for Jesus College and Cambridge University in the Boat Races in 1882 and 1883, his team losing on both occasions to Oxford University. He might have taken his competitive career further, but responsibility called, and Fairbairn returned to Australia to familiarise himself with family business interests. Whenever he had the opportunity, however, Fairbairn returned to England, and he rowed in the Jesus College Boat Club eight that won the Grand Challenge Cup in 1885 at the Henley Royal Regatta.

When Fairbairn returned to read postgraduate law, he quickly stepped back into the boat at Jesus College and rowed for Cambridge in the Boat Race in 1886 and 1887, settling old scores by rowing to victory on both occasions.

Graduating from law, Fairbairn was admitted to the Bar but never practised, instead becoming more involved in the Fairbairn family business. He returned to Australia from 1897 to 1904, managing interests from Victoria to Queensland. The draw of the Mother Country, however, was deep in Fairbairn's rich blue blood and, backed by family wealth, he did what every other rowing tragic would do and returned to England in 1905, a young wife in tow, to pursue his first true love.

In England, Fairbairn worked for the multinational Dalgety agricultural institution and immersed himself in the sport of rowing, focused on capturing the genie of rowing and coaching.

There is some irony in the fact that in an amateur sport such as rowing, Fairbairn's considerable means meant that he, along with many other well-heeled or titled Englishmen rowing as amateurs, could avoid the distractions of menial labour and uphold the sports' lofty ideals simply because they could afford to do so. From 1905 till his death in 1937 Fairbairn remained in England and became ostentatiously more English than the English.

Fairbairn's approach to coaching and rowing was a fabled mix of homespun philosophies, a deep belief in the natural order, and the pursuit of Victorian-era ideals of manliness, forbearance and stoicism.

He wrote several testaments on rowing called *Rowing Notes* or *Chats*. These epistles on coaching philosophy soon morphed, in world rowing circles, into a quasi-rowing religion called 'Fairbairnism'. They included religious-sounding pronouncements such as, 'You face your stretcher, as you face your God.' 'Fairbairnism' generated an endless stream of critics but attracted as many dedicated rowing disciples and devotees, who stoically carried their rowing bible into the boat.

Fairbairn didn't really set out to proselytise, but he believed his philosophy and vision were more about the instilling of deep life values than simply the mechanics of rowing. 'Fairbairnism' was anchored in vocation, ambition, excellence and nature, all rolled into the one watery elemental discipline that was to be executed both on and off the water. Perhaps the best summation of his rowing philosophy came from the great man himself:

> The true view of rowing is that it consists in the cultivation of the sense of touch, timing, control and balance, which is the secret of success in every form of athletics; and the main principle is, there must be no effort; if you can't do it easily you can't do it at all.[6]

An oarsman had to subjugate him- or herself to the boat, the water and to the crew, 'There is a boat. There is an oar. Move the boat. Your natural way will be the best way.'[7]

This is not so radical in itself, but it was diametrically opposed to the accepted 'English Orthodox' rowing style. English Orthodoxy, in itself, wasn't so much a philosophy, but more a long-held English social and stylistic convention bound by traditional rowing 'class' values. The ideal of the English Orthodox style was the whole crew looking perfectly angled and in sync, much like a well-drilled military parade or a German goosestep.

Even with the innovation of the sliding seat in the late 19th century in North America – a quantum leap in rowing physics that ultimately redefined the sport by propelling crews even faster down a rowing course – the purists of English Orthodoxy rigidly applied their traditional fixed-seat, straight-backed rowing technique and principles to the sliding seat. English Orthodoxy didn't effectively utilise the more powerful leg drive that the sliding seat enabled.[8] Fairbairn, in contrast, embraced this new rowing technology. He immediately saw its potential for increased leg drive and power and dedicated himself to capturing a suitable new rowing technique.

Not that Fairbairn ever prescribed how one should row. He was more concerned about the blade and what the oar was doing in and out of the water. The oarsman's body, in Fairbairn's opinion, should be allowed to twist and turn as it desired, so long as the timing of the blade work was perfection. For Fairbairn, the aim of the oarsman was to become 'an extra part of the oar'.[9]

For the stiff-upper-lipped, crusty old English adherents of amateurism, class order and English Orthodoxy, one should never step out of the boat. Fairbairn did, and often. He didn't care what anyone said and loved to make a splash. He enjoyed the attention, adored the controversy and craved the adulation of his rowing disciples. Fairbairn chased the ephemeral moment when the ecstasy of submersion in equal parts effort and ease fill the exhausted mind with flowering bliss. When he was asked how a perfect oarsman should look, Fairbairn admitted he didn't know what rowing should look like; all he knew was that the oarsman should blend themselves seamlessly into the humanity, the boat, the oar and the water.

> One can never really row, I mean, one can never become a perfect
> example of an oarsman; one can only illustrate in a boat what
> one thinks rowing is.[10]

What Fairbairn was espousing was 'new age' stuff in a dawning era of groundbreaking thought, science and philosophy, and the breakdown of Victorian class distinctions. His views rankled the orthodoxy of the privileged rowing establishment and challenged their views on manual labour and working-class values.

He was a man ahead of his time, unafraid to ruffle feathers, and soon after meeting him, the oarsmen of the AIF Rowing Section hated his guts.

ROWING MEN IN THE KHAKI

TOP LEFT Harry Hauenstein circa 1910.

CENTRE LEFT Headline from *The Referee*, 28 June 1916.

TOP RIGHT Private Thomas Whyte (left) and Sergeant John Rutherford Gordon sitting on The Great Pyramid, Giza.

CENTRE RIGHT Illustration from *The Sporting Globe*, 22 April 1931.

BOTTOM An early AIF rowing squad outside Oak House, Putney, March 1919. Underneath the photo, it read, 'Good fighters and the best of sports'.

TOP LEFT Captain Keith Heritage MC, 19th Battalion. Killed in action at Pozières, 26 July 1916.

CENTRE LEFT Harry Hauenstein's 1912 Grand Challenge Cup winner's medallion.

TOP RIGHT Harry Ross-Soden (left) with Harry Hauenstein in Putney, May 1919.

BOTTOM The AIF Rowing Section outside London Rowing Club, Putney.
Left to right: Disher, Ross-Soden, Tulloch, McGill, Fairbairn, Audsley, House, Davis, Robb, Smedley. Hauenstein had stormed off for a few days.

TOP The 1912 Henley Royal Regatta. British spectators 'toss' their oars and paddles in salute as King George V, Queen Mary and the royal barge row up the Henley course.

CENTRE Sydney Rowing Club (far shed), before it was squeezed out of Circular Quay, with Fort Macquarie to the right. The same site, Bennelong Point, is where the Sydney Opera House stands today.

BOTTOM Weekend crowds gather outside London Rowing Club to watch the Australian, New Zealand and Canadian crews train from the Putney Embankment rowing clubs.

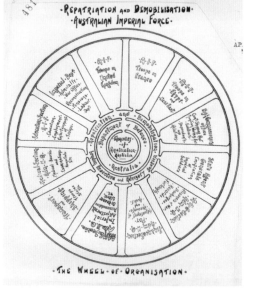

TOP LEFT AIF oarsmen at Oak
House, March 1919.

TOP RIGHT Oak House, Putney.

CENTRE The AIF Wheel of
Organisation, Repatriation and
Demobilisation.

BOTTOM The early AIF No.1
crew on the River Thames, Putney.
Left to right: Robb, House,
Tulloch, Audsley, Hauenstein,
Jonsson, Ross-Soden, Disher,
Smedley. House is scratching his
head as to why he was bumped
from the stroke seat.

TOP LEFT Major Sydney Albert Middleton DSO, OBE, 19th Battalion, 5th Brigade, 2nd Division.

TOP RIGHT Marion Streatfeild.

CENTRE The AIF Rowing Section take a break from training outside London Rowing Club, Putney.

BOTTOM The 'scratch' eight with Lieutenant-Colonel Norman Marshall DSO, MC (7) and Syd Middleton (6) at Putney.

TOP The AIF No. 1 crew take out the *Q.L. Deloitte* from London Rowing Club, Putney.

CENTRE LEFT Lieutenant Tom McGill, 20th Battalion, No. 3 in the AIF No.1 crew.

CENTRE RIGHT Major Eric W. Tulloch coaching at Putney.

BOTTOM The AIF Rowing Section hoisting Lieutenant-General William Birdwood's Anzac corps headquarters flag at Wharfe House, Henley. It flew at Gallipoli and the Western Front.

TOP LEFT Scotty the 'funmaker' at Wharfe House, Henley.

TOP RIGHT Gig Smedley with Kanga the mascot at Henley.

CENTRE LEFT Captain Harold Clive Disher.

CENTRE RIGHT Smedley, Scotty and Eric Harrison feed the swans at Wharfe House, Henley.

BOTTOM The AIF Rowing Section digs at Wharfe House, Henley.

TOP The 1910 Wallabies Rugby Union team. Seated third from left is Syd Middleton (captain) with hand on ball.

CENTRE J. 'Chung' Howieson amusing the diggers with the hose on the lawn at Wharfe House.

BOTTOM A rare photo of the AIF No. 2 crew out for a training row on the River Thames, and passing the iconic Henley waterfront houses that are still there today.

TOP AIF Rowing Section guests of Lady Stapleton.

CENTRE The AIF Rowing Section with Major-General E. Tivey, Lieutenant-General J.J. Talbot Hobbs, Brigadier-General Thomas Blamey, supporters, diggers and old mates on the lawn of Wharfe House, Henley, June 1919.

BOTTOM Lieutenants H.A. 'Brum' White and Fred House paddle during the Royal Henley Peace Regatta. The parasol is more for rain.

TOP The AIF No. 1 crew (before final selection) training on Henley Reach, approaching Temple Island.

CENTRE The King's Cup, Grand Challenge Cup and assorted silverware under serious security at Phyllis Court.

BOTTOM Thousands of spectators in punts line the booms of the Henley course.

TOP The iconic AIF rising sun emblem with crossed oars embroidered on Archie Robb's AIF Rowing Section blazer pocket.

CENTRE AIF oarsmen in blazers and flannels mingle with diggers and guests on the lawn of Wharfe House, Henley during the regatta.

BOTTOM The YMCA 'Australians Only' stand erected for visiting AIF digger spectators during the Royal Henley Peace Regatta. 'Buckshee', thatta way.

TOP The AIF No. 1 crew holding off a final challenge from the Cambridge University Service Crew in a King's Cup semi-final.

CENTRE LEFT The King's Cup.

CENTRE RIGHT Tasmanian wartime volunteer Carine Pennefather, who led the party of wounded and amputee diggers to the Royal Henley Peace Regatta.

BOTTOM The AIF No. 1 claim victory over the Cambridge Army Service Crew in a King's Cup semi-final, 4 July 1919.

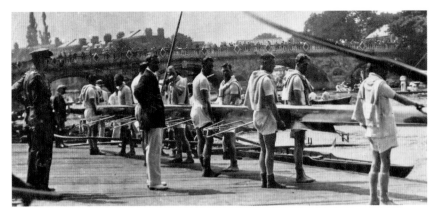

TOP The AIF No. 1 crew waiting to boat from the regatta boat enclosure, Henley, 5 July 1919. Note the installed timber decking and 'Dinkum Aussie' flag dangling from the 'sneak' at the bow.

CENTRE The AIF No. 1 crew on the water prior to paddling to start the King's Cup, Henley, 5 July 1919.

BOTTOM The AIF No. 1 crew in action during the King's Cup final, Henley, 5 July 1919. Note the bow of the Oxford crew, pictured right. The winning time of 7 minutes 7 seconds was the fastest at the regatta.

TOP The finish of the King's Cup final, 5 July 1919. Oxford slump as they drift past the line.

CENTRE LEFT AIF supporters cheer the AIF victory from the stand erected on the lawn of Wharfe House, Henley.

CENTRE RIGHT Illustration from *Henley Races* by Sir Theodore Cook.

BOTTOM The finish of the King's Cup final showing the course and spectators. This photo was taken from the St Mary's Church tower, Henley-on-Thames.

LONDON AMAZED

A.I.F. in the Fields of Sport

Official Programme

FRIDAY JULY 4th.

Royal Henley Peace Regatta 1919.

Price 1/-

HERMON TURNER SERIES A2. No. 7002

TOP The AIF No.1 crew at Wharfe House, Henley, 5 July 1919. Back row, left to right: Marshall, House, McGill, Smedley, Scott, Robb, Ross-Soden. Seated, left to right: Middleton, Disher, Mettam, Hauenstein.

LEFT Headline from *The Sun*, 28 August 1919; the official programme cover for the Royal Henley Peace Regatta.

BOTTOM The Royal Henley Peace Regatta medallion presented to Gig Smedley.

TOP LEFT Syd Middleton, with Marion, at Buckingham Palace to receive his OBE.

TOP RIGHT The 'Dinkum Aussie' flag that flew on the bow of the winning AIF No. 1 crew in the King's Cup final.

CENTRE A photograph of HMT *Euripides* with autographs of AIF athletes, including Albert Jacka VC and Jack Ryan VC.

BOTTOM Archie Robb's oar from the King's Cup victory hangs in pride of place.

17

Trouble in the boat

At water level, Fairbairn's sharp-eyed observations and rowing acumen were intuitive and decisive. The workings of a boat, the rowing cycle, the mind of an oarsman – he could peer inside and see things others could easily miss. His first and most emphatic observation of the crew was about the big man, the number 5, Harry Hauenstein. Straight away, Fairbairn knew he was going to build the crew around him.

Even though Harry was a little past his prewar rowing peak fitness, he was still a powerful oar. Hauenstein rowed like his life depended on it. The intense focus and sheer power that Harry brought to a crew was impressive. If any coach had eight Hauensteins, they would be indestructible on the water.

The Times incorrectly identified Hauenstein as a 'Mr. Hohlstein' and added six years to his age when it reported that he was over forty but nonetheless 'a magnificent oar with a perfect blade and finish'.[1] Then again, what Harry had seen and carried deep inside him from Pozières undoubtedly did add years onto him.

One can only imagine what desperate horrors Hauenstein recalled from those sleepless nights at Pozières. He was possibly also preoccupied with his brother, Paddy, who was languishing in the bottom few of the squad, often standing on the shore as an 'emergency'. He cut a lonely figure, watching the boat paddle by, and seemed to be deeply affected by his wounds, both mental and physical.

But for Fairbairn, Harry Hauenstein's temperament and spirit were a rowing 'force majeure' that could be harnessed like a wild brumby. He was determined that Hauenstein was to be the central immutable rock of the crew and everyone else had to be moulded around him to build a solid foundation. He was definitely worth the risk.

Fairbairn put the AIF rowing squad to work straightaway. Long rows twice daily, long walks, time sunk into the Thames R.C. rowing tank and plenty of rhetoric and poetry about the 'karma' of rowing. But there was time to relax and tour the local area. Not far from Putney were Kew Gardens and further east the vast hunting grounds of Henry VIII, situated on the high ground of Richmond Park, where herds of royal deer still roamed free. These grasslands are one of the highest elevated points in London and AIF oarsmen visited them, accompanied by many female friends and acquaintances.

The rowing squad were just as interested in the other inter-Allied sports competitions that were being held, most notably the rugby. Twickenham rugby ground was only a few miles further up the Thames. On 19 April, the prestigious King's Cup for rugby was played at Twickenham between New Zealand and England. The winner of the match not only won the cup, presented by King George V himself, but also the opportunity to play an international 'Test' match with France. As Major Audsley reported:

> Last Wednesday afternoon I went out with [family friends] the
> Fells to see the football match between NZ and the Mother
> Country at Twickenham it was the deciding game as to who
> should win the services competition and a fine match it was NZ
> won by 9 points to 3 much to the home people's disgust.[2]

By mid-April, after the decision not to row in Paris had been settled, Disher returned to the fold. He had been bumped down to rowing in the four (equivalent to being sent to Coventry), then stroked the AIF

No. 2 crew, then worked his way back into the bow end of the AIF No. 1 boat, in the number 2 seat, with Freddie House back in the stroke seat. Disher was a little humbler now about his status in the boat. He had high but guarded hopes for Fairbairn as 'he is not attempting to Anglicise us if that is correct term to use'.[3] But Disher still rated Fairbairn well below his old rowing coach Charlie Donald.

Meanwhile, Middleton had started to plan ahead for the modified Henley Royal Regatta. He knew that suitable accommodation in Henley was paramount to keep the camaraderie tight. Audsley was detailed to motor to Henley and recce the town for suitable quarters. He reported that 'Henley is a very pretty place and while I was there I had a look at the course which is fine – fresh water of course and straight as a die for a mile and a half.'[4]

On 27 April, the Paris Regatta on the River Seine was just the opposite. The regatta course was a crooked mile and a half, starting from the Pont Royal near the Tuileries Palace and rowed to the Pont de l'Alma in the shadow of the Eiffel Tower. In a poignant commemoration of the recent fallen of the Great War, the Alma Bridge was guarded by four large statues of Crimean War soldiers, at one end a Zouave and a grenadier, and at the other a skirmisher and an artilleryman.

Six Allied Army crews were entered: New Zealand, France, Portugal, Newfoundland, the newly 'liberated' Alsace-Lorraine and the United States.

The US crew were keen to compete at Henley and were hard at work training on the Seine under the watchful eye of Major Paul Withington, a legendary Harvard dual letterman in both rowing and American football. He was an alumni of the Union Boat Club crew in the Grand Challenge Cup final and as a sculler in the Diamond Sculls at the American-dominated 1914 Henley Royal Regatta. Their coach was just as intimidating: Captain Charles D. Wiman, who was in charge of the American Expeditionary Force (AEF) rowing squad, and himself an experienced 1914 Grand Challenge Cup oarsman and Yale alumni.

The United States, with characteristic postwar enthusiasm and cash, approached their training at full tilt, sparing no expense. French flâneurs strolling the riverbanks would have been bemused by the sight of the American rowing squad in training. As they ploughed through the waters of the Seine, Captain Charles D. Wiman as a coaching film auteur, followed the crew along the riverbank in an 'ornery flivver [a cheap car], which coughed madly along the river banks and occasionally dashed through three feet of water',[5] all while shouting orders into a megaphone as the vehicle rattled over the cobblestones.

In another chase car, like a scene out of the 'Keystone Cops', a squad of movie men followed with a newfangled hand-cranked movie camera, capturing footage of the racing team in action. This touch of American 'Hollywood' ingenuity was courtesy of Wiman, who had the idea that the best way for the oarsmen to correct and blend their different varsity rowing techniques was to see themselves in action on the big screen. It proved an invaluable advantage for the Americans and was possibly the first instance of filmed footage being used in elite sports training.

The Americans were dead keen on Henley; several of the AEF squad had rowed in the 1914 Henley Royal Regatta and they knew it was the traditional home of rowing. The only hiccup was that the dates of the Inter-Allied Games the Americans were organising – from 22 June to 6 July 1919 – clashed with the Royal Henley Regatta, which was being held on 2–5 July. It was going to be a tough choice for the Americans, but for now they had the Seine to contend with.

With the crews having to row in supplied fixed-seat clinker boats, making their way through the six low-arched bridges along the fast-flowing River Seine, it was more a dodgem boat race than a formal regatta course. But, as was probably acknowledged, it was not always about the rowing. For the Parisians, the regatta was an excuse for a public holiday. Two heats were held with three crews each, with the top two placegetters going through to a four-boat final. After the two heats, New Zealand, the United States, France and Newfoundland had qualified for the final in front of New Zealand prime minister Bill Massey and 500,000 excited Parisians lining the banks of the Seine.[6]

In an exciting final, the four Allied military crews ducked and weaved down the Seine with the strapping New Zealand eight stroked by the legendary Union Club, Whanganui oarsman Clarrie Healey. The final was closely contested by the Americans and the New Zealanders and was 'a gruelling race throughout, the two shells alternating in the lead'. The New Zealanders 'nosed out the Americans in a heartbreaking sprint in the last 50 yards', winning by a desperate 8 feet in front of a wild crowd.[7]

Small French naval monitors blasted salvos from their guns into the air and French bi-planes dipped and flew low over the Seine as the victorious New Zealand crew swept under the Pont de l'Alma finish line. The French sure knew how to put on a spectacular show.

A beautiful half-metre high porcelain Sèvres vase worth £100 was presented to the New Zealand crew by French president Georges 'The Tiger' Clemenceau. Afterwards, the New Zealanders celebrated hard with their Anzac mates at the Hotel Majestic in Paris.[8] Victory is always sweet. The New Zealanders' victory, the Americans noted, 'was not expected by those who had followed the preparations of both crews. The New Zealanders were quartered at Putney within the environment of England's best professional oarsmen and were given every facility in order to turn out an unbeatable crew.'[9]

Perhaps the Americans didn't quite understand the difference between professionalism and amateurism in rowing. Perhaps they thought only a professional crew could beat their AEF crew, and that simple 'amateurs' could never be that good.

The New Zealanders returned to Putney buoyed by their victory, and with much-deserved boasting rights, as a serious contender for the King's Cup. Having captained the first ever Wallaby victory over the New Zealanders in the 1910 Rugby Union Test series, Middleton would have taken note of their victory, but not let it rattle him. Ever taciturn, he would have locked the New Zealand win into the vault and turned his attention to the big prize: winning the King's Cup at Henley on a proper regatta course.

Fairbairn had some pretty good men on hand in the AIF squad – Middleton had scoured the entire AIF to get them. It was hard for Middleton and the rowing selectors to decide who was in or out and sometimes old allegiances swayed decisions. Not so for Fairbairn; he had dealt with this type of decision for years, and in countless crews. He had some difficult personalities to manage, though, regardless of the quality of their oarsmanship or the extent of their elite rowing experience. The first flash of fireworks occurred almost immediately. Fred House, as stroke of the crew, wanted his fellow Tasmanian and Derwent Rowing Club wingman Archie Robb to move into the key number 7 seat in place of Ross-Soden. His objection to Ross-Soden was 'not on the grounds of the latter's incompetency as an oarsman, but … his lack of condition and the presence of a "girth"'.[10] He argued that Ross-Soden would not be able to get into form in time. Nonetheless, Middleton overruled House and gave Ross-Soden, his 1912 HRR Grand Challenge Cup crewmate, the time to get back into shape and up to race fitness. House was not happy with Ross-Soden in the number 7 seat and offered to both move out of the stroke seat and quite possibly out of the whole crew. Middleton rejigged the crew, taking the bold step of moving Disher from the number 2 seat back into the stroke seat and dropping Freddie House in the process.

House was a proud Tasmanian who had stroked the Tasmanian crew to its victory at the 1914 Interstate Regatta on the Yarra River. If there had been an Olympics in Berlin in 1916, Fred would have been a serious contender to stroke the crew. House didn't throw a tantrum – he would never do that – but Archie Robb bluntly told the selectors that if House went, he went too.

Ever since the crew had been at Putney, Archie pretty much had a mortgage on the bow seat of the AIF No. 1 boat. No one could hold a candle to Archie; no one else had the finesse and innate sense of timing that is essential for a 'bow' rower.

Many bow rowers would tell you that after the stroke, the bow seat is the most important one in the boat. A bow man can affect the pull or direction of a 60-foot-plus boat, as they sit closest to the bow and furthest from the rudder. There, if they are either too late or too early into the water, they can incrementally change the course of the boat. It's only ever a matter of inches, perhaps fractions of inches, but over a distance of a mile and a half, over the 250 strokes it takes a crew to row the distance, all those inches add up, with the coxswain having to make repeated and boat-slowing steering corrections.

The shortest distance between two points (the start and the finish line) is a straight line. A fast boat is a straight boat. A boat going straight means the coxswain does not need to apply any rudder to correct the pull of a yawing boat to keep a straight course. Every time a coxswain applies rudder, it is like applying a brake, particularly when all eight oars are out of the water; the boat may slightly yaw or roll to one side and the boat speed slows. It also means a crew is rowing further than it has to as the boat meanders up a course like a wriggling water snake.

Fairbairn knew the value of a good bow man like Archie Robb, so he moved Fred House into the number 3 seat. It wasn't ideal, as House was now rowing the opposite of his preferred side and did not yet feel as comfortable but, crucially, he was still in the crew. The AIF No. 1 crew now comprised Archie Robb (bow); W. A. 'John' Begg (2); Fred House (3); Alan Audsley (4); Harry Hauenstein (5); Eric Tulloch – filling in for John Jonsonn (6); Harry Ross-Soden (7); and Clive Disher (stroke), with Ossie Wood in the coxswain seat.

The selection still wasn't perfect. Each man had their pros and cons regarding physical shape, experience and fitness but the new combination seemed to have immediate results. Disher was now getting excited about the improving performance of the crew.

> Altogether the 8 has been rowing well; better each day until
> Wednesday when we had a magnificent row. Fairbairn was
> inwardly pleased. Easily the best row I have had for ages if not
> the best ever.[11]

But Fairbairn was like a mad scientist, forever tinkering with his formula; he always felt he could go one better and perfect the delicate balance of oarsmen and machine.

The next day, Fairbairn dropped John Begg and brought in a Victorian oarsman, the former 1914 Victorian state sculling champion and 1912–13 Interstate Eight-oared representative, Lyndsey 'Lyn' Davis from the 'emergency' standbys, parachuting him into the number 2 seat of the AIF No. 1 crew.

Hauenstein lost it. Davis was a very good sculler, and to be a good sculler sometimes you have to be opinionated, because there's no one else to chip in except yourself. Several times during the month Davis had been in the crew with Hauenstein, trying out for a seat, he had talked a lot from inside the boat, criticising crew members and giving opinions about how to move the boat better. It probably started off as mildly irritating, but after several rows together, Davis became downright aggravating for someone like Hauenstein, the strong and silent type who knew when to shut up and row. Now, with the prospect of Lyn Davis more permanently in the boat, Hauenstein refused to even get in and 'went off his nut'.[12]

The crew was probably standing around, wondering what the hell was going on, drumming their fingers on the hull inside the shed while waiting to get on the water, as Hauenstein, Ross-Soden and Disher were hurriedly pulled aside by Fairbairn to find out the cause of the delay. Hauenstein flatly admitted his intense dislike of Davis and after a great deal of argument refused to row and stormed off.

These are the times when an opportunity arises for another oarsman to seize the moment and fill the gap. As a truculent Hauenstein disappeared into the London R.C. shed to collect his gear and headed back to Oak House, the selectors quickly grabbed Tom McGill to jump into his seat. No one had been prepared for this kind of trouble in the boat. Disher commented in a missive to his former rowing coach John Lang that 'Hauenstein is a man of most peculiar temperament and has frequently done things like that with other crews but comes back a sorry man after a few days.'

Middleton was in the Sports Section office at Horseferry Road when he received an urgent telephone call from Ross-Soden, Ossie Wood, Tulloch and Disher informing him that Hauenstein had walked. His first reaction was probably to hang his head, knowing the inevitable had just happened. Middleton knew Hauenstein was not afraid to speak his mind and didn't respond well to unjustified crew changes – it was going to be up to him to sort it out. Harry, described by Disher as 'a child in many ways', was sent to Horseferry Road like a petulant schoolboy being sent to the headmaster's office, the prospect of getting expelled looming.[13]

When Hauenstein arrived at Horseferry Road, Middleton knew there was probably little he could do. Hauenstein railed about there being way too many Victorians in the crew with their 'un-Australian' style of rowing. When Middleton asked who Harry would replace Davis with, he replied that Lieutenant Harold White – a glamour flyboy in the Royal Flying Corps – perhaps could sit in. Middleton probably didn't have the nerve to tell him that even though White had enlisted in Perth, Western Australia, he had grown up in Melbourne and gone to school at Melbourne Grammar, the same school Ross-Soden had attended.[14]

The best solution Middleton could think of was the same one he had given Disher when he had bowled into Room 38. He suggested that Harry take a few days off to think it over and then decide. Of course, at the same time, Middleton would have reminded Hauenstein that his only other option would be to send both him and his brother Paddy back to their Pioneer unit in whatever wet and miserable camp they were based, to await repatriation. Being sent to a base depot somewhere was an option Harry would not have liked at all. There were still well over 100,000 diggers languishing in England and the lists and repatriation preferences would likely mean a long wait for Harry and Paddy in desperate camp conditions. Oak House seemed a much more comfortable alternative. Disher, probably aware of the scarring psychological effects of war, wrote that:

> This man is a magnificent oar but has a kink in his brain says he won't row if a certain person is kept in the boat; the committee are trying to smooth him over, but I am afraid it will end by him staying out.[15]

Hauenstein stood fast by his decision about Davis and refused to row. Disher was worried that the news of this trouble had been leaked by Harry Ross-Soden to a pesky journalist and was going to be reported in the Australian newspapers. He did not want the reputation of the AIF Rowing Section tarnished. Disher wrote to John Lang saying that there was another side to the argument, and advising him to discount any scuttlebutt he might read in the Australian newspapers. Hauenstein's sudden disappearance from the crew did draw attention back in Australia: 'It is noticed that the Olympic oarsman Lieutenant H. Hauensetin [sic] is not in the crew, he evidently not being available, though in the original selection.'[16]

Disher – now part of the selection committee, as his position as stroke permitted – thought that Harry's objection was 'not altogether without reason. Davis has adopted a rather loud method of talking which has caused some little ill feeling ... that style of talking doesn't go down.' Even though Davis was 'a very good man', the prevailing feeling was that if Hauenstein wasn't in the crew, it would cruel their chances of winning the King's Cup. Disher didn't have anything personal against Davis, but he admired Hauenstein's impact as an oarsman. 'I never thought before that one man could make such a difference to a boat. I do believe it now.'[17] His absence was going to be a real setback. Even though the young, quiet and determined Tom McGill was up to the task, the AIF No. 1 was going to miss Hauenstein's sheer output of power – he was the beating heart of the crew. Disher wrote that Hauenstein

> to my mind has proved himself a super oarsmen and I don't think
> that anyone does not consider him by far and away the best
> man in the boat in fact the nucleus in whose work Fairbairn has
> openly expressed his intention of building the crew.[18]

For the next week the AIF No. 1 crew simply wasn't rowing as well as it had been. The AIF No. 2 crew were doing much better, much to the No. 1 crew's chagrin. They were also dealing with extra administrative and equipment problems such as getting a coaching launch that could keep up with the crews, so that Fairbairn didn't have to do his work while cycling madly along the Thames towpath.

Middleton was emphatic that they should just get back into the hard work and not focus on Hauenstein coming back. Everything seemed a bit grim, even the climate, turning on snaps of cold and blustery wind as only English weather can. The water was choppy and swirling. The mercury dropped, it started to rain, and training sessions were also held in difficult and even snowy conditions.[19]

Paddy might have tried to encourage Harry to get back in the boat – it's hard to say. The prognosis for the AIF No. 1 crew, though, was not good. Writing to his parents, Disher commented:

> The coach Mr. Fairbairn considered that the crew would be a
> better crew than the Australian Olympic eight in 1912 but now
> he is not prepared to say it will be without this man in, who in a
> way definitely influenced the whole rowing.[20]

Disher wasn't sure if Davis had any suspicion that he was the root cause of the trouble. The job to have a quiet word to Davis was flicked to a recent arrival, another Victorian oarsman at Oak House, Horace Stevens, who knew Davis well from rowing days before the war.

No one is sure what, if anything, was said, but Davis did pipe down and was 'most pitifully quiet all day'.[21] Then, after several days, there was a sudden change of heart and Hauenstein inexplicably returned to the fold, probably very much cap in hand, as far as Harry could be contrite. Middleton had once again read the situation correctly; he had managed to avert yet another crisis and get the rowing squad back on the water. Hauenstein conceded on his objection to Davis and settled back into his number 5 seat and Davis remained, cowed and mute, in the number 2 seat, with Freddie House in number 3.

Fairbairn still had crew selection issues during early May 1919. The AIF rowing squad only had eight weeks to go till Henley and the AIF No. 1 crew was still unsettled. Now that Fairbairn had more power with Hauenstein, he wanted the boat to go faster. The number 4 seat was still in doubt, as Audsley seemed to be more interested in the London social scene than rowing – socialising, attending picture shows and gala events and heading to the airfields with Harold White for a possible 'flip' in a biplane. He was in danger of losing his seat but 'the trouble is to replace him.'[22] White was tall, young, smart and with good length; he was a contender but was considered inclined to be erratic. There was always Scotty, powering away like a steam engine in the No. 2 crew; Disher considered Scotty 'a very powerful man but ... somewhat muscle bound and clumsy but determined efforts are to be made immediately to remedy this if it can be done.'[23]

The ideal would be to match Hauenstein's raw power on the bowside of the boat with raw power from another strong oarsman on the stroke side. The trouble would be finding a match for Hauenstein. But this would not prove to be Fairbairn's greatest challenge. There was further trouble brewing in the boat.

18

Anzac Day

Disher, by default by as much as Syd Middleton's shrewd planning, became the Rowing Section's unofficial RMO. He certainly had the experience after his attachment to the 4th Field Artillery Brigade in France on 16 March 1918.

Disher might not have been attached to the exclusive Royal College of Surgeons or the Royal College of Physicians, but he did have his own de facto general practice operating out of Oak House, and the requisite medical experience to keep a clean, hygienic and healthy house. In any sports squad there are always going to be blisters, muscle strains, twists, twinges, aches and pains. They were easy to treat with ice or sunlamps and prescription drugs were also on hand. There was also another deadly round of Spanish flu hitting London in 1919, meaning an even greater need for hygiene and preventative medicine. The physical contact, common bathing areas, coughing and shared utensils of the athletes' communal living meant a large risk of spreading infection. If anyone was up to keeping the Rowing Section in tiptop shape and the best of health, it would have to be Clive Disher.

Knowing the pressures and strains of team sport, Middleton had also ensured the squad had a specialist team masseur in residence. He had contracted AIF Sergeant C. H. 'Duke' Mullins, who had been the personal trainer and masseur for African American heavyweight boxer Jack Johnson during his drawcard world championship bout at the Sydney Stadium in Australia. On Boxing Day, 1908 Johnson had snatched the world heavyweight title from the great but diminutive Canadian boxer Tommy Burns, who had welcomed all comers.

The Duke was in great demand with all the Peace Games sports teams – particularly with the AIF's boxing team, also based in Warwick Square – but Middleton made sure he was always on hand for the Rowing Section too. It is sometimes said by top rowing coaches that there is no such thing as overtraining, but there is such a thing as under-recovery. Duke's healing hands helped the oarsmen recover from the strenuous demands of training.

These AIF oarsmen, however, hadn't arrived at Putney as fit, healthy, bulked-up elite athletes. They had stepped straight out of the most brutal industrialised war ever conducted. They had slept in mud, shivered with cold, been shot at, blown up, gassed, gone hungry, been shredded by barbed wire, deafened by barrages, splattered with gore, copped shrapnel, almost drowned in flooded shell holes and, for days on end, had little or next to no sleep. Not quite the training camps oarsmen and -women enjoy today.

The AIF oarsmen carried with them into Putney all kinds of physical and psychological wounds that required constant treatment and management. Tom McGill had pieces of shrapnel left lodged near the base of his spine, and likely needed some regular painkillers to relieve the discomfort – not to mention the constant reminder of having no teeth and scars healing on his cheeks. The serious gunshot wound to his left thigh would also need attention from the Duke. George Mettam required extensive physiotherapy for a hand he had lacerated, especially as the injury could be exacerbated by gripping an oar for long training sessions and handling heavy timber boats. Disher probably had to check on Fred House and listen to his chest regularly to monitor his gas-impaired lung capacity – House needed to be fit enough to endure extended periods of high aerobic output.

There was little Disher could do for Archie and his hearing loss, except to speak up – or talk about him behind his back then smile and wave. Archie's regular bow seat was the furthest point away from the coxswain yelling orders; he must have remained oblivious to the calls, in his own world of muffled silence. (Many would say bowmen and -women are in the same state today.) The oarsman in the number 2 seat would have had to regularly turn around and relay the coach's or coxswain's messages to Archie regarding what was happening next, or if he was required to 'touch' the boat around.

Of course, no one had a problem with the rowing squad puffing away on copious cigarettes; if anything, the smokes calmed their nerves and stopped the trembling of their fingers.

At times, the physician was required to heal himself. For days on end Disher experienced neuralgia and extreme headaches. These debilitating attacks caused him to lose weight, and to feel 'pretty off'.[1] On top of the neuralgia, Disher broke a tooth biting into some toffee and this resulted in an abscess and a trip to the dentist, where he eventually had his tooth capped.

The Australians also found themselves in a bind when it came to Harry Ross-Soden. Harry was giving 100 per cent, both on and off the water. He was heavily involved in crew selections, coaching and managing the Rowing Section, but he was also determined to row in the AIF No. 1 crew and regain his old number 7 seat. Without a doubt, he was among the squad's greatest assets – except, that is, on the water.

Ross-Soden hadn't been in the best of health for over a year and his persistent bladder stones had left him bloated and out of condition. With his health rather fragile, Ross-Soden had also suffered an attack of the Spanish flu and took some time off training to recover.[2] Mentally, he was as acute as ever, but his health 'had not been all that would be desired' and no-one was really prepared to confront him about it – not even Middleton, who had relied on him so much during the formative days to pull the Rowing Section together.[3] Bonds between crewmates die hard. Ross-Soden had an armoury of Henley racing knowledge, experience and know-how, and he stoically turned up for training each and every day. But the last thing a crew who wanted to win needed was to be carrying a man who – despite his best efforts – wasn't pulling his weight.

With two training sessions a day, and plenty of walking to and from Oak House and London R.C., it must have felt to the oarsmen that life revolved entirely around rowing. The squad were getting along but there were times when they knew an individual needed to be left alone. The oarsmen shared rooms with two or three others and had nice soft beds; in comparison to the battlefield, Oak House was pure luxury, and couldn't be much better.

Life at Putney also meant the rowing squad could make frequent trips into Soho, Westminster or Shaftesbury Avenue, which had plenty of entertainment and night-time distractions. In central London the men could find theatre, shows, music halls, the Anzac Buffet, AIF Administration Headquarters at Horseferry Road and private clubs, and could catch up with comrades and distant relatives. After a routine day's training the squad had dinner 'and afterwards usually picture theatres etc. to fill in the evening'.[4]

Disher was also actively involved in organising a gala formal 'smoke' dinner for all the old Scotch College boys, or 'old Scotchies', who were either living in the UK or had served in the AIF and were still not repatriated. This was potentially a big gathering as, 'Over twelve hundred Scotch Collegians, more than enough to make up a battalion, enlisted in the war of 1914–18.'[5] Overall, the private schools from Melbourne did more than their part volunteering in the AIF, with over 4700 ex-students enlisting and 756 either dying or being killed in action. The proud 'Scotchies' were scattered right through the AIF, all the way up to the great man himself, General Sir John Monash, and when this band of brothers got together at a dinner it would be quite a bash.

The day after the great Hauenstein blow-up was the most sacred of days for the AIF, even at that time – Anzac Day, 25 April. The AIF had immediately appreciated the poignant but proud significance of Anzac Day, before it had been recognised back home.

A parade – another means of occupying a huge chunk of the diggers in England – was to be held. A huge contingent of the AIF, numbering roughly 5000 diggers, was selected to march on Anzac Day, four abreast down the Strand. An Anzac Day parade of this magnitude in the centre of London didn't just get thrown together at the last minute and planning would have taken weeks, selecting the best men of the AIF battalions and getting back into lockstep marching for the special day.

His Royal Highness the Prince of Wales, accompanied by his brother, Prince Albert, took the salute standing in front of Australia House and the dignitaries present included the Australian High Commissioner, Andrew Fisher; the revered General Douglas Haig; and Anzac champion Lieutenant-General William Birdwood.

There was no way Major Audsley was going to miss this parade and – more importantly – the evening of festivities and dancing to follow.

The diggers, beautifully turned out, were permitted to parade through the Mall and the Strand with fixed bayonets, an honour not even allowed the prestigious Grenadiers, Royal Marines and Guards Division. It was probably the farewell AIF march-past for the diggers in London and they were not going to miss the opportunity to put on show with all the military hardware available, followed by some truly hair-raising aerobatics. Audsley enthused to his family:

> Our chaps in the planes followed the route and treated the
> Londoners to an exhibition of stunt flying such as they had never
> seen before and all the newspapers made a tremendous mouthful
> of the whole show.[6]

One daring Australian Flying Corps pilot, nicknamed the 'Red Devil' in his red Sopwith Camel, 'travelled at terrible speed, and looped and nose-dived almost amongst the chimney pots ... which caused women to scream.'[7] On the ground there were all sorts of horse-drawn gun carriages paraded through the streets of Westminster. Mounted greys pulled columns of 18-pounder field guns and the Australian Light Horse Brigades, emu feathers flapping, also trotted in tight formation down the Strand.

Anzac Day 1919 was colourful and cosmopolitan, an inspiration for the future world order. In the streets of London, the world – or the victors, at least – came together. While the parade was spectacular, it was first and foremost a solemn day of respect and remembrance of the fallen. Four years of war added up, and the recent death and loss weighed upon everyone. Of course, once the formal parade was over, the tone changed. There were undoubtedly massive games of two-up, and hotels and bars filled with diggers enjoying a drink or ten before heading back to base or sleeping it off under a River Thames bridge.

Major Audsley had already organised his dates for the evening: young and pretty family friends, the sisters Janet and Marie Fell. Together, they attended a big AIF dance at the grand Piccadilly Hotel in Regent Street. At the dance, Audsley was in his element. He revelled in his status as a major, with a couple of attractive girls on his arms, and after an enjoyable evening of dancing, smoking and socialising made to accompany his dates safely home. As he waited for the women to collect their coats and stoles from the cloak room, Audsley felt someone grab him by the arm:

> General Birdwood was also there waiting for Lady Birdwood
> and Nancy and he came over to me and grabbed me by the
> arm and started yarning. Janet and Marie came out first, [and]
> I was able to introduce them to him. Old Birdie always seems
> to remember my name and always has a yarn when he gets
> the chance.[8]

As well as the venues of central London, there was plenty of entertainment along the high street down Putney Hill from their digs in Carlton Road. After a hard day's work out on the water, the oarsmen needed distraction, recreation, and plenty of opportunities to kick back and unwind. Major Audsley, wrote:

> It is quite a treat to see all the womenfolk turning out in summer
> togs because you know it is mostly all coats and skirts and furs
> galore ... Last night a crowd of us from the house patronised the

Putney Hippodrome, a bit of a music hall in the vicinity and it
was quite a good show, with a lot of good turns in it.[9]

An evening of theatre at the Putney Hippodrome was great light
entertainment but only cast into the shadows the veil of depression that
could envelop the oarsmen at any time.

The financing of the regatta posed a serious problem for the committee
of management of the Henley Royal Regatta. Inflation, rising costs
and the demise of active rowing members affected the coffers of
Leander Club and other English rowing clubs. The financing of the
1914 Royal Henley Regatta had cost £3,046 2s including £214 13s for
'arson insurance'. As early as 1913, a social and political movement
had been sweeping England and inciting fear and fire – the Suffragists.
Varnished and highly combustible timber boats were popular targets.
The Suffragists were seen by the quaking Henley stewards as

> so busy just before the regatta, and had done much damage at
> Oxford and other places by the way of destruction of boathouses,
> etc., that the Committee of Management were wise in taking
> every precaution... By next year perhaps the militant Suffragists
> will have seen the error of their ways.[10]

They didn't. In 1914, the Henley stewards still held somewhat
alarmist concerns about the 'Militant Suffragists' who were allegedly
blazing their way across the English countryside 'setting fire to all sorts
of things, including Wargrave Church, and fears were entertained that
they might try to burn the boat tents'.[11] The stoic gentlemen of Henley
prepared themselves for any eventuality. In 1919, with plans for the
modified regatta well underway, if it wasn't the Suffragists to be wary
of, then it could also be the Bolsheviks sparking the fires of anarchy.

The Henley stewards anticipated that with rising regatta costs
(including the spectre of arson), forward projections for inflation,

rising unionised labour costs, supplies and materials, the estimated cost of the 1919 Regatta was somewhere between a hefty £5000 to £6000. In reality it actually blew out to a staggering £8,243 19s 7d.[12]

The difficulty with rowing was that any spectator could stroll along the riverbank to watch the regatta without having to pay an entrance fee. Unlike Royal Ascot, where a racecourse could be enclosed, or a cricket pitch surrounded by a grandstand such as at Lord's, or the lawn tennis discreetly hidden by ivy-covered fences at Wimbledon, the towpath at Henley was a public space that could not be fenced off. This access to both river and riverbank contributed to rowing's popularity as a spectacle, but it meant that it was difficult to generate income necessary to cover running costs such as booming and piling the course, and building boat enclosures, grandstands and planked boat staging ramps.

At their April meeting, the committee of management proposed a course of action that was unanimously carried, and a resolution was passed: 'That an enclosure to be called the Henley Stewards' Enclosure be provided for the use of members and their friends.' Considering that there were only thirty-five or so Henley stewards, it was proposed to elect 300 new members of the new and exclusive Stewards' Enclosure. In this way, the Henley stewards could maintain exclusivity through a process of nomination and seconding, but also charge entrance fees to new, well-to-do members and their guests. Since its establishment in 1919, the Stewards' Enclosure has appeared annually and provided a vital financial lifeline to the Henley Royal Regatta. The Henley stewards also decided on a name for the modified regatta, calling it 'the Royal Henley Peace Regatta'.[13]

19

Mutiny in the boat

Pedalling up and down the Thames towpath was good exercise but hard work, even for Steve Fairbairn. The option of hiring a coaching boat was complicated by availability, and the cost of hire, petrol and a driver. As a result, Fairbairn coached the boat as a whole, which works for some oarsmen but not for others. Disher, for example, was frustrated that he wasn't receiving personal attention:

> I wish Fairbairn would do more individual coaching than he
> does. He rarely speaks individually. Personally, I know I am not
> rowing as well as I should be and am sure I am not improving but
> I can't get anything out of him.[1]

Fairbairn also wasn't above losing his cool when the crew weren't listening, beyond earshot of his tin loudhailer, or didn't understand what he was trying to convey. There were times when his loudhailer probably hit the dirt – hard.

The AIF No. 1 crew wasn't quite coming together and growing frustrations within the boat meant it felt 'as if a baby elephant was wobbling down the slide and falling out of the boat at times'.[2] Another

157

object of Disher's frustration was Major Audsley, in the number 4 seat. Audsley was a big unit and a good powerful match for Hauenstein, but he seemed to be 'going mad' at times, shifting his weight as he came up the slide in the recovery of each stroke, making the boat less stable.

The AIF were being flogged by Fairbairn twice a day, sometimes in atrocious rowing conditions. As Audsley wrote to his family:

> I am afraid we have kept fairly well on the go this last week
> doing two solid rows a day and by the time these are finished one
> does not feel inclined to do much I can tell you.[3]

The Q.L. was also perhaps not quite suited to the No. 1 crew – the feedback was that it was 'very springy', making it hard work for the crew to sit up the boat.[4]

Middleton often made the trip from his office at Horseferry Road to keep an eye on things, offering some individual coaching tips and taking 'a very live interest in it'.[5] No doubt Middleton and Fairbairn conferred often, talking selections and combinations as the crew went about their strenuous work.

Frustrated with the progress of the AIF squad rowing one unified style Fairbairn broke the squad down into pair-oar boats so that he could target specific bad technique and supervise the oarsmen at an individual level. He then went even further, fixing the boats by rope to the staging ramp on the Putney Embankment and coaching the men from the river's edge. Hovering over them as they pulled heavy dead water, he extolled them to think about their blade work both in the air and water rather than what their damn bodies were doing. The AIF oarsmen were beginning to find Fairbairn's 'back to basics' approach to coaching and rowing galling. Even the Australian newspapers suspected that something might be amiss with this rowing 're-education':

> It is a matter of doubt whether Mr. Fairbairn, whose rowing is
> on English lines, will prove a suitable coach for an Australian
> crew. He is coaching the crew in pairs, which would lead to the

impression that he is endeavouring to teach the men to row the English style.[6]

Fairbairn's supercilious demeanour was perceived as patronising and officious, a little too English to be palatable to these battle-hardened veterans who had spilled blood and survived a terrible war. The AIF squad began to resent it – especially Hauenstein, who simply believed in putting in the work when the blade was in the water and giving every stroke maximum 'shove'. Harry had represented his country on the water at the Stockholm Olympics; rowed to victory in the Grand Challenge at Henley; fought on behalf of Mother England for Australia on the battlefield; won a Military Medal for bravery at Pozières; and now here he was being treated like a schoolboy rower. With his short fuse, he was not going to be able to handle it much longer.

And explode he did. Fairbairn, the focal point of Hauenstein's ire, copped the full blast. Harry confronted Fairbairn upstairs in the London R.C. One can imagine him storming back and forth in the boardroom as Fairbairn watched, feeling somewhat shell-shocked at Hauenstein's tirade. Finally, 'with lurid Australian adjectives Hauenstein told Fairbairn he had no intention of continuing to row with him, put on his coat and walked out'.[7] Fairbairn had probably never experienced anything like it in his life. No oarsman would have talked down or raised his voice to Fairbairn – ever. But to be fair, Fairbairn did understand what loss meant, and how the war impacted men, rarely for the better.

His position was now untenable. He had lost the confidence of the AIF squad and could not continue in his role. The official line was that Fairbairn was ill and couldn't continue coaching due to his poor health. This result wasn't what Fairbairn had envisaged, but, to his credit, the departure never diminished his opinion of the Australian rowing crew as a force to be reckoned with.

It had always been a risk to engage Fairbairn as coach, but it was a good idea at the time – he was brilliant, a risk-taker, a legend. He was probably more disappointed by his ousting than anybody. He had a real affinity for the Australians, because he was one. But the Australia that Fairbairn knew and had grown up in was a colonial Australia that

159

saw itself, at heart, as British. The Great War had drawn an indelible line between pre- and postwar Australia: a new, self-reliant, resilient, slouch-hatted national identity had been forged on the fatal shores of Gallipoli.

The AIF now saw themselves as Australians who, while on the same side as their former colonial masters, were happy to show them up in any way they could. At a straightforward coaching level, Middleton's insistence on the Australians being coached along 'Australian' lines in the 'Australian' style meant Fairbairn, who was more English than Australian in the squad's eyes, could never fulfil the Rowing Section's essential selection criteria.

And so, just weeks out from the regatta, Fairbairn walked away from the squad. The oarsmen of the AIF rowing team were treading water once again.

PART 3

The Regatta

Yet my courage, strategy and intelligence found a way out for us
even from there; and I am sure that this too will be a memory
for us one day. So now let us all agree to do exactly as I say.
Oarsmen, stay at your oars, striking hard with your blades
through the deep swell, in the hope that Zeus allows us to escape
disaster and come out of this alive.

Homer, *The Odyssey*

20

Picking up the pieces

Interest was building and entries were streaming in for the Royal Henley Peace Regatta.

There were all kinds of rumours as to which English crews would enter. Leander Club was considering entering. The newly formed Royal Air Force (RAF) were said to be trying to raise an eight, but seemed more interested in playing rugby. There was talk of an 'Army of the Rhine' crew coming together and entering but they hadn't materialised. A. F. R. Wiggins, the 1914 Oxford University Boat Club president and exceptional oarsman who had served in the Grenadier Guards, was invited to raise a service crew of university oarsmen.[1]

The French were, of course, training in France and the Americans were keeping their powder dry and training away from the public eye on the Seine. As it was, only the Australians, New Zealanders and Canadians were hard at it at Putney. At the May meeting of the committee of management, the Henley stewards decided to extend the program to include more university and school events, which meant the regatta increased from two days to three. There had been a groundswell of enthusiasm from the schools and universities, especially for the smaller boat classes.

There were two events for 'service' eights proposed. One was the King's Cup, for the Allies' Service Eights, and the other was the Fawley Cup, which was for senior eights that could be military club crews as long as they were locally registered Amateur Rowing Association eights.[2]

The AIF Rowing Section was again without a dedicated coach. Major Eric Tulloch had also taken early repatriation, leaving the AIF squad even more in the lurch. 'I think [it] won't be much loss though [he was] a decent enough chap,' Disher opined.[3] What Fairbairn had promised now seemed clearly out of reach.

But the ace up the sleeve was Middleton. For him, the loss of the coach was just a misstep, like a mistimed rugby pass. He knew that when you make a mistake, you forget about it and make your next move bigger, focusing on the outcome. It's never over till the final whistle. Disher thought Middleton 'strong enough to be autocratic' – and that's exactly what was needed to get the AIF rowing squad back on track.[4]

Disher suggested that perhaps Middleton could row but it was out of the question. With Australian troops returning to England and repatriation now in full swing, the need for sports competitions in France may have been dwindling, but Middleton was still flat out raising funds and organising all the AIF team sports underway throughout England. Middleton was also extremely busy liaising with American Lieutenant-Colonel David Goodrich, Assistant Chief Athletic Officer of the AEF, about the sports for the Inter-Allied Games in Paris and hosting sports superstar Major Paul Withington, who was sent to Horseferry Road to organise American rowing squad arrangements for Henley. Middleton later informed Goodrich that Withington 'knew all there was to know about his job, and had already seen Sims re a boat for your crew'.[5] All the teams had to be housed, kitted out and transported to and from venues resulting in logistical problems not dissimilar to those encountered when moving an entire brigade.

Middleton had the AIF tennis team of Norman E. 'The Wizard' Brookes, Randolph Lycett, Hector 'Pat' O'Hara Wood and future 1920 Australian Olympic tennis representative Gerald Patterson competing at Wimbledon and elsewhere, sweeping teams from the US, France and England before them. The tennis team paired with some quality

British female tennis players, including Mrs Winifred McNair, Mrs Phyllis Satterthwaite and Mrs Madeleine O'Neill for the mixed doubles with Lycett. Middleston also had two rugby teams on tour. The No. 1 team included quality players such as Lieutenant Ernest Austin 'Bill' Cody and Captain Bruce 'Jackie' Beith, under the management of Major Wally Matthews and Lieutenant Leslie Seaborn MC. They were competing for their own King's Cup for rugby and playing as far away as Bradford, Leicester, Gloucester and Twickenham. The AIF reserve rugby team also toured England, drawing thousands of spectators to watch them play against armed forces teams and clubs from London to Wales. The AIF cricket team, featuring current and future Test cricketers, played thirty-four matches at ovals such as Lord's, the Oval and Glasgow. Then there was the AIF rifle shooting team competing at Bisley, about 30 miles from London, plus boxing, golf, cross country and athletics.

The AIF rowing squad spent the last week of May at Putney doing the best they could. Middleton stayed in London, organising teams and tours and, no doubt, continuing his secret tryst with Marion. A revolving roster of coaches was assembled to look after the two AIF eights, a four and a pair-oar, and Alma Cox was to compete as the single sculler.

Horace Stevens had been asked to step up and take on coaching duties but according to Disher: 'Stevens failed us a couple of times being unable to turn up and Harry Ross-Soden has had them the last sessions twice.'[6] Ross-Soden, Middleton and even Disher were coaching in between jumping into boats. Word that Lieutenant-Colonel Norman Marshall would accompany the squad to Henley to coach was welcomed. Disher wrote: 'We are in hopes of Norman Marshall coming along to Henley with us and he will be able to do both 8s for us since Middleton says he can't get up with us.'[7]

The AIF No. 1 boat was struggling; a sense of defeat was creeping into the crew psyche. 'The 1st eight is going well but that is all I can say for it. It certainly is not the crew it promised at one time to be. However, there is time enough yet on which to come on.'[8] The vigour, expectation and excitement that squads experience when they first form often peters away into self-doubt. Trying to rebuild a team's confidence once it has been shaken is difficult. Even harder than starting is starting again. Disher lamented:

> As it is it won't be a bad crew but it is lacking in a blind confidence as regards its coach, committee, and perhaps I might add, stroke. I am not going to say that there isn't confidence in any one of these but it is not a blind one which to my mind is essential for the *best*.[9]

The entry deadline for the Peace Regatta was 21 June 1919 at noon precisely. The Rowing Section were going to enter the AIF No. 1 eight into the King's Cup; the AIF No. 2 eight (which was rowing in the Marlow Victory Regatta the week before) for the Fawley Cup; and a coxless military service four-oar crew for the Leander Cup. Alma Cox would race the singles in the Kingswood Sculls.

The New Zealanders and the Canadians were also entering the King's Cup, and of course the Americans and French were entered, but there was still little sign of the English crews. The local Upper Thames rowing clubs such as London R.C. and Thames R.C. weren't feeling confident enough they could put together crews of sufficient excellence to have a crack at the King's Cup. The English selectors still hoped an Army of the Rhine crew might materialise, but where or from what arm of the services an English 'service' crew would appear remained a mystery.

Most of the work that Middleton had been putting in on the AIF Sports Control Board could not have happened without serious money. The Australian Comfort Fund committee's financial contribution was vital but the reality was that funding the combined sports teams required some serious cashflow. Middleton's working relationship with Australian mining tycoon and political influencer W. S. Robinson had developed to the extent that W.S. was happy to contribute to the costs of the board. The Australians were lucky to have W.S. as a benefactor and Middleton knew it. Even though the rowing was often patchy and tensions were getting high in the boat, it was important to know where the money was coming from and nurture those relationships. Being able to entertain the men, keep them fed and requisition supplies as needed was critical to keeping a steady ship.

The Robinsons lived at Bourne End, a beautiful country mansion on the Thames, not far from Henley. Before the team packed up for Henley, Middleton, along with W.S.'s fellow 'Scotchie', Clive Disher, went up to pay the Robinson family a visit. Disher reported:

> This afternoon 3 of us went up to Bourne End in one of the
> AIF cars on semi-business to see a Mr. Robinson up there. He
> is an old Scotch Collegian by the way is very wealthy. Spends
> thousands of pounds on Australians over here. He is taking a
> lot of interest in the Sports that the AIF are taking part in and
> particularly so in the rowing. He is helping us financially and
> in lots of other ways. We had afternoon tea at his weekend
> house there and met Mrs. Robinson and the daughter. They are
> exceedingly nice people.[10]

It's not hard to imagine a thick envelope changing hands, along with a firm handshake and a pat on the back. W.S. knew that Middleton would do the right thing and spend the money on winning the postwar Peace Games.

Middleton knew that timing was everything, especially making sure the crew's performance peaked in time for the Royal Henley Peace Regatta. The risk of moving up to Henley too soon was that after the coaching disasters, personal irritations and growing frustrations among the Rowing Section at Putney, the squad could suffer from staleness if too long at Henley before the regatta. A change could be as good as a rest, but too much of that change could lead to further unrest. It was a microcosm of the larger issues Monash was facing as he repatriated the AIF: keeping the men occupied and in line were big challenges at every level in 1919.

21

New digs, new coach

Major Audsley's early reconnaissance of Henley had been spot on. He had scoped the layout of Henley and the Reach, and recommended suitable quarters for the squad that was definitely on the luxury end of available Henley rentals.

At the end of May 1919, the AIF Rowing Section moved into a three-storey freestanding Mock Tudor brick mansion. Situated on grounds that stretched to the Thames riverbank, Wharfe House was a rambling expanse of rooms and staircases, built on a grand scale. It was also private, tucked away behind tall, ivy-covered walls at the end of its own private laneway, Wharfe Lane, off New Street. The squad would live and train in style.

The ground floor of the house boasted a huge kitchen, and there were ample mess rooms, pantries, bathing amenities, reading rooms, a sweeping staircase, and salons and full-size billiard room which looked onto the Thames. On the upper level and in the attics were six large bedrooms with casement windows that could comfortably billet four or five oarsmen each. The rooms also looked out across the Thames and each had a balcony on which the oarsmen could recline, relax and watch the activity on the water. The well-trimmed lawn in the rear swept smoothly down to the river's edge and it was literally a 20-yard stroll from the rear patio to put boat to water for training. Audsley reported:

> The place we are in is a magnificent spot right at the finish of the course and with a lawn down to water's edge, all we had to do was to level a pontoon and make the existing boat shed longer and were easily able to get all our boats in. Our fleet of ships consists of two racing eights, 1 racing 4, 1 practice 4 and two sculling boats.[1]

Among the advantages of Wharfe House's location were the proximity of Brakspear's Brewery and the quaint and cosy Crown Hotel, located just around the corner from Wharfe Lane. The Crown would become a regular team bonding and carbo-loading ale station at the end of thirsty sessions on the water. It was all very idyllic – for oarsmen who'd spent the last few years dodging ordnance in flea-infested trenches, it would have seemed like paradise.

When the Australians arrived at Henley, they discovered the Americans had already secretly slipped in from Paris and were hard at work training on the still waters of the Henley Reach. The Americans had left their training camp at Asnières-sur-Seine, about 7 kilometres north-east of the centre of Paris, for Henley-on-Thames on 20 May.[2] The *New York Times* reported that the American Army would be represented at Henley for the first time. Their late arrival in England meant they had missed out on Wharfe House, but they had quickly found quarters at Greencroft House in Vicarage Road, from which it was about a ten-minute stroll to the boat enclosures. Although the Americans were a smaller squad by actual number, consisting of just the one King's Cup eight, two sweep four-oared crews aiming to win the Leander Cup, and two scullers, selected from both the eight and the coaching team, they were big men and well fed. They were rowing as guests out of the Leander Club and made the daily trip across Henley Bridge to train.

This American rowing squad was different from the Australian squad in two distinct ways. Firstly, whereas the Australian crews were made up of all ranks, from gunners to majors, the American rowing squad members were all officers and graduates of the high-profile American Ivy League universities. Secondly, they were flush with money and military support to the extent that they could bring little pieces of American comfort with them, including steaks, baseball kits and American footballs. The Australians had limited funds and often had to rely upon the generosity of strangers.

Following on from the Paris Regatta, the AEF team remained under the coaching command of Captain Charles Wiman, with Major Paul Withington still his right-hand man, chief trainer and physical conditioner of the AEF rowing squad. If there was any American all-round sports star equivalent of the dual Olympian Major Syd Middleton, it had to be Major Withington, whose superb multi-code athleticism had shone out at Harvard and beyond. He had also coached football at the University of Wisconsin. Withington believed that in rowing all the hard work should be done early, so that a crew could taper off and do lighter work. In his book, *The Book of Athletics*, he proposed that

> Many a good crew has been found sadly lacking, when it came to the final endurance because, as one great coach said, 'They had left all their rowing on the water by too much practice.'[3]

As we saw earlier, Major Withington also had Henley Royal Regatta racing experience, having competed in the 1914 Grand Challenge Cup final, and as a sculler in the Diamond Sculls. The other crew members included (bow) Lieutenant C. J. Coe (Yale); (2) Captain Royal R. Pullen (Washington); (3) Captain Louis Penney (California); (4) Major Paul Withington; (5) Lieutenant J. Amory Jefferies (Harvard); (6) Major Herman L. Rogers (Yale and Captain of Boats); (7) Lieutenant J. Howard McHenry (Yale); (stroke) Captain Douglas Kingsland (Cornell); and Lieutenant Guy Gale (California) on the ropes as coxswain.[4] The American squad's Henley crew was a very different one to the crew that had raced on the River Seine in April. Only three members of that crew remained: McHenry, Pullen and Gale.[5]

The Americans had vast numbers of men in France and had drawn upon their overwhelming depth to improve their crew. Each and every one of them had served on the Western Front (Lieutenant Jeffries had been wounded in Champagne) and had rowed in the American Varsity eights; they were enthusiastic and experienced oarsmen. On the water, as the Australian and American crews rowed past each other, they sized up their opposition. Disher observed that:

> The Americans are a big strong looking lot. Row well sometimes, with an awkward semi-English style and at other times row badly. They are improving but any first-class crew could beat them. Trouble is we are not first class as yet.[6]

The Americans in return noted that 'The Australians have been together since last winter. They have shown formidably in practice ...' They also noted that the American and New Zealand boats 'are so evenly matched that a thrilling finish between the two may be expected at Henley'.[7]

The Americans were pretty sporty in general and made the most of English facilities, often playing golf at the Henley Golf Club.[8] After a late afternoon training session, having washed down their Sims boat and put it away inside the Leander shed, the Americans would sometimes grab their baseball kit and mark out a rough baseball diamond on Lion Meadow to play ball. The distinctive whack of the bat would have rung out across the Thames. From Wharfe House, the Australians could see through the trees the Americans running around Lion Meadow. English children crept nearer for a closer look, and there was great interest in having a go at this strange ball game with a round bat. Major Withington would later recall that:

> [the] adaptability of the Briton toward any line of sport was shown at Henley, where we were training for the regatta ... the English boys would come to us in the evening and borrow the bats and balls and gloves ... Although cricket holds first place

in the hearts of the English, they were much impressed with baseball as a sport.[9]

It is easy to imagine a kind of international rowing 'field of dreams' in which the English, New Zealand and Australians crews, never shy to whack a ball, were shown how to stand and face the pitcher or wear strange pad-like gloves to catch a high ball.

The squad had begun their move to Henley on Tuesday 27 May. The next day they were taken to Oxford to mix with the heart of amateur rowing in England, at 'The Bumps'. The Bumps had started in Oxford in 1815 and usually took several days to race, during the 'Torpids' in March or the 'Summer Eights' in May. They are the aquatic equivalent of British Bulldog or 'tag' and are incredibly nerve-racking as they are held on a winding and narrow reach of the Isis. After some qualifying races, seeded boats line up bow to stern and as a crew sets off, they are chased by the following crew, separated by about a length and a half. The aim is to bump the stern of the boat ahead, which must then drop out, allowing the faster crew to bump the crews further ahead. It must be hell for the stroke to watch the bow of a speeding boat bearing down upon their stern. Bumps are rowed in both Oxford and Cambridge.

Disher arrived in Oxford looking forward to seeing an old college rowing mate: 'MacNeil who used to row at Scotch and Ormond is at one of the Colleges there and is sure to be rowing.'[10] Lieutenant Neil Harcourt MacNeil was indeed back in the boat, rowing for the Balliol College crew. While in Oxford, the AIF rowing squad were also entertained to dinner by Dr Hugh K. Ward, another expat Australian and former crewmate of Middleton, Hauenstein and Ross-Soden in the Australian 1912 Stockholm Olympic crew.[11]

The genteel university world of Oxford, with its aristocratic and well-heeled students reading law, ancient Greek, Latin or medicine striding in black gowns across college quadrangles, was chalk and cheese to the world of rowing in Australia. In Australia, rowing was much more a club system, where if you put the time and effort in, you could participate. Anyone with the talent and inclination could walk into a rowing club, join up, pay their subs, get into the club spirit, step into a boat and row. The New South Wales Rowing Association (NSWRA) had removed the ban on manual labourer amateurs in 1903, pretty much opening rowing to all classes and types of workers.

Disher's old rowing alma mater, Melbourne University R.C., situated on the Yarra River – itself a copy of the Putney Embankment in the heart of Melbourne – was perhaps an exception, modelling itself more closely on the English university rowing system. With its well-established student colleges such as Ormond College, Melbourne University students studied in well-furnished 'rooms' that were filled with sporting trophies and luxurious essentials from rural Victoria or upmarket Toorak. The 'wet bob' college students rowed for their respective colleges first before being selected into the Melbourne University representative crew. The rowing community in Melbourne fondly tried to emulate the English heartland, holding regattas such as the prestigious Henley-on-Yarra Regatta, a hugely popular and well-attended rowing spectacle that attracted tens of thousands of Melburnians turned out in all their finery.

Predominantly, though, the Melbourne-based rowing clubs were community-based clubs founded by oarsmen who just wanted to pull an oar rather than replicate the amateur sporting ideals of the English class system. In Australia, 'amateur' was much more loosely interpreted than it was by the Henley stewards in England.

Sydney-based rowing clubs like Sydney Rowing Club, Enterprise, Balmain, North Shore, Glebe, Mercantile and Leichhardt were also community-based rowing clubs, often founded by groups of like-minded businessmen who wanted to promote physical activity and manly sports. These community rowing clubs generally took all (male) takers, including private school, GPS-educated oarsmen. The only exceptions were the openly declared professional oarsmen who rowed for prize money and side wagers – not that they didn't sometimes paddle 'ex officio' or have 'honorary' club membership granted to them out of a local Sydney-based rowing club. The professional scullers even had their own rowing club and shed, later named the Parramatta River Professional Sculling Club, which was situated at the end of Wharf Road in Gladesville.

The professional Australian oarsmen of the late 19th century and early 20th century were often manual labourers, farmers, boatmen, boatbuilders, watermen and 'menial labourers' who rowed as single scullers. Most were based in New South Wales, where the big money events were. Rowing as a single sculler meant they didn't have to split prize money, as they would were they in a crew boat. As single scullers they simply sourced (or built) their own sculling boat or skiff and found a long, flat stretch of water to train on. These professional oarsmen were also canny, streetwise self-promoters, tapping into nationalistic pride, and built up legions of followers (and SP bookmakers) for the drawcard races, just as professional boxers did for their heavily promoted drawcard bouts. Their world professional championship races had stakes sometimes in excess of a tidy £500 for a side wager, and one can only wonder what money changed hands through private bets and starting price odds.

Peter Kemp, for example, a professional sculler and world sculling champion from 1889 to 1890, could live, train and scull on the Colo River in the north-west of Sydney, away from the hustle of central Sydney. World champion professional sculler George Towns could be found up the north New South Wales coast, near the town of Maitland, where he had first learned to pull an oar. Down the coast from Sydney, the British-born professional sculler William 'Bill' Beach lived and farmed in Dapto and trained on Lake Illawarra.

But these big events were the exception, rather than a regular weekend round of competition. Large steam ferries and boats filled to capacity lined the courses, often with said vessels listing dangerously to one side as spectators crowded over the ship's railings for a view of the race. Steamers filled with well-heeled paying spectators could follow the race and buy the best view. Often the NSWRA, or even the governor of New South Wales, would hold civic receptions for victorious world sculling champions when they returned from overseas or successfully defended a title. In late 19th century and into the 20th century, sculling in Australia was high profile, incredibly popular and not exclusive in any way. Those were the days.

The larger community rowing clubs in Sydney Harbour, which at first congregated around the working maritime hubs of Circular Quay, Walsh Bay, Woolloomooloo Bay and thereabouts, were places where city-based working oarsmen could stroll down Pitt Street and go for a row after work. These Sydney crew oarsmen were arguably more akin to the hard-working Thames watermen based near the Isle of Dogs in East London. Eventually, as prosperity and commerce grew, the Sydney CBD–based rowing clubs such as Sydney Rowing Club, founded in 1870, and first situated where Sydney Opera House stands today, were pushed out of Circular Quay and west into numerous cosy little bays, quiet creeks or coves along the furthest reaches of the Parramatta and Lane Cove rivers.

Along the western reaches of the Parramatta River, suburbs and landmarks were named after River Thames landmarks such as Greenwich, Henley, Woolwich, Putney and Mortlake. These western waters, where Sydney Harbour merged into the Parramatta River, provided dozens of nice, calm stretches of water upon which to row. Rowing was also not exclusively the preserve of males – though their clubhouses were. Many rowing clubs staged women's or girls' rowing events as part of their regatta schedule. By 1917 there were six amateur ladies rowing clubs around Sydney, and vigorous competition between them.

The egalitarian nature of rowing in Australia was reflected in the make-up of the AIF Rowing Section. Private school or university educated oarsmen were clearly in the minority. For example, Tom McGill's family was in the haulage business (read truck driver); Harry Hauenstein had been a constable in the NSW police force (or 'public servant', as he was graciously deemed by the 1912 HRR committee of management) and then worked as a carpenter; Sydney Middleton had grown up on the mean dockside streets of Pyrmont; Alan Audsley and Ossie Wood were office clerks; and Gig Smedley was a signwriter.

Elsewhere across Australia, Scotty was a steam locomotive fireman on the railways; Eric Harrison (later a Nationalist Party MP and then Sir Eric Harrison, Australian High Commissioner in London) had left school at thirteen and first worked in haberdashery; George Mettam was a cadet in a bank; Archie Robb was a shop floor engineer; Freddie House was an office clerk; Harold Newall was an importer; Harry Goyen, the son of a Tasmanian quarryman, was a printer; and the list of non-professional and 'menial' labouring or office occupations of the AIF Rowing Section went on and on.

These oarsmen came from all walks of life, trades and callings and displayed a healthy disrespect for authority or social class. That's not to say that a diluted and bastardised form of a class system did not exist in Australia; it just meant very few people respected it in the way the British adhered to their class distinctions.

The educated oarsmen of the AIF Rowing Section did, however, seem to emanate mainly from Victoria, with Clive Disher (a doctor) and Harry Ross-Soden (a solicitor) being among a few university-qualified and private school educated oarsmen in the AIF Rowing Section. But fundamentally, the worth of an oarsman was predicated on his ability to grab an oar, sit in a boat and row himself out all the way to the finish line.

The Americans would be formidable competition in the Royal Henley Peace Regatta, but the ace up the Australians' sleeve was their new coach, Lieutenant-Colonel Norman Marshall MC, DSO and two Bars.

Norman Marshall was a dead-set legend. He was born in Callander, Scotland but grew up in Melbourne from the age of two and was educated at Scotch College, Melbourne. He was an all-round athlete and footballer, and also rowed for the Scotch College eight.

Marshall had volunteered on 17 August 1914, not long after the outbreak of war, and served with the AIF 5th Battalion in Gallipoli, where he rose rapidly through the ranks and was awarded the Military Cross for bravery at Krithia. At Lone Pine, his resourcefulness and rat cunning led him to develop an early form of IED (improvised explosive device), a 'hairbrush' bomb improvised from gun cotton and a paddle of wood that blew up a whole Turkish outpost. After the Gallipoli campaign ended, when the 'great schism' of battalions occurred in Egypt, Marshall was attached to the 57th Battalion and served on the Western Front, notably at the disastrous operation at Fromelles, but with distinction. He also served with the 60th Battalion and his stellar service and numerous occasions of bravery were acknowledged with the DSO and two bars, and frequent mentions in dispatches. Effectively, Marshall seemed downright indestructible, and a force of nature equal to the great Fairbairn.

After the squad returned from Oxford, Marshall took charge of whipping the AIF squad into shape in Henley. Every man in the AIF knew of Marshall's brilliant military career. Without displaying one shred of conceit or arrogance, he commanded the utmost respect from the men, and probably, to an admirable degree, fear. He was also still a formidable oarsmen. At Putney, Norman Marshall had jumped into a scratch eight with Middleton and his technique and skill were immediately apparent. Disher reported: 'we now have a 3rd Eight, a scratch one in which Middleton and Norman Marshall row and we have hopes that Middleton will end up in the 1st Eight. Some 8 then believe me. Marshall is rowing damn well and is worth a seat in any boat'.[12]

Middleton, who was still motoring up from Horseferry Road (and likely from Marion's flat in Sloane Square), was still run ragged with his AIF sports responsibilities. Between himself and Marshall, in consultation with Ross-Soden, Disher and Hauenstein, he had now selected two AIF eights. They were still undecided on the crew for a coxswainless four in the Leander Cup; had outsourced the Hambleden Pairs entry to the AIF Wattle Club; and were now settled on Alma Cox as the single sculler for the wonderfully Australian sounding 'not the' Kingswood Sculls.

The AIF No. 2 crew comprised 'Nip' Newall as stroke; Johnny Begg in 7; 'Googly' Cogle in the rhythm seat of 6; young Tom McGill in the 5 seat; 'Brum' White in 4; Eric Harrison in 3; 'Blue' Penny in 2; and the man from the west, George Mettam, in bow; with 'Gig' Smedley steering. These men were a classic bunch of quiet achievers and were rowing exceptionally well. Middleton, Marshall and the AIF No. 1 crew certainly were not underestimating them.

> They went over the course [yesterday afternoon] in roughly
> 6 seconds faster time than we did an hour later. They are further
> advanced than we are, and I don't think came down below
> 30 during any part of the row whereas we came over at 28 and
> only at the finish went up to 31.[13]

With Middleton being far too distracted and busy with his Sports Control Board duties in Horseferry Road, as a coach and selector, he and Marshall kept swapping between McGill, Begg and Scotty in the number 6 seat as well as throughout the AIF No. 1 crew. This coaching indecision was taking its toll on the confidence of the crew members. The crew had good pedigree and physical size but there was something missing. On the water, the crew often took to arguing and calling out fellow crew members for on-water errors such as not pulling their weight, shooting the slide, being either too slow or too fast at the catch or finish of the stroke. But when Middleton arrived in Henley something transformative took hold.

Disher and several others, including Hauenstein and Ross-Soden, had for weeks been flippantly suggesting that Middleton should row, and now they might just see it happen. As always, with the highly muscled Hauenstein powering away in the number 5 seat, the No. 1 crew needed the raw power to balance him. Middleton was the same height and had the same reach; the war had burnt off his softness and he was now closer to his competitive weight during his elite rugby and rowing days.

The war had ravaged Middleton in many ways. His gruffness towards those in the Sports Section was legendary. When Disher spoke with Middleton during their rowing debriefs, he found him irascible, with little time for petty grievances or inconsequential details. The only company that seemed to cheer him up was that of his beau – and it's possible that when it came to deciding to row in the No. 1 crew, the motivating factor was Marion. In 1919, Middleton was thirty-five years of age and Marion was ten years younger. Perhaps Middleton wanted to demonstrate his physical prowess; maybe he wanted to impress Marion by taking the boat all the way and winning the damned King's Cup for Australia. Whatever, it was, Middleton began to waver, and then he buckled. He stepped back into the boat, back into the number 6 seat. *His* seat. Audsley, distracted by his retinue of lady friends (and the awarding of a DSO) had once again been clinging onto his number 4 seat but had long seen the moment coming.

> We are working fairly hard up here now and old Syd Middleton
> has at last decided to row in the 1st crew, at present I am the
> one to be kicked out of it, and I am now rowing 5 in the second
> eight, however the selectors have not decided yet so there is still
> a chance, the second crew however is just as fast, if not a little
> faster than the first, so you will see there is not much in it and
> our first race is at Marlow in about a fortnights time.[14]

The squad finally had an oarsman who could balance out the raw physicality of star rower Hauenstein. The challenge for Hauenstein would be to balance his own temperament before the race.

Hauenstein had been struggling to keep his mind together. The experience of Pozières and the bloody battle that followed had deeply affected all veterans of that battle. Some could lock it away and function on a day-to-day basis; some managed by self-medicating. Hauenstein's fondness for the bottle was lost on nobody in the squad.

But the one thing that did hold Harry together was the boat. In an eight, Harry felt bolted into his seat. He owned the number 5 seat. He cut a striking figure as he carried his oar down the pontoon, crewmates parting like the Red Sea as he went straight to the middle of the boat, pulled the handle and oar collar through the poppet rigger and settled into his seat. Any crew would have felt relieved that Hauenstein was in their boat and that they weren't up against him.

On the Henley Reach, Harry was in his element. Henley, even though it was worlds away from the hardscrabble neighbourhood he'd learned to row in, would have been like returning home for him.

He was a born oarsman, an Olympic-level competitor who could trounce any takers. If he'd been born into money, he would have been a world champion, but his legacy had been tarnished by his need to make a living by hustling on the water back in Sydney. At the time, the distinctions between 'amateur' and 'professional' were rigorously policed. An athlete choosing to compete for money was scandalous, even though financial hardship and the need to earn a living was likely the driving factors.

Hauenstein had already suffered the indignity of his amateur status being called into question by the stewards at the 1912 Henley Royal Regatta, but on that occasion it was due to his being a former policeman, and then deemed a 'menial' labourer. The Australian officials worked hard behind the scenes with the committee of management and, 'agreed to put his case before Mr. Steward, which was done and who agreed to waive objections.'[15]

What was worse for the NSWRA – and for rowing in Australia, for that matter – was when news broke in England that Harry Hauenstein and another rower, Stuart Amess, had allegedly 'gone over' from the amateur ranks.

Hauenstein must have been tempted to row for pay. He had sacrificed his career, and his Olympic stipend was now finished. He needed money and the opportunity to further himself. As the only Sydney oarsman to have won three Interstate Eight-oared Championship titles, Hauenstein seriously considered switching to the professional ranks. The temptation to cross over ramped up when professional oarsman and promoter Archie Priddle actually listed a proposed Parramatta River Professional Sculling Club sweep oar four-man crew, including Harry Hauenstein, to challenge any other crew to a race on the Parramatta River for an enticing sum of £50 per man. This was what started the rumour that Harry Hauenstein and Stuart Amess had crossed over into the professional ranks.

Hauenstein was seriously annoyed and had to slap down the rumour and public innuendo that he was turning professional. Maybe he simply got cold feet; maybe he had seriously thought about it as an option, but was counselled out of it by his very close friend and coxswain Ossie Wood, who was the persuasive and influential secretary of the NSWRA. What Haunestein said publicly to Sydney's *Daily Telegraph* was:

> I know nothing about it, and never gave any permission for my
> name to be used, or my consent to row with the crew. I have
> never had any intention of turning professional, and have none
> now ... I am no professional, and have no idea of becoming one.[16]

After 1912, he had reasonably expected that he would never see Henley again but here he was again strolling over the Henley Bridge, peering over the stone railing above the head of Tamesis and watching crews emerge from the arches, heaving and splashing their way up and down the River Thames.

It wasn't only Hauenstein who was having trouble with his mental health. Each day was riddled with outbursts and irrational behaviour. Men had to give each other space or rally around; sometimes it was difficult to tell which worked best. Often these outbursts were downplayed with grim humour. As a medical doctor, Disher knew that even though this new condition may have been given a label – 'neurasthenia' or 'shell shock' – there was no cure or ointment that made it feel better. If these episodes struck, caused by something seemingly insignificant like a sudden loud noise, the walls of Wharfe House could close in on the men like the collapsing dugouts, bunkers and trenches of Pozières, and it was often a case of every man for himself. Disher observed:

> It is rather amusing in a way the members of the 8 seem to have
> periodic attacks of nerves, [a] rather interesting study of human
> nature. I had quite a burst about 10 days ago and now Harry
> Ross-Soden is having [one,] a couple of others too have had a go
> and of course everybody else is most superior about it, forgetting
> that all have their turns.[17]

22

The two crews

Perhaps the defining difference between the two AIF rowing crews was that the No. 2 crew was more relaxed. They were not expected to make the finals of the Kings Cup and so weren't under as much pressure to live up to Middleton's great expectations. His impact within the No. 1 boat was obvious but the question of why they were not getting the relevant speed up was a quandary. Hauenstein and Middleton probably had their own ideas about what to do but for the moment they kept them under wraps. As Middleton grew even more irritated with their scratchy and lacklustre rows, he and Marshall knew there needed to be some major surgery – but the diagnosis had to be correct.

Smedley, coxing the No. 2 crew, was probably adding to the carnival air of his boat with his droll asides and rapid-fire quips, typical of a canny coxswain trying to psych out the opposition. When the two crews rowed over the course at capped rates or practised short trail sprints to the Barrier mark or the Fawley mark, the AIF No. 2 were faster almost every time. Every time the No. 1 crew were beaten, it was back to the drawing board. The last thing a No. 1 crew wants is a No. 2 crew (or second eight, ostensibly a back-up crew) constantly beating them, thereby making a solid case for being the No. 1 crew. Usually that kind of rivalry ends in tears at best, or a full-on punch-up at worst.

The No. 2 crew had Scotty muscling his way in the middle of the boat, now teamed with Audsley in the number 5 seat. Audsley was only now adding some much-needed weight to the crew, likely with the intention of trying to force his way back into the No. 1 crew. As Disher noted:

It is quite possible that they will be entered for the King's Cup at Henley as well as ourselves. It would be rather a nasty jinx? To be beaten by them.[1]

He also wrote of the No. 2 crew:

... they are a far happier crowd than we are. I am no paragon of virtues myself these days and don't know that others are. Middleton is about the worst tempered thing I have seen for months and the very sight of him makes me want to say something sarcastic or unpleasant; though I am more than thankful to have him in the boat. There he is invaluable.[2]

With New Zealand's win of the King's Cup for rugby, by the middle of May the rugby competitions were winding down.

Middleton – now that many of the other sports competitions were either underway and in the hands of capable AIF administrators, or finishing – could finally see his schedule opening up. He drove the 33-mile return journey to Henley from London each day, and didn't always arrive in Henley in good humour.

Middleton's earlier experience of Henley had generated many pleasant memories, unadulterated by the violent intrusions of war. The 1912 crew was the finest crew he had ever rowed in. It was a perfect blend of raw power and orchestral rhythm. Every crew member owned their seat and had earned their place in the boat. They had transcended borders and states and come together as an Australian crew rowing a homegrown Australian style. To combine nine volatile and wilful individuals into a vessel and have them become a single masterful crew went far beyond the arithmetic of heights and weights of oarsmen, or the angle of their oars. Perhaps Middleton thought that the waters of Henley could wash away the blood, grime and terror of four years of war and allow that internal peace to return.

The latest incarnation of the No. 1 crew was Clive Disher as stroke; Harry Ross-Soden backing him up in the 7 seat; Middleton back in his familiar 6 seat, with Hauenstein in 5; House back on the stroke side in 4; Begg in 3; Davis in 2; Robb, as usual, in the silent world of his bow seat; and Ossie Wood steering. On paper, the AIF No. 1 crew looked the goods, but on the water the crew just didn't click. Hauenstein was still wrestling with his demons and was difficult to handle, especially with cheap alcohol available at the Crown Hotel as a form of self-medication.

Middleton's commuting days ended when he moved to Henley. Disher noted that:

> Middleton has now come down to the House to live and I hope it will improve his temper. House unfortunately has developed a bad throat but I expect will be better by Monday. Hauenstein has been giving a bit of trouble lately but is better again.[3]

In fact, the members of the No. 1 crew were fighting like dogs on the water. The much sought after 'boat run' between strokes was missing during their daily rows. Each time they took a stroke, instead of the boat lifting and running along the top of the water, it felt as if they were lugging the heavy cedar boat along a few yards. Occasionally, between strokes, the run would magically appear, tempting them to repeat their work, but as soon as they took the next stroke the run was gone and they were back to the repetitive grind of shoving the boat a few yards and plonk; shove and plonk; shove and plonk.

As they rowed up past Temple Island, the murmur of the breeze in the branches, the distant screech of a kite and the frenzied sound of ducks hurrying out of the path of an oncoming eight were drowned out by the syncopated sounds of oars, grunts and yells emanating from the boat. Everyone in the boat considered themselves an expert and almost everyone thought they knew exactly what the problem was, though the wisest kept their opinions to themselves. As Sydney's *Daily Mirror* reported it:

> In the boat there was no rank. Each called the other by
> Christian name. At times one of the gunners was likely to let
> out a full-blooded blast at some lieutenant who was shooting
> his slide. Only man to escape any kind of back chat was
> Middleton … Middleton was a 'tough guy' who was just as
> likely to turn on a colonel as a private if he thought he was
> 'being done in'.[4]

Lieutenant-Colonel Marshall needed to take control of the AIF No. 1 crew, and quickly. There was griping and squabbling among the men; tensions were rising along, with the growing sense of frustration about why the combination was not working.

Meanwhile, the Henley stewards and committee of management were well underway with their plans for the Royal Henley Peace Regatta. One major work that defines the regatta is the rowing course, which is boomed and piled into a straight for the last mile. Workers on barges methodically and with great precision drove timber poles into the riverbed at set intervals, parallel down both sides of the course. With the piles set deep and secure into the riverbed, hundreds of floating timber booms were then linked between the piles, and boom by boom the regatta course materialised – from the start on the Oxfordshire side of Temple Island, sweeping in a gentle right-hand bend just clear of the island, then into the straight and down towards Henley Bridge, finishing just past the new Stewards' Enclosure.

The committee of management was also busy supervising the large boat enclosure, comprising deep canvas tents erected to accommodate the many boats and oars that would be sheltered for the duration of the Royal Henley Peace Regatta.

Timber grandstands and platforms were constructed; picket fences were planted, stark white against colourful flower boxes arranged around pavilions, tea stations and a rotunda where a brass band would play at lunch and tea intervals.

Rowing often attracts spectators hoping to while away a few hours alongside a riverbank, watching the crews push off and train on the water. During the weeks at Henley, hundreds of soldiers and supporters of many different nationalities caught the train from London in order to stroll along the towpath beside the Thames and watch the bustling activity on the water.

From the town centre, visiting soldiers on a day trip could share an ale or two at the Angel on the Bridge, then stroll a few yards to the Henley Bridge and catch the first glimpses of those coming and going from the Boat Enclosure – boats and crews of all shapes, nationalities and sizes. All of this activity was open to the public; visitors could peer into the beautifully crafted boats stored on racks or resting on wooden trestles in the Boat Enclosure before setting off for a pleasant stroll down the Thames towpath. For the hundreds of diggers who travelled daily to Henley the sight of the AIF crews rowing up and down the Henley Reach was great entertainment. Not least, the diggers 'delighted to hear the collection of military ranks in No.1 crew abusing each other'.[5]

The walk down the towpath is shaded by trees until it opens out at Temple Meadows into the wide, flat, green grazing lands. All along the riverbank the water teemed with birdlife such as moorhens, parakeets, spotted flycatchers and swifts. The King's white swans cruised the summer waters with cygnets in tow, columns of Canadian geese gatecrashed the river party and tufted ducks paddled furiously in convoy, only stopping to duck-dive while foraging for food. All in all, a trip to Henley to watch the international crews train amidst the gentle refrain of the river, woods and wildlife was a very pleasant day out.

Even as the days grew more and more pleasant, threats and challenges for the AIF oarsmen mounted on all sides. From mid-June 1919, fresh school or university crews and Allied crews from across the dominion were arriving in Henley almost daily.

23

Six to one

The activity, on and off the Thames, was intensifying, and Henley now crawled with foreigners and military personnel from all the Allied armies. The New Zealanders and Canadians took up quarters at Eversley House in Hart Street and Mattlands in Vicarage Road respectively. The English crews who were expected might still enter the King's Cup were the Army of the Rhine; Sandhurst Military College; the RAF; the Tank Corps; a Thames Rowing Club Service Crew; Oxford University; Cambridge University; and a Leander Club Service Crew. As the Australians, Americans, Canadians and New Zealanders practised over the Henley Reach, some voiced concerns that the local club crews had not yet entered or made an appearance on the water.

The reality was that many of the Upper Thames rowing clubs had realised they could not gather enough service oarsmen from their sadly depleted ranks to enter crews in the increasingly competitive King's Cup. Hopes for a RAF crew were abandoned, 'owing to the impossibility of securing sufficient first-class oarsmen'.[1] It's possible they had focused all their athletic attention on their giant-killing rugby team.

Instead, English sports authorities stayed with the option of smaller boat crew events, such as pairs or four-oared events, or at best a more rudimentary clinker eight-oar crew. Only the rowing club bastion of Leander remained hopeful of entering a quality eight of returned servicemen in the King's Cup. The dominion crews kept a keen eye out for the appearance of the fabled cerise colours of Leander Club on the Henley Reach; a Leander team would be stiff competition for any crew on the water.

English rowing could, however, rely upon the age-old traditional nurseries of rowing at the cloistered colleges and hallowed halls of Oxford and Cambridge universities. Students who had ridden out the war at home enthusiastically grasped the chance to win glory on the water. The university students swelled the regatta entries, and an additional day was added to the racing program, extending it from three to four days. The interest from university rowing clubs made some of the English rowing pundits snort that:

> the college crews are quite as numerous as in the old days; but it must be confessed that quality is sadly lacking, which is scarcely surprising, in view of the heavy sacrifice made by oarsmen in the war ... To see crews with every fault known to the rowing critic ... may be painful to old hands, but after all, we have been through the greatest war in history, and rowing cannot be reconstructed on former lines without a long period of apprenticeship.[2]

It was no surprise that eventually the Leander Club abandoned all hope of entering a competitive eight-oared crew for the King's Cup. The Australians, Disher quipped, were disappointed to hear that such a venerable rowing institution had 'scratched worse luck. I am not an admirer of the English Sporting spirit'.[3] Perhaps the Leander Club, who 'do call upon the pick of university oarsmen year after year', weighed up their diminishing options, took into consideration the selection needs of the two King's Cup university service crews, and wanted to avoid the savaging they might receive from the press for entering a half-rate military eight-oared crew.[4]

The *Henley Standard* was somewhat bleak about the English chances of winning the King's Cup, reporting that the central plank of the Leander Club had 'failed to get a Service eight together to row for the King's Cup ... and it is practically certain that the trophy will leave England'.[5]

As a member of the Henley Regatta committee of management, Mr Harcourt 'Tarka' Gold was compelled to make the King's Cup eight-oared event as competitive and successful as possible. The King's Cup event for the Allied service eights might have been a one-off in place of the prestigious Grand Challenge Cup but the lure of the impressive gold trophy was having its desired effect.

The Henley Royal Regatta relied on having a grand eights event as a drawcard, and the Peace Regatta was no different in that respect. Tarka loved a tussle and had already been in cahoots with the towering Major Ewart D. Horsfall MC, DFC – university past boat club president and Great War veteran – gathering the best Oxford University service oarsmen from active duty. For several weeks, Tarka had his Oxford squad secretly training on their home waters of the Isis before arriving in Henley and settling into West Hill House. The Oxford crew that Tarka had selected included some quality oarsmen from prewar Henley days but also some emerging freshmen oarsmen from the ranks of Eton and Magdalen colleges. The Oxford crew was a great mix of young guns, war heroes and salty old sea dogs.

Their arrival at Henley was a great relief for the foreigners and the *Henley Standard* reported that 'the Oxford crews brought their practice on the home waters to a conclusion on Saturday and proceeded to Henley, where they did some smart work ... being a treat to watch'.[6] The AIF were not surprised to see sitting in the number 2 seat of the Oxford University service crew their Australian 'Bumps' host and former Victorian state oarsman Neil MacNeil. Calling the shots from inside the Oxford University service crew boat was Horsfall, who had an impeccable rowing pedigree, having won the 1912 Boat Race and been in the Great Britain Olympic crew (Leander Club) that defeated the Australians at the 1912 Stockholm Olympics and went on to win the gold medal.

Tarka Gold was one of English rowing's coaching greats. A proponent of English Orthodoxy to whom Fairbairnism was anathema, Tarka ruled his crews with a big stick and was always looking for the subtle winning edge. With a slight following wind, the Oxford crew showed they had some horsepower, with a reasonable time of 7 minutes 19 seconds down the course. This jolted the AIF No. 1 crew, who had been struggling with times between 7 minutes 30 seconds to 40 seconds. Disher thought they were 'a jolly good crew and will take a lot of beating ... [and] are to be feared'.[7]

Throughout June 1919, the Americans flexed their muscles and powered through the course in their George Sims–built racing eight, followed by Captain Wiman and Major Withington in the coaching launch. The local pundits noted that the Americans had improved and that 'there is plenty of power in the boat, and although the Americans have not the pace or finish of the Australians at the present time, they are likely to improve'.[8] Disher recorded that:

> U.S.A. went over it last time in 7.22. They are a powerful lot and
> will take some beating. They are rowing in swivels and I find
> it hard to judge. They are no mugs anyway. Have a very good
> swing indeed but are in a way rough, yet they get pace.[9]

With the weather yielding gorgeous summer days, the River Thames was now a wonderful tableau of crisscrossing boats, clattering oars and drenched men messing about on the water. With spectators and visitors wanting to get a close-up view of the action, the canny boatmen of Henley hiked the hiring fees of skiffs and punts and 'all sorts of fancy prices were being asked'.[10]

Eventually all the King's Cup crews were assembled. Disher noted:

> Canadians have only just arrived, and I have not seen them. N.Z.
> arrived too and look the same as they were at Putney. French
> Army not yet seen nor Army of Occupation. Cambridge 1st Eight
> is not a very good crew as yet.[11]

But first appearances can be deceptive. The Cambridge University crew moved into their Henley quarters, Roslyn House, St Mark's Road, and were soon training steadily on the water under the guidance of a young Australian member of Australian parliament, Stanley 'Janey' Melbourne Bruce. Bruce was born in 1883, educated at Melbourne Grammar School and rowed in their senior eight crew. Following the death of his father, he moved with his mother to England and attended Trinity Hall, Cambridge where he read law and won a Cambridge Blue for rowing, 'and in 1904 won a place in the Cambridge boat ... which beat Oxford by 4½ lengths'.[12]

When the Great War began, Bruce, who was back in Australia, chose to travel back to England and gain a commission in the British Army. He joined the Worcester regiment and saw service at Gallipoli with the 2nd Battalion, Royal Fusiliers. He was wounded there at Krithia on 3 June 1915, then badly wounded in the knee at Suvla Bay in August 1915, and then again in France in 1916, and was eventually discharged 18 months later with 'a noticeable limp and heavily dragged foot'.[13] He was later awarded the Military Cross and Croix de Guerre. Returning to Australia, Bruce won the outer Melbourne seat of Flinders for the Nationalist Party in a by-election and entered Federal parliament. However, in 1919, family business interests necessitated Bruce's return to England, where he stepped forward to coach the Cambridge University Army service crew. Fellow Cambridge coach Steve Fairbairn, who was closely following the progress of the crew, thought highly of Bruce, who had also coached rowing at Jesus College, and wrote:

> Overdoing the forward swing means cutting the finish, but forcing the forward swing is young brother to murder. Thank goodness, Stanley Bruce is taking on the Cambridge rowing, as he strongly insists on rowing one stroke out before starting the next. This is swinging truly and swinging comparatively.[14]

Stanley Bruce was a very accomplished oarsman and coach. After being prime minister of Australia, Bruce readily admitted that his

Cambridge Blue 'gave me more satisfaction than did the Australian Premiership'.[15] Bruce's commitment to rowing was to give the Australians the biggest shake of their Royal Henley Peace Regatta campaign.

As the opening day of the regatta neared, the whole river frontage of Lion Meadow was taken up with specially erected separate viewing enclosures. The Boat Enclosure was closest to the Leander Club. Next there was the private gated lawn for the rarefied Henley rowing illuminati, the Committee of Management Enclosure. Then there was the cash cow of the innovative Stewards' Enclosure, and finally the public enclosure, and grandstands that the YMCA and Henley stewards erected for the visiting New Zealand and Canadian troops, and other English rowing clubs. The New Zealanders, fresh from their King's Cup for rugby win, were expected to descend on Henley in their thousands to watch their crew of 'All Blacks' win their second King's Cup. The Australians hoped that after the New Zealand crew's win in April on the Seine, they wouldn't be able to make it three from three.

But the New Zealanders had an ace up their rowing sleeves: the indomitable sculler Sergeant Darcy Hadfield. The New Zealander was highly muscular and had a handshake like a vice. He was also extremely modest, warm and greeted everyone with a huge grin. There was little doubt that Sergeant Hadfield was going to cut his way through the early heats of the Royal Henley Peace Regatta. It was just a question as to who was going to take him on in the final of the Kingwood Sculls.

The Australians were not the only ones experimenting with combinations. As America's Captain Wiman and Major Withington found additional oarsmen in France, they brought them over straight away. One of the new recruits was the talented Harvard oarsman Lieutenant Henry S. Middendorf, who had raced with his twin brother, John William Middendorf, in the winning Harvard Athletic crew boat at the 1914 HRR Grand Challenge Cup final against his now Peace Regatta coach Major Withington. Henry Middendorf served in the 310th Field Artillery. After the Armistice, the multi-talented sportsman studied at the University of Clermont-Ferrand and tried out for the AEF tennis team.

The Americans also availed themselves of noted Oxford oarsman and English coach Guy Nickalls, who had coached at Yale and was now a consultant trying to 'perfect the fine points of their oarsmanship'.[16] The Americans had now settled on a much more powerful crew, with (bow) Lieutenant R. C. Coe; (2) Captain Royal Pullen; (3) Lieutenant J. Howard McHenry; (4) Henry Middendorf; (5) Captain Louis Penney; (6) Major Herman Rogers; (7) Lieutenant J. Amory Jefferies; (stroke) Captain Douglas Kingsland; and Lieutenant Guy Gale as coxswain.[17]

Two of the crew members, Rogers and McHenry, had also raced at the 1914 Henley Royal Regatta, rowing for Yale in the university eights, so they were not completely ignorant of the eccentric English rowing ways.[18] The attitude of the Americans generally was remarkably upbeat; they were hopeful 'of giving a good account of themselves on the famous reach, where their compatriots so worthily upheld the best traditions of American oarsmanship in the memorable regatta of 1914'.[19]

The American contingent wouldn't require much room in the stands and enclosures overlooking the course. Because the US-bankrolled Inter-Allied Games in Paris would be in progress at the same time as the Royal Henley Peace Regatta, there were actually very few American servicemen in England to cheer on the AEF rowing squad. Unlike their overwhelming presence at the 'All American' 1914 Henley Royal Regatta, spectators waving 'Old Glory' were somewhat thin on the ground. The Americans settled for hiring a large multi-decked houseboat christened 'Dreamland'[20] to watch the regatta, and to entertain their modest number of diplomatic, US military and civilian guests.

In the dark hours of the short summer nights, Wharfe House heaved and breathed. With over thirty restless diggers spread through the dark rabbit warren of rooms, lying in their bunks or twisted in swags, the black dog must have prowled the corridors, its toenails clicking on the hardwood floors, edging its nose into the rooms of the sleeping men.

Small dots of red light glowed and faded as pyjama-clad oarsmen gathered their thoughts while sneaking a cigarette or two on the balcony under the Southern Cross-less stars and listening to the chatter of the dark flowing Thames. The darkness put to sleep the daily realities of wounds, memory and loss, but at the same time might unleash other horrors of the night.

The dangerous switch of mood was always there. For some of the oarsmen, a simple sharp breath or flick of the eye was enough to hint at the suppressed memories and psychological trauma that lurked like a second skin beneath the façades of friendly banter, wickedly funny sledging and polite manners.

The AIF entries were now in for the Marlow Victory Regatta on Saturday 21 June and the Royal Henley Peace Regatta starting on Wednesday 2 July 1919.

The AIF No. 1 crew was entered for the King's Cup for the Allied eights. The AIF No. 2 crew was entered for the senior eights at the Marlow Victory Regatta and the Fawley Cup for senior eights at the Royal Henley Peace Regatta. The Fawley Cup was open to senior eight-oared crews already registered with clubs of the local National Amateur Rowing Association of England. As the AIF had effectively been fighting a continental war on England's behalf for four years the stewards had accepted the Australians into the event. It seemed, though, that they might be having second thoughts.

But the oarsmen's days on the water at Henley were not all grind and worry. And there were ways to hold such concerns at bay. After a long morning session on the water, sometimes stretching over three hours, the oarsmen lifted their boat off the pontoon at Wharfe House and would then spend some time on the lawn rerigging, repairing breakages or adjusting rigger heights. Then they often dropped into the Crown Hotel for a glass of stout. On one particular occasion, the over-confident publican approached the Australians, saying cockily, 'I'll lay a case of champagne to nothing the King's Cup stays in England.'[21]

Gig recognised the opportunity for a sting with some serious financial benefits. The Henley locals surrounded the AIF Rowing Squad like a pack of wolves, offering them 'six to one that the cup would not leave England', so dismal were Australia's chances. Rising to this challenge, 'the crew made its bets'.[22]

24

The Marlow
Victory Regatta

The Marlow Victory Regatta was upon the AIF oarsmen. The course was shorter than the Peace Regatta's, being just under a mile in length, but the event was almost as prestigious, and success here would be a bellwether of Australia's chances in the King's Cup. The key competition was expected to be the Americans, who were also using the Marlow Victory Regatta to gain experience racing in the smaller class of boats. Paul Withington entered the single sculls and was also back-up stroke for the American senior four crew.

On the day before the regatta, half the AIF rowing squad motored by road down to Marlow for a row over the course while the other half rowed the boats down the River Thames 9 miles through Hambleden, Temple and Hurley Locks.

The plan was for the AIF No. 2 crew to race in the Allied Forces eight event; a clinker four; and a coxless four in the senior fours. The No. 2 crew was (bow) George Mettam; (2) 'Blue' Penny; (3) Eric Harrison; (4) Scotty; (5) Audsley; (6) 'Googly' Cogle; (7) McGill; (stroke) 'Nip' Newall; and (cox) 'Gig' Smedley. The AIF crew for the clinker fours (services) was (bow) J. Howieson; (2) 'Brum' White; (3) H. K. Goyen; (stroke) R. J. Clarke; with Gig Smedley once again steering.

A new combination was being tried out for the senior four event with (bow) Archie Robb; (2) Syd Middleton; (3) Harry Hauenstein; and (stroke) Freddie House. Alma Cox had been entered in the single sculls. An AIF Wattle Club eight was also racing in the clinker eights. The Wattle Club was a registered National Amateur Rowing Association (NARA) services rowing club formed by the AIF Administrative HQ for officers and NCOs (non-commissioned officers) based in Horseferry Road. The blades of the Wattle Club's oars were lovingly painted in the distinctive dark green with a gold kangaroo.

The peculiarity for Middleton and his crew in the senior fours was that there was no coxswain to steer the boat. A coxless boat is steered by an oarsman using a movable foot plate on his foot stretcher, attached to a system of pulleys and wires that run down inside the boat and are attached to the rudder. A subtle movement of the foot one way or the other moves the rudder. The chief difficulty is maintaining a straight course while you are rowing flat out. To do that the steersman has to line up two landmarks or points to the stern, for example a steeple and a building, and try to keep them visually in line. Another complication is that the bow oarsman has to turn around occasionally for a sneaky look in the direction the boat is heading to make sure it doesn't hit anything and relay the information to the oarsman steering the boat. Middleton had the boat rigged for him to do the steering from the number 2 seat and Archie was to keep a lookout.

Middleton had never rowed this type of boat before but that said a lot more about his confidence than his actual competence. To say the Australian senior four had any real experience in coxless rowing (about six practice outings) would be a major overstatement.

The next day, Saturday 21 June 1919, the Marlow Victory Regatta was underway. The weather was overcast but the rain held off. In order to address the expected thousands of spectators, the organisers had moved the finish line 250 yards, from just above the Marlow suspension bridge to within the spacious Higginson Park. This served to eliminate a slight final bend as well as accommodate the larger crowd, who could then better see the finish. The crews boated from the Marlow R.C., situated just in the shadow of the Marlow bridge.

On the big day, punts, barges and wherries full of spectators lined the Thames riverbank. It was more a picnic-style regatta, full of boaters, blazers and parasols, with strolling families and couples and English rowing pundits eager to see the Antipodean crews. The Marlow Victory regatta also included rowing events for ladies eight-oared crews as well as the innovative idea of crews of blind soldiers from St Dunstan's Hospital in four-oared boats coxed by their nurses, competing against able-bodied crews. It would take almost until the Invictus Games in the next century before this kind of competition was again given equal footing.

The events at the Marlow Victory Regatta were a match racing format, the same format as the Royal Henley Peace Regatta would use. The suspension bridge next to the church provided a scenic backdrop to the regatta, but for the Australians taking in the view the regatta was a big wake-up call.

In the senior fours event, Middleton's handpicked crew were in a heat first up against a New Zealand service crew. At the gun, Freddie House took off like lightning, but the Australians were soon zigzagging down the course. It was a comedy of errors as Middleton, rowing blind and steering with his feet, overcorrected either one way or the other. The Australians were a crack heavyweight crew and should have smoked the second-string New Zealanders but the men in black raced ahead simply by rowing a straighter course.

Eventually the Australians careered across the course and collided with the New Zealanders. The race umpire, who must have been almost doubling up trying not to laugh, stopped the race only a quarter of a mile from the finish.

With likely a few mumbled expletives, the two crews extricated their oars, separated like two punch-drunk boxers and angrily lined up once more. The umpire restarted the race; even though the Australians had clearly caused the foul, he cut them some slack. He must have felt sympathetic to Middleton's attempts at steering, which bordered on farcical. When the two crews were finally a safe distance apart, the umpire dropped his flag and yelled 'Go!'

Over the distance remaining, only another thirty to forty strokes, the Australians, with the strength and power of Middleton and Hauenstein in the middle of the boat, sprinted away and claimed the victory, much to the New Zealanders' chagrin. In fact, the New Zealanders were never going to forget it.

When it came to steering, the first heat of coxswainless four racing didn't help the Australians in the next heat, up against Thames R.C. Once again Freddie House leapt out of the gate at a rate of knots and they had themselves well in front of the Thames crew. It looked good for a second but soon the Australians lost the race for themselves in spectacular fashion. Halfway through the race they simply careered off the course and ran almost at right angles into a punt full of spectators moored next to the bank.

Finally, the multi-talented athlete Middleton realised there was one thing he could not do – steer. It would have been funny if it was not so tragic, especially as their key bowman, Archie Robb, injured his back falling hard off his seat when they came to a dead stop.[1] The two coxswains, Gig Smedley and Ossie Wood, stood on the riverbank watching Middleton's AIF senior four come to grief and shook their heads. They both knew it was coxswains who actually win the races – the rowers are simply the horsepower.

The Thames R.C. crew met the Americans, who had defeated Granta R.C. earlier in the day, in the senior fours final. The Americans – crewed by Lieutenant H. S. Dillon (bow), Captain Billings Wilson (2), and the two senior members of the American rowing squad, the coach Captain Douglas Wiman (3) and trainer supremo, Major Paul Withington (stroke) – rowed with all the experience of wily veterans but, despite their best efforts, they were dispatched by the formidable crew of the Thames R.C.

Only two crews entered the Allied Forces eight at Marlow so it was a straight final. Here was the opportunity for the Australians to size up the New Zealanders after their big win in April on the River Seine.

The New Zealand crew, stroked by Clarrie Healey and with Arthur Thrussell in the coxswain's cockpit, both Whanganui Boat Club members, were pretty much the crew the Australians thought the New Zealanders would be using for the King's Cup. The AIF No. 2 were also a pretty solid crew; they had the grunt of Scotty and Audsley in the middle of the boat, the cunning Nip Newall in the stroke seat and unassuming but hardworking George Mettam in the bow.

The No. 2 crew had been outclassing the No. 1 crew for so long now that the squad thought they were assured to dust the New Zealanders. They thought it would be a hard and fast race but that they would be too good not to win. Any outcome other than victory would not say much about the current form of the AIF No. 1 crew.

From the blast of the starter's gun, the Australians blitzed the start and jumped out at a lightning 42 strokes a minute. The New Zealanders were shocked at the furious intensity of the Australians, who, as the race progressed, wound it up to a backbreaking strike rate of 44.

There was no way the Australians could possibly sustain such a strike rate and all the New Zealanders had to do was wait for the AIF to blow up. As Disher later commented, 'Nuff said. No crew on earth can do it and get length.'[2] The Australian crew simply faded away until they were dead on the water. Spectators were treated to Scotty calling out for more effort, McGill grunting support and George trying to row his way out of the pickle they were in, all for naught.

The irrepressible New Zealand stroke Clarrie Healey held his nerve, length and metronomic stroke rate for the bulk of the race, leaving enough gas in the tank for a final sprint, with Australia choking on their wake.

The Australians had completely underestimated their opponent's ability and arrogantly overestimated their own. As Audsley wrote to his family:

today we are all disgusted with ourselves as we reckon we
should have beaten the N.Z. crew if we had rowed our race a bit
different and it has been rowed over again several times, anyhow
they are a jolly fine crew and proved themselves the best on the
day ... The N.Z. crew was the same as that which won over in
Paris a month or so ago. We jumped out, in the lead at the start,
but could not hold it to the finish and were beaten by about a
canvas after one of the hardest races I have ever rowed, they are

extremely good crew and our first 8 will have to go some to beat them for the Kings Cup.[3]

Of course, the future iron man of New Zealand rowing, Clarrie Healey, and his coxswain, Arthur Thrussell, were no fools when it came to racing and proved that slow and steady could win the race.

In the third heat of single sculls, the Australian, Alma Cox, came up against the New Zealand man mountain, Darcy Hadfield, who soon staked his claim as the sculler to watch at the Royal Henley Peace Regatta. Hadfield thrashed Cox, who now realised just how good Hadfield was as a sculler.

In the final, Hadfield met the seasoned and resilient American 1914 Henley Royal Regatta sculling veteran Paul Withington, who was also rowing in the sweep oar senior fours. It was a case of youth versus experience, except in this case the youth, a farm boy from New Zealand, completely outranked his opponent, winning the Marlow Singles Final in convincing fashion. The single Silver Fern, Sergeant Darcy Hadfield, had made his mark.

The AIF rowing squad returned to Henley cowed, shattered and with their tail between their legs. The motor trip home was likely silent and brooding. For the lads rowing the boats, it must have felt twice as long as it was.

One of two modest highlights from a day of serious lowlights was that the AIF clinker fours (services) crew salvaged a modicum of pride, beating the New Zealanders in their final; and the Wattle Club thrashed their way to a win in the splash-and-dash clinker eights.

Now back in Wharfe House licking their wounds after Marlow, Middleton and Marshall were prepared to bunker down in the war room and rethink their strategy and selection. If the AIF No. 2 crew could not defeat the New Zealand crew, then the writing was on the wall for them at the Royal Henley Peace Regatta. 'We came home a sorry but a lot wiser mob … N.Z. never say die.'[4]

There was no time to be lost in trying out a new combination to improve the AIF No. 1 crew. Former 1912 Olympians Middleton, Hauenstein and Ross-Soden intimately knew the consequences of

last-minute crew selections, which had cruelled their chances of gold at
the 1912 Stockholm Olympics, one long world war ago.

Archie Robb had to take a few days off to recover from his back
injury, so the rest of the crew were effectively on down time. The rowing
squad had been invited to spend a day or two up at W. S. Robinson's
place at Birchington for a quick break and to forget their Marlow woes.
W.S.'s estate boasted an artificial lake and manicured gardens. Swans
and peacocks strolled the lawns and the garden must have seemed a
colourful wonderland compared to the detritus and death of the fields
that they knew more intimately.

W.S. supplied bottled beer and a spread was laid out on a garden
table. The crew wore their military blue blazers with the pocket
featuring an embroidered AIF rising sun emblem, the rays made up of
bayonets, framing King George V's crown over a pair of crossed gold
oars. Ties, white shoes and flannels completed their outfits. Around
the table were aristocratic ladies keen to acquaint themselves with the
crewmen. These 'days in the country' put on by W.S. at his own expense
were difficult not to enjoy. His hospitality was the perfect antidote to
the grind of training.

Upon their return to Wharfe House, the rowing squad received
word about their entry into the Fawley Cup, and the word was not
good. The Henley stewards had inexplicably changed their minds and
were refusing the AIF entry. The AIF Rowing Section was informed
that the crew members did not fit the criteria set out by the Amateur
Rowing Association (ARA – as distinct from the NARA) for the Fawley
event. Middleton, disgruntled about their losses at Marlow (and his
inability to steer), was likely now furious.

The criteria of a Fawley Cup entry was: 'Open to any crew of
amateur oarsmen from the United Kingdom who are members of his
Majesty's Navy, Army, Air Force, or who are members of any amateur
club having its headquarters in the United Kingdom.'[5] The AIF Rowing
Section oarsmen were now quickly made official paid-up members of
the long-established AIF Wattle Rowing Club, based in Hammersmith,
so as to satisfy the 'local' membership criteria of the entry rules. As
Clive Disher reported:

We have been trying to get the 2nd eight entered for the Fawley Cup at Henley. The Henley people first said it would be alright and then at the last moment said no. So, we got them made members of the Wattle Club. That beat them for a while ... but now they won't accept them at any price. Fact of the matter is the Henley people think we can win the Cup and they don't want it to go outside England. It is still in the air though entries have closed. I learn to love the English sporting spirit more every day.[6]

Following some tense negotiation between Middleton and the Henley stewards, they held firm on their rejection for the Fawley Cup but opened up an entry for the King's Cup – there were at the time only seven entries – to round it up to the eight entries required for four two-crew King's Cup match racing heats on Thursday 3 July.

The AIF rowing squad was now in the unenviable position of possibly having one of its crews squaring off against the other in a fight between Wharfe House stablemates for the King's Cup. Or, ideally, if the two AIF crews were drawn on either side of the event draw, there could be the possibility of an all-Australian final.

The AIF Wattle Club was also having its own run-in with the Henley stewards over its entry into the Remenham Cup event for club clinker eights. The Peace Regatta committee was happily accepting service entries from the British Tank Corps and the Cambridge Naval Officers, but now inexplicably rejected the entry of the AIF Wattle Club clinker eight crew.

There was apparently a profound divide in English rowing between the definitions of 'amateurism' used by the lofty National Amateur Rowing Association (NARA) and the even loftier Amateur Rowing Association (ARA). The AIF Wattle Club and the AIF Rowing Section were aligned with NARA and its definition of amateurism, but the Henley stewards abided by the definition used by the ARA. The Australians were furious about the ARA's specious and counterintuitive definition of the word 'amateur.'

What's more, the ARA definition of 'amateurism' that so completely stumped the 'foreigners' was equally confounding to the rowing community. *The Times* found it just as confusing, and a contradiction in terms.

> When the whole of the rowing world and all lovers of honest
> sport are looking forward to the revival of the Henley Regatta,
> it seems a profound pity that the festival should be marred
> by the action of the Regatta Committee ... the status of the
> amateur in rowing is more strictly conditioned than in any
> other sport, where amateurs, as opposed to professional, are
> merely those who do not make and never have made a living
> out of their skill. But in rowing, by the rule which governs the
> proceedings at Henley, an amateur is more than an ordinary
> 'gentleman,' for he must be one who earns his living by no form
> of manual labour whatsoever; and the consequence is that many
> men, who can truly be called amateurs in other sports, dare not
> aspire to that name if they happen to be oarsmen ... The crew
> of the National Amateur Rowing Association – a vain title it
> would seem ... are not 'gentlemen' enough for old fashioned
> rowing circles.[7]

The disagreement between the Wattle Club and the Henley stewards went about as public as it could in those days with a very stern letter written by George Dunstan of the Wattle Club general committee to the editor of the venerable *Times*.

> We entered for the Remenham Cup as laid down and complied
> with every detail. On June 23 we received a letter from the
> secretary, stating that the Committee could not accept our
> nomination ... What we want to know is why we have been
> refused, as we comply with everything as laid down by this body.

> Are we not English? Or are they afraid we are too good for our
> opponent? Hoping you will give this matter as much publication
> as possible.[8]

Even before the war, there had been conflict about what to do about the pesky foreigners entering the Henley Royal Regatta. Now, with the world at peace, there might have been a xenophobic creep from the Henley stewards in their attempt to restrict which 'foreign' rowing clubs could enter which particular Peace Regatta events, with the implicit aim of limiting the export overseas of the silverware.

With a reciprocal whiff of composed cool, a matter-of-fact reply to Dunstan's diatribe appeared in *The Times*, written by Mr Fred I. Pitman, chairman of the committee of management, Royal Henley Peace Regatta. He observed that the NARA had refused to verify the crew's status as amateur according to the rules of the ARA, by which the Henley stewards abide.

Sorting out the definition of amateurism in English rowing was an ongoing concern. The NARA wanted the ARA to modify their rules so that they did 'not exclude men who are only disqualified by reason of their having rowed with or against mechanics classes'. At best this would allow a two-tier system of amateurism where NARA would 'represent the people and the A.R.A. the aristocracy'.[9] In a postwar world, after the British Pals, conscripts and volunteers had fought and died en masse, side by side with the commissioned officer class, often in execrable conditions, one might hope that the class differences between the survivors – the mechanics, the professionals, the aristocrats, the suffragettes – would be tossed aside to create a society that was egalitarian and accepting. However, citing the fact that the other entries had been received and entries were now closed, the Henley stewards had dismissed the request.

25

Tough choices

It was crunch time for the AIF No. 1 crew. Heads were going to roll. Middleton and Marshall, probably also in consultation with Disher, Hauenstein, Ross-Soden and Nip Newall, held the equivalent of what could be called a rowing star chamber.

In the first instance, Ross-Soden was in no state to row. Having struggled over the last six weeks during the intense training, relying heavily on the loyal support of his 1912 Grand Challenge crewmates, it was clear to all, especially Ross-Soden himself, that he was a detriment to the team on the water. In a true moment of sporting self-sacrifice, he jumped rather than be pushed. That is not to say he upped and left. Ross-Soden knew he could still contribute to the AIF rowing squad by assisting coach Marshall in the coach's launch, drawing upon his useful Henley experience and giving the AIF No. 2 crew much-needed personalised coaching.

In the final analysis, Johnny Begg in the number 3 seat and Lyn Davis in number 2, who had both given 100 per cent to the crew, were now on the chopping block to make way for more power, more youth, and more resolve. In contemporary Australian rowing vernacular, the number 3 seat is referred to as the ejector seat or the FTG, the 'first to go.' Johnny Begg was strong and keen, but he was nuggety and lacked the length required to grab hold of the water at the catch and propel the boat through the full length of the stroke. Davis had obviously tempered the talkative style that had raised the ire of Harry Hauenstein, but as the AIF No. 1 struggled to outpace the AIF No. 2 at Henley, it is hard not to imagine Davis chipping in with his two bits.

The elephant in the Wharfe House war room was 'the funster', Arthur Scott. Scotty had been happily basking in the Henley sunshine; playing the prankster as a Morris dancer with a pitchfork; dangling his legs over the riverbank, feeding the King's white swans; riling up the other men; and displaying a dismissive, devil-may-care demeanour.

Though he was thought clumsy, Scotty was powerfully built and born to be an oarsman. A blemished AIF service record, with an egregious court-martial, may have been a factor in his exclusion. Not that Scotty's court-martial was due to cowardice or ill-discipline. Scotty had heard that his brother Edward, who served in the 48th Battalion, had been wounded in action on 28 March 1918, and died the next day in hospital at Camiers. Scotty put in for leave to attend to his brother's affairs, but at the time, during the German offensive Operation Michael, all leave had been cancelled as the AIF scrambled to defend their lines on 6 April 1918. And he wasn't the only one on the crew to have had run-ins with the AIF military hierarchy; perhaps it was the fact that Scotty had more or less joined the AIF to abandon his wife and his son Walter.

Scotty was certainly no paragon of virtue. But at the Marlow Regatta he had proved, racing in the AIF No. 2 crew, that he could perform at an intense strike rate, and he brought to the crew a physical dominance and stamina that was relentless. The AIF No. 2 crew's defeat at Marlow was likely due to some of the other crew members not being able to keep up with Scotty's locomotive-like coal-shovelling stroke rate in the middle of the boat, and his ability to mercilessly rip the blade through the water right through to the finish. His oar puddles foamed like boiling water from his fiery exertion.

Nip Newall, who had been stroking the AIF No. 2 crew, had for some time been extolling to Middleton, Disher and the rowing selection committee the virtues of the quiet West Australian backing him up in the number 7 seat. George Mettam was not an overly wordy type of man. What he did do was get in the boat, shut up and meticulously mirror the stroke man, taking a huge load of the work off Nip and allowing him to work the oar and rate to the bejesus.

Nip was a good club man through and through. Since the two AIF crews were now possibly going to meet each other in the King's Cup, a lesser man might have kept the stronger assets to himself, but not Nip. He was interested in seeing the AIF as a whole win the King's Cup. Nip told Middleton and Marshall what he thought and left it up to them. A good club man is often the backbone of the club and they paid close attention to what Nip had to say.

Tom McGill, who had been knocking on the door of the AIF No. 1 crew, was now pounding away for inclusion. He was relatively young (compared to Hauenstein and Middleton at least) and his resilience in springing back from numerous serious gunshot and shrapnel wounds to his face, arms and leg was astonishing.

And always hovering and smiling, with his irrepressible grin and sense of camaraderie, was Gig Smedley. He had a lot of respect for what the AIF rowing squad was doing, irrespective of his love of a laugh, a stout or two at the Crown and geeing up the odds with the publican. Gig wanted the AIF rowing squad to have a stuffed toy kangaroo as a mascot. Another idea that was likely Gig's, perhaps inspired by the massive Birdwood Flag flying on the edge of Wharfe House, was to create a blue ensign 'Dinkum Aussie Flag', about 10 by 8 inches and made of satin, to fly on the bow of the boat. Anything that would build pride and unite a crew was important to Gig.

Middleton and Marshall likely thought Gig the type of coxswain who, regardless of his small stature, owned the crew on the water with the intimidating parade ground demeanour of a sergeant, which of course, he was. Now, to inject the No. 1 crew with some water rat cunning, Gig Smedley, the risk taker, slid into the AIF No. 1 coxswain's seat. As Clive Disher wrote to John Lang:

The other suggestion as put forward by Middleton was the crew to be placed as follows building up the 1st eight. Smedley

cox Disher stroke McGill 7 Middleton 6 Hauenstein 5 Scott
4 Mettam 3 House 2 Robb bow. That meant dropping out Ross-
Soden, Davis and Begg and taking in Scott, Mettam and McGill.
My opinion about it was that it was a chance and a chance
worth taking. I did not consider that the 2nd 8 though they were
faster than the 1st would be fast enough to win the King's Cup
and, also, I did not think that they would be likely to get much
more pace than they already had. In the main I think we agreed
on that.[1]

This was major surgery and opened up all sorts of recriminations
about late changes to a crew that, regardless of their internal difficulties,
could still come through on the day.

Back in 1912, the Australian crew that was selected as 'Sydney Rowing
Club' for the HRR Grand Challenge Cup was Jack Ryrie (bow); Simon
Fraser (2); Keith Heritage (3); Thomas Parker (4); Harry Hauenstein
(5); Syd Middleton (6); Harry Ross-Soden (7); Roger Fitzhardinge
(stroke); and Robert G. K. Waley as coxswain. Syd's older brother Bill
was coach and Alex Thomson was team manager.

The Grand Challenge Cup is only open to club crews and not inter-
national representative or national eight-oared crews. The way Leander
Club navigated this was by inviting (selecting) the best rowers from
Cambridge or Oxford Universities to become members of Leander
Club. Effectively, Leander Club was often a proxy national Great
Britain crew, such was the quality of its club members and oarsmen.

The Australian crew lost considerable fitness during the passage
to England but coach Bill Middleton, soon after arriving in London,
initiated a strict training regime to get them back to peak fitness,

Our training consists of getting out of bed at 6 o'clock, a long
walk of six or seven miles, then to the cricket ground and run
six laps of 500 yards each. After a shower, we have breakfast,

and then do a six-mile row. In the afternoon we do another good solid row and take long walking exercise in the evening.[2]

The Leander Club Grand Challenge Cup eight had some great oarsmen who seemed to be able to row for ever. Sitting the bow seat was the indomitable S. E. Swann; (2) C. E. Tinne; (3) L. G. Wormald; (4) E. D. Horsfall; (5) J. A. Gillan; (6) A. S. Garton; (7) A. G. Kirby; (stroke) P. Fleming; and H. B. Wells as coxswain.[3] They were under the wily guidance of the master English coach Harcourt 'Tarka' Gold.

The 1912 HRR was about as royal a regatta as one could imagine, with the attendance on the final day of His Majesty King George V, Queen Mary and Princess Mary. It was estimated a record 130,000 people were present to watch the finals and Grand Challenge Cup. The royal entourage were rowed in the royal barge under the central arch of the Henley Bridge to the Henley Royal Enclosure, where they sat in the royal balcony to watch the rowing.

In the final of the Grand Challenge Cup, the colonials from Sydney Rowing Club defeated the cream of English rowing, the privileged and handpicked Leander Club crew. Leander Club was not happy, particularly Tarka. The increasing intrusion of the 'foreigners' who were starting to muddy the waters of Henley required urgent attention, to put them back in their proper Antipodean place.

For the British Olympic campaign that same month, Leander Club reshuffled their crew. This threw the normally composed Australian coach, and Bill Middleton called Leander's bluff and followed suit with a crew change of his own. Without any consultation, and at the eleventh hour, Bill dropped Keith Heritage in favour of local Oxford University oarsman Dr H. K. Ward, a stroke side oarsman now sitting in Heritage's seat on bow side. The change evoked comment from George Towns himself: 'It is always dangerous, the men being well, to alter a successful crew. The time was too short to allow of Ward becoming an "Australian rower" again.'[4]

Upon his return to Australia, Harry Hauenstein fumed about the replacement.

Personally, I think the Henley crew should not have been altered. Dr. Ward had not had sufficient training and was not in the condition he should have been in for such a race as this, Heritage had trained assiduously as any member of the crew, and, I think, would have lasted the Stockholm course better than Dr. Ward.[5]

The Australians raced Great Britain in the semi-finals and lost by the smallest of margins. Many years later, 1912 Olympic number 3 oarsman Tom Parker was holding court to an invited gathering at the Railway Hotel, Glen Innes, and this was his version of events:

Australia were leading the English crew by 60 feet, when Ward cracked up under the strain. The Australians stopped momentarily to allow him to recover. The Leander crew pulled level and drew 15 feet ahead. The Australians determinedly chased them. They were overtaking Leander with every pull of the flashing blades – another three yards and the race was won. The fatal gun spoke – and Australia had lost the world's title by two feet.[6]

When the Australian rowing squad returned, there was huge interest in the reasons for the HRR win and the Olympics loss. The sports reporters smelled blood in the water. Meanwhile, Bill Middleton stood by his decision to replace Heritage with Dr Ward and maintained that the Stockholm course was unfair as one crew had to move out wide to pass through an arch of a bridge at a critical moment before the finish. For his part, Keith Heritage didn't say a word about the whole affair, apart for an emphatic: 'The other can say what they choose. I will say nothing.'[7] The controversial loss weighed heavily on Australia's first Olympic oarsmen for many years and was still a sore point between members of that Olympic crew.[8]

When it came to the 1919 Royal Henley Peace Regatta, the proof was going to be in the pudding. The new crew list looked impressive on paper but how would it work on the water? Here they were, only about ten days out from the King's Cup final, and it was like they were just starting out. Four months of training could be down the drain. But the great advantage of having a personal boat shed on your own back lawn was that you could slip out for a row without being too conspicuous as you passed the Angel Hotel, crossed Henley Bridge, walked past Leander Club and entered the Boat Enclosure. The bush telegraph was pretty active in Henley. This trial row needed to be a top-secret military operation.

The plan hatched by Marshall and Middleton was to trial the new crew combination one evening about 7 pm, after the wind had dropped, when the water was flat and glassy and every other crew had packed away their boats and strolled home to their billets for dinner. They would paddle down to the start, spin around and row a full piece down the course. The crew was now (bow seat) Archie Robb; (2) Fred House; (3) George Mettam; (4) Scotty; (5) Hauenstein; (6) Middleton; (7) Tom McGill; (stroke) Disher; and Gig in the coxswain seat.

The two AIF crews waited until the Thames was silent and sleeping. Both crews laid their oars on the lawn near the river's edge. The No. 1 crew carried their boat to the floating pontoon and quickly put it onto the water. As bow-side held the boat, stroke-side gathered the oars and together they threaded the oar handles from the outside of the poppet rowlocks, twisted the well-greased half-moon leather buttons through the poppet and stepped into the boat. Together stroke-side pushed off and, 'Silently the boat was pulled down river.'[9] The No. 2 crew quickly boated and pushed off following the No. 1 crew.

Temple Island was perfectly mirrored in the still water of the Thames. As the No. 1 crew approached the island, the eight oars caught the water with each stroke, the legs of the oarsmen pushed off the stretcher, their backs rocked over to the finish, they tapped out and together they reached forward for more inert water. As they easy-oared and let the boat run tottering on its wafer-thin keel, the thin bow sliced the water into a 'V' for victory–shaped wave that peeled off like two shavings of water towards the reedy riverbanks till Gig called 'Lower!'

Both crews roughly lined up at the start of the course. What happened on the return run down the Henley Reach was beyond words. All eyes of the new No. 1 crew gazed toward the stern of the *Q.L.* From Gig's call of 'Row', the legs, shoulders and arms of the oarsmen were in unison as they gripped the oar handles, pushed their legs down and squeezed the boat forward, with their blades finishing out of the water together as one. From this very first stroke, which gently heaved the shell out of the water, the No. 1 crew fell silent and all eyes and ears remained focused inside the boat. The clunk of the eight greased leather collars, spinning and locking flat against the bottom of the poppet rowlock, was one sound. Then all eight feathered oars skimmed at an equal height above the water as the oarsmen approached the catch and locked their razor sharp blades into the wine-dark water as one.

To blend and subvert the unbending wills of nine damaged men filled with resentment, sorrow and wrath required a subservience of each individual will to the greater good of the many, damn the consequences to self. This was the true heart of war. Although on the cool, still, flat waters of Henley Reach nobody would die. The rattling rush and adrenalin of going over the top into battle now morphed into rhythm and movement in concert.

As the oarsmen activated every muscle fibre of their bodies, their cores locking their leg drive to their upper body, they created the swing of the stroke. First, the oars clamped in the water in a foaming tumult, then the oarsmen glided their oars through the air like an airfoil, creating lift, reducing wind resistance and allowing the unleashed boat to run across the water's surface. Not one oarsman wasted his breath on crass slurs or colourful invective. For once the noise of the oars rolling into the rowlocks, the metallic glide of the brass wheels on the brass rails and the dance of clattering air bubbles running down the hull of the boat were all that existed.

Between strokes the shell lifted and shot through the dead calm water. By the time they reached the finish of the Reach, more than a length ahead of the No. 2 crew, everyone who was anyone in Henley was present in dinghies, in wherries, standing along the towpath with binoculars, leaning over the stone railing of Henley Bridge, gawking at them like tourists. Word had indeed passed around Henley about the Australian crew putting to water. The crews that had aimed for discretion now 'had as much privacy as a nude in Trafalgar Square'.[10] It was not until the boat was lifted from the water that the first smirks and friendly banter from the No. 1 crew began, as they carried the boat across the trimmed green lawn of Wharfe House and back into the shed.

During the week leading up to the final weekend and the draw for the King's Cup, Middleton and Marshall set a tough training schedule and experimented like crazy with the crew. The AIF No. 1 crew now had some good power with Mettam, Scotty, Hauenstein and Middleton in the middle of the boat. The crew were doing some strenuous pieces but it still didn't quite feel right. As Disher wrote:

> Thursday morning we went for a long row against the wind and
> we came back torn limb from limb, + muscle from muscle. In
> the afternoon, we did another course and we did in 7'.9" despite
> being obstructed near the finish. The last half of the row in each
> case was the better part and really encouraged us. Friday we
> really began to get together and on Saturday we did some minute
> pieces in good style.[11]

There was now time to take stock and study the King's Cup competition and observe their form up close on the water. Marshall and Ross-Soden would have often grabbed their stopwatches and timed the pieces of the other Allied crews as they drew past. They noted the strike rate and observed the distances between the tell-tale puddles between strokes. A key indicator of boat speed relative to stroke rate is the distance between the bow man's puddle, swirling in the river, and where the stroke man places his oar in the water to create his puddle. This demonstrates how far the boat has moved through the water.

The aim is for the bow man's puddle to clear the stern of the boat before the crew catches the water for the next stroke. To the expert eye, the puddles of different crews tell no lies. Of course, it is always handy just to time a piece between two points and count the stroke rate. The numbers do not lie either.

The draw for the regatta is traditionally held on the Saturday before the start week, inside the Baroque-inspired Henley Town Hall. On 28 June 1919, from about 2.30 pm, the coaches, the schoolboys, the clubs, the service crews and interested supporters walked up the steps to the Henley Town Hall and then filed either left or right up two sweeping staircases that lead to the spacious upper-floor hall under a barrel-vaulted ceiling. The draw would take place at 3 pm. Slips of paper with the names of crews written on them are placed into the Grand Challenge Cup, and selected by the chairman of the committee of management.

For each race, one crew races in either the 'Bucks' station (Buckinghamshire) side of the regatta course, and the other in the 'Berks' station (Berkshire) side. In the first draw for the King's Cup event, whether by bad luck or as a result of brilliant stage management, the AIF No. 1 crew was drawn in the Berks station against the AIF No. 2 crew in the Bucks station in the first heat, scheduled for 11.05 am on Thursday 3 July. The draws for the other three heats to be raced on the Thursday were the Canadian Army crew against Oxford University service crew at 11.10 am; the French Army crew against the American Army crew at 3.45 pm; and the New Zealand Army crew against the Cambridge University service crew at 4.20 pm.

As the stewards moved on to the next event, the Australians shuffled out of the Henley Town Hall, at best bemused by the luck of the draw but possibly suspicious that there had been some sleight of hand. As Disher wrote:

> Well the heats were drawn yesterday and of course we drew the
> 2nd Australian crew to row against. Pretty rotten luck isn't it?[12]

The combinations of the final two AIF crews had now been settled. Johnny Begg, having been dropped from the AIF No. 1 crew, had slipped into the number 6 seat of the No. 2 crew; Lyn Davis had decided not to row in the No. 2 crew, stepping aside for Begg. The AIF rowing squad had worked together for so long that there were no recriminations or sour grapes between the Wharfe House stablemates. In fact, the communication and goodwill between the two crews was as good as ever. All the AIF rowing squad were working together with the express aim that one of the two AIF crews would win the King's Cup. The No. 1 crew were now in perfect sync and were settled. The right oarsmen had been identified and elevated into the crew and the work on the water was exceptional. Middleton, after endless crew reshuffles, had now found the perfect combination and finally 'The crew, with Middleton in command, was rowing like a machine'.[13]

Which did not mean there was no time for a minor readjustment or a further tweak. Looking across from one boat to the other as they trained side by side on the Henley Reach allowed shrewd observations and ideas to flow freely between the boats.

> On showing the crew to Newall who is stroke of the 2nd eight, he suggested Mettam (West Australia) as '7' in place of McGill and as it was a day of experiments we experimented and so there we are still with him at 7 and I am quite satisfied. Yea 200% more satisfied than [when] Harry Soden [was] there. You may want to know why Harry was kicked out, well, have it that his condition wasn't satisfactory. He is now coaching us, and we are benefiting by it. The change has been justified if for that reason alone.[14]

Ross-Soden had indeed proved himself a huge asset as coach and manager of the two crews.

George Mettam slotted effortlessly into the number 7 seat behind Disher, and McGill moved into the number 3 seat. The rowing jigsaw puzzle was now almost complete. The only question now was whether the AIF No. 1 crew should persevere with the *Q.L. Deloitte* boat.

The crew had often found the boat springy and it twisted noticeably with this heavier, stronger crew, which took away crucial boat speed. It was a heart-wrenching moment for the New South Wales members of the crew. The boat was like their baby. It had been rediscovered, cared for, sheltered, washed, repaired and admired, but the Cambridge boat that had been hired for the No. 2 crew was firmer and had less twist.

Middleton was not someone to attach himself to something for reasons of sentimentality and it was an easy decision. The defining question for elite rowing crews is always 'Will it make the boat go faster?' A firmer, stiffer boat would make the crew go faster. Disher reported:

The first 8 is not the using the Q.L. Deloitte. It was a wrench for the NSW personnel to get out of her but I think the Cambridge boat we have though not nearly so well made is the faster boat. It is being polished at present.[15]

Problem solved.

26

The Royal Henley
Peace Regatta

Wednesday 2 July was the first day of the Royal Henley Peace Regatta, and crowds of supporters and soldiers began to pour into Henley from London and surrounds. The Henley stewards had applied the finishing touches to the brand new Stewards' Enclosure – from which one could view almost the whole length of the Henley course – and it looked quite the picture, with its whitewashed picket fences, raked viewing stands, and rows of deck chairs for the 300 new Regatta members and their guests. The dress code was strict: gentlemen were required to wear a suit coat or rowing club blazers and tie, and the ladies dressed in their finery, ideally with hats and stoles. It was the place to be seen.

> The Management Committee may be congratulated on the
> excellence of the arrangements. Several improvements on 1914
> had been carried out in addition to the provision of the Stewards'
> Enclosure with its gay flower beds and dwarf trees.[1]

The enclosure was an immediate success with the diehard old Cambridge, Oxford and Leander oarsmen and their guests. If there's one thing the English do well, it is to stage a lavish garden party – perhaps even with some rowing thrown in.

Not that the diggers, along with the numerous other Allied troops who were also stranded in Britain and France, were allowed into the Steward's Enclosure, or cared at all. The diggers had plenty of free time (if on leave), were cashed-up and looking for ways to occupy the dragging days till their long-awaited repatriation. The YMCA had set up tea stands and just being in the English countryside was plenty to enjoy compared to trenches and field kitchens under fire. The natural surrounds were beautiful, the sound of the River Thames was soothing and all the Australians looked forward to a chance of victory in the King's Cup.

The AIF crews were not scheduled to race for the King's Cup until the following day. During the afternoon of 2 July, the oarsmen from both crews gathered and mixed freely with guests and mates on the lawn of Wharfe House, dressed in their flannels and blue blazers and carrying on as usual, joking and not taking things too seriously. After all they had been through, they were still mates.

Now that the selection for the AIF No. 1 crew was finally settled, after weeks of deliberation, the AIF No. 2 crew was represented by (bow seat) Lieutenant J. 'Chung' Howieson; (2) Sergeant Gideon 'Blue' Penny; (3) Sergeant Eric Harrison; (4) Lieutenant H. A. 'Brum' White; (5) Major W. A. 'Alan' Audsley; (6) Corporal Jack 'Googly' Cogle; (7) Gunner W. J. A. 'Johnny' Begg; (stroke) Lieutenant Harry R. 'Nip' Newall; and Lieutenant O. J. 'Ossie' Wood on the rudder.

At 11 am on Thursday 3 July, the two AIF crews backed down their sterns to the official boat holders, who held the boats in line by leaning over the gunwales of the moored dinghies. The Henley Boat Race umpire, from his launch, warned the crews that they would start soon, and left them to prepare and straighten their line to the first turn into the boomed straight of the Henley Reach rowing course.

Inside the umpire's launch, Ross-Soden sat on the Bucks side and Marshall sat on the Berks side, along with top AIF brass, to follow the race and watch it at close quarters.

At the gun, the two AIF crews took off and all the trials, readjustments and myriad combinations unfolded as expected. The row was solid but the AIF No. 1 crew were in control. At the first signal, where the boat race official hoisted the number of the boat that reached the mark first, the No. 1 crew led by a quarter of a length and then increased the lead slowly to half a length. It was best to keep in touch with the trailing crew to measure their performance and the run of the boat. The No. 1 crew crossed the line three quarters of a length ahead in a leisurely time of 7 minutes 31 seconds. It was not a fast race, but it did not need to be. There was no animosity about the result.

If anything, a weight had been lifted and the rowing squad could pull together. The true measure of their worth would be winning the King's Cup as a squad and not as a single crew. Now that it was settled, the Australians had to wait until 4.20 pm to see who would win the heat between Cambridge University and the impressive New Zealand Army service crew.

Immediately after the Australians, the Oxford University service crew took on the Canadians. The Canadians had some experienced Winnipeg Rowing Club oarsmen in their crew – men who had competed in the 1914 Henley Royal Regatta such as Lieutenant Albert D. Spragge and the coxswain Sergeant Robert A. Preston – but they were no match for Tarka's Oxford men in dark blue. Both crews shot out of the start, striking 40 or over, but Oxford pressed ahead and led by three quarters of a length at the Fawley mark, at a speedy 3 minutes 32 seconds. Oxford cruised into the next round, finishing two lengths ahead of the shattered Canadians.

Later that day, as the King's Cup American and French service crew eights took to the water from the Boat Enclosure, they were greeted with applause by the enthusiastic crowd. Both crews tightened their foot stretchers and checked their equipment and then began their paddle to the start.

It was obvious that the English rowing crews had strong class ties, but the American crew was perhaps even more exclusive, with each of them an officer and the product of an Ivy League education. Still in the crew were varsity oarsmen McHenry and Rogers, who had been coached at Yale by coach for hire Gully Nickalls; Middendorf, who with his twin brother J.W. had rowed to 1914 HRR Grand Challenge victory in the All-American final in the Harvard Boat Club crew; and Jefferies, another Harvard alumni. During the war, the coxswain, Gale, was 'an expert aviator and pilot'.[2] Royal Pullen, though a graduate of Washington University, hailed from the tough, frozen backwoods of the Alaskan Klondike. He was a remarkable soldier and his brothers had also fought in the Great War. General Pershing had once said, 'I wish I had a regiment of Pullens.'[3]

Up against them and vastly outweighed, though selected with a far greater spirit of 'liberté, égalité and fraternité', were the French crew, who did have some very experienced oarsmen among its officers and ranks. In the bow seat was Second Lieutenant H. Lefebvre; (2) Private Gabriel Poix; (3) Second Lieutenant M. Baudechon; (4) Sergeant I. Cordier; (5) Second-Lieutenant Touvet Barrelet; (6) Lieutenant A. Conbarieu; (7) Private P. Vaganay; (stroke) Sergeant M. Bouton; and Lieutenant E. Flament was coxswain.

As each crew rowed past the Steward's Enclosure, the band in the rotunda struck up the 'Marseillaise' then 'The Star-Spangled Banner'. These two international crews had the fewest soldiers and supporters on hand but were welcomed by thousands of locals, Allied troops and spectators.

The race was pretty much a one-horse show. The Americans, as expected, dominated and took the lead early, striking a lively 39 strokes per minutes to the slightly slower stroke rate of 37 from the French. The French had obviously suffered greatly from years of deprivation and the loss of some of their best oarsmen. Physically they were smaller and less robust, but what they lacked in size they made up for in technique; they knew how to row.

As the two crews rounded the first curve into the straight at Temple Island, 'the Americans let out and increased their lead to a length, but rowing with great power. Later the French got within a length, but the Americans increased their lead to two lengths at the mile post.'[4] From there on in, the French Army service crew, with their portly coxswain, Second Lieutenant E. Flament (9 stone 9 pounds, or 61 kilograms) could not keep within touch of the American crew. The Americans 'won an easy race by three lengths in 7 minutes and 40 seconds'.[5] The stage was now set for the Americans to meet the Oxford University Army service crew the next day.

At 4.20 pm, the gun fired for the Cambridge University and New Zealand crews. Even with the addition of Darcy Hadfield in the New Zealand eight, the crew was about half a stone (3 kilograms) lighter than the Stanley Bruce–coached Cambridge crew. From the start, however, the New Zealanders showed their remarkable turn of speed; they led up to Temple Island and had increased their lead to half a length over Cambridge by the half mile mark. But here Cambridge made their move, reducing the margin to one quarter length at the Fawley mark and continuing to push through, overtaking the New Zealand crew and finishing three quarters of a length ahead in a brisk time of 7 minutes 17 seconds. The New Zealanders were out of the King's Cup – except for their Leander Cup crew, and Hadfield in the Kingswood Sculls.

At 5 pm, the Leander Cup heat for Allied fours between Middleton's AIF crew and New Zealand was a rerun of the coxswainless four-oared event at the Marlow Regatta. George Mettam replaced Archie Robb in the bow seat; in the number 2 seat Major Sydney Middleton steered; number 3 was Lieutenant Henry Hauenstein; and stroke was Lieutenant Fred House. The New Zealand crew was Sergeant H. H. Prideaux (bow); Sergeant G. L. Croll at number 2; Sergeant F. V. Horne at number 3; and Sergeant J. Fry as stroke. There was no love lost between these two Antipodean crews; the New Zealanders had felt unfairly treated at Marlow after the AIF crew had careered into them.

From the start, the Australians were all over the place and within the first 30 strokes, they ran bang into the New Zealanders.[6] A series of arms shot up, claiming the foul. The Australians were not going to get away with it twice. The Henley umpires immediately disqualified the Australians. Competing in the coxswainless four-oar was always a bold move for the Australians but their hopelessness at steering did have an upside. As George Mettam wrote, 'I was surprised at their action but it was for the best as it allowed us to concentrate our efforts on the eight.'[7]

The next day, 4 July, was Independence Day for the Americans. For the Australians it was a fresh chance to thumb their noses at their one-time colonial masters.

The AIF crew walked over the Henley Bridge early. The start time for their Heat 5 against Cambridge University service crew was scheduled for just before lunch at 12.50 pm. The Australians had drawn the Berks station and Cambridge had drawn the Bucks station, closer to the middle of the stream.

The enclosure tent was now a little less busy as the number of crews and boats competing in the regatta were being reduced by a half each day, but crowds were already growing outside in the marshalling yard, especially the keen student supporters of the Cambridge crew. There were plenty of Cambridge college caps and blazers waiting for their champions to emerge from the enclosure.

The AIF crew started their knee bends and half rolls as a warm-up and coach Marshall and Ross-Soden had an encouraging word to each of the crew. Across the enclosure, Stanley Bruce, with his trademark limp, had his Cambridge men preparing. The squads gave each other no more than the most cursory sideways glance, if they looked at all.

The AIF No. 1 crew had at first arrogantly dismissed Cambridge as blow-ins, underprepared and crewed with several oarsmen who looked more like boys than men. Unlike many sporting codes, competitive rowing is a sport where competitors peak later in life, as decades of hard-won muscle are driven on by the discipline and mental toughness that only comes with age.

Now they saw their physical fitness up close, the youth and vitality of the younger men such as recent Eton first eight graduates H. Peake (1917) and H. O. C. Boret (1918) in among old hands and decorated war heroes such as the accomplished rowing brothers Lieutenant M. V. Buxton MC and Major Clarence E. V. Buxton MC, alongside Lieutenant Alfred Swann DSO and expat Geelong Grammar old boy Private John A. Campbell from Victoria. The other nagging factor was that Mr Bruce knew the Australians very well, perhaps too well, and his presence as coach was starting to raise some doubts among the Australians about their ability to hold this wiry pack of old dogs and young pups.

From the gun, Cambridge University went out at a cracking strike rate of 42, compared to Australia's more restrained rate of 40. The two crews approached the first bend that led into the boomed part of the course, and seeing the exuberance of the Cambridge crew, but with half a length to spare by the end of Temple Island, Gig gauged the situation and decided to play hardball. The Australians would have to run a slightly wider course into the straight and Gig was having none of that. 'With years of coxing, [he] knew all the tricks of the sport. He also knew all the rules', and he steered the AIF No. 1 boat into the middle of the river, 'to cut the corner slightly'.[8] His aim was to push the Cambridge boat just enough towards the Buck's side booms and squeeze their line for the straight. The Cambridge coxswain, Private R. Johnston, immediately recognised what Gig was up to and raised his arm in protest.

The umpire, seeing Australia's skulduggery, got on his loudhailer, warning the Australians off, and then held a white flag to his left, indicating that Australia should move back into their Berks station. Disher, the stroke, seeing the umpire's white flag waving wildly, was panicked about how close they were to the Cambridge crew. As the two crews converged Gig kept his boat in the middle and the Australians side-washed the Cambridge crew.

Slowly the Australian blades came closer to the Cambridge oars. Then they overlapped.[9] Disher was nearing a state of apoplexy and between strokes was grunting and urging Gig to get back over to his station:

for some time we were much closer to them than we should have been they certainly got some of our wash which is most regrettable and no one is more sorry or vexed than I was, however the cox was alone to blame; he would not go over in spite of being told several times.[10]

As Sydney's *Daily Mirror* reported it: 'As the Cambridge blades left the water, the Australians' dipped in. The oars windmilled one over the other, but never touched.' The umpire was calling the Australians over and over. The risk of Gig's move was enormous. If the Australians, who were out of their own water, touched or clipped the Cambridge crew's oars, the umpire would raise his red flag and disqualify them. But just before this happened, Gig, with impeccable timing, broke contact and straightened up. But before reaching the Fawley mark, Gig went over again into Cambridge's water, putting them once more under pressure.

Gig's gamble paid off and by the three quarter mile mark, the Australians had increased their lead to three quarters of a length. But the Cambridge crew were not in any way finished. With a length or so lead, Gig again steered a course to wash off Cambridge. *Referee* recorded:

The Light Blues were rowing well, and at the three-quarter mile Australia's lead had been reduced to a third of a length, with the coxswain keeping his boat as far over in Cambridge's water as possible.[11]

Over the last quarter mile, the Australians were mentally and physically drained by the intense pressure applied by Cambridge in this watery dogfight but they hung on – just. The Cambridge stroke, Captain Hartley, made a final splendid effort and the Cambridge crew gave it their best shot, but it was not enough. The crowd exploded as the Australians crossed the line, winning by a half of a length and in a time of 7 minutes 24 seconds. But Disher, as stroke, felt let down by the crew's finish:

I expected Cambridge who were almost a length behind to go for us soon after the mile mark but hoped that as in previous dozens no appreciable effect would be noted; they did go for us and started slowly to come up I let them a little and about 200 yards from home called on the crew who had up till then been rowing

very well. It started off alright but there was not the response
there should have been, and I feel it couldn't last so dropped it
down again slightly and prayed hard for the finishing line ...
I was disappointed in the crew's finish which I had thought
would be a strong point and I felt that I had rather confirmed a
lingering suspicion that we were short of a gallop; well we had it
then and a damn hard one.[12]

There was little sense of elation when the AIF No. 1 crew lifted
their boat off the water and staggered inside the Boat Enclosure,
surprised by Gig's gambit, but relieved it had paid off. Marshall was
scratching his head; Disher was red-faced and ropable; George Mettam
was physically shattered and later wrote:

This was the hardest race we had and it *was* hard. We hopped
away from them at the start and just held them off all the way
over the course. Hard it was ... one of the severest goes I have yet
rowed but it turned out our way.[13]

At 3 pm, the Americans pushed off from the staging ramp and
started their paddle down the Henley Reach to Temple Island. A few
minutes later the Oxford University service crew emerged from the
enclosure and carried their boat to the water, followed by the silent and
watchful Tarka. A distant refrain of 'The Star-Spangled Banner' struck
up and floated across the water as the Americans were swallowed up
by the throng of wherries and punts skittering and poling across the
surface of the Thames. A large gathering of loyal Oxford supporters,
students and reserve crew members formed a tunnel for the Oxford
University crew as they carried their boat to the water, threaded their
oars through and pushed off.

At 3.40 pm the starter's gun fired, and the two eights squeezed their
first stroke, and then rapidly shortened to lift their boats out of the
water. The Americans, displaying their power, steadily increased their
boat speed, using their strength and weight to muscle ahead. Oxford
were striking at a higher rate and moving the boat well but knew that

once the Americans had attained maximum speed, they would be difficult to crack if they could maintain their composure.

By the first signal, the Americans were leading by half a length and then increased their lead to three quarters of a length by the Fawley mark, reaching it in 3 minutes 34 seconds. Oxford had to hold their nerve; Tarka would have stressed to his stroke man, Lieutenant-Colonel E. A. Berrisford MC, that he must hold his length and rhythm no matter how far ahead the Americans were; they were big and brash, but ultimately did not have the finer rhythm or swing. Tarka, with Guy Nickalls, likely knew the Ivy League oarsmen brought into their boat their clashing varsity rowing styles. As the *New York Herald* reported, 'With almost as many [rowing] systems to encounter as colleges represented, the difficulties encountered were much greater than if men had been taught the same system in college competition.'[14] The United States of America, it would appear, did not easily morph into a united state of rowing inside their expertly crafted George Sims boat.

After the crews passed the Fawley mark, the rugged power of the Americans reached its apogee and Oxford began to claw back, reducing the margin to a few feet at the Mile Post.

In the last quarter of a mile the dominant American crew, stroked by Cornell oarsman Captain Douglas Kingsland, cracked, and what power and grit they held in reserve simply leached uselessly into the bottom of the boat as panic set in. Under pressure, the individual varsity oarsmen reverted to their natural styles. The Oxford University service crew, under Tarka's stoic guidance and with their years of rowing English Orthodoxy, held their swing and rhythm and drew away from the Americans, crossing the finish line by a convincing margin of one and a quarter lengths in a respectable but not blistering time of 7 minutes 25 seconds.[15]

Too late, American leader Major Withington recognised that the coaches who worked in the big money varsity rowing programs did not readily share their coaching expertise or rowing techniques unless paid to do so. He observed that 'the absence of the professional coach in English rowing as the American knows him makes of rowing in the British Isles an open book'.[16] The English Orthodox style was widespread and everyone was familiar with the same system. Withington also noted that, for American crews, 'more emphasis is placed on winning. New features that help for speed in crew, if discovered, are maintained a secret.'[17] It should not be so surprising that the unholy matrimony of professionalism and sport cuts both ways.

27

The King's Cup

Carine Pennefather awoke early on Saturday 5 July. As usual she was well prepared for the day ahead, with her clothes laid out along with all that she would require for a long day touring the country. Soon she was dressed and hatted, her hair pulled back into a no-nonsense bun, and, equipped with her bag, she was out the door of her Maida Hill flat on her way to King George Hospital, Waterloo. She had a little day trip planned to Henley-on-Thames.

Carine was born and bred a proud Tasmanian. She had sailed to London in 1914, with plans to travel the world. But when war broke out and she saw the wounded soldiers streaming back to England from Europe and Gallipoli, she immediately knew her calling was to provide what comfort she could for the sick, wounded and dying. She stayed put and volunteered her considerable resources to the cause.

She arrived at King George Hospital before 6 am and immediately set about mustering her troops. The day before, six double amputee Australian soldiers had arrived at King George from Dartford and they were assembled in wheelchairs, dressed, ready and waiting.

All up it was an impressive party of twenty-four seriously wounded men, four able orderlies and one strong-minded, unflappable woman heading for Henley. By 7 am they were out the door. They caught the train to Charing Cross station, where they were met by a large motor bus. The bus detoured to Pennefather's favourite restaurant, where she collected a large pre-ordered hamper of Cornish pasties and gooseberry turnovers. All set, all loaded, they were finally on the road to Henley-on-Thames, ready to lunch on the way.[1]

On the Royal Henley Peace Regatta finals day, Syd Middleton woke early after a fitful sleep and peered through the curtains across the gently flowing River Thames. Locked up in Wharfe House with the lads, the victim of his own training regime, he was tired above all. His first thoughts these days were, of course, about Marion. He thought about her now more than ever. Meanwhile, he looked skyward and checked the weather. The sky was grey and overcast.

Across the river, he saw there was already some early activity in the Boat Enclosure. He watched as a racing eight and a set of oars were carried out of the boat tent, loaded onto a farmer's dray hitched to a team of draught horses and lashed tight. He could tell from the military uniforms of the hands loading the boat and the imposing figure of Tarka Gold, who was closely supervising the boat loading, that it was the Oxford University boat.

Sneaky buggers. They were going to sneak their boat by cart to the start at Temple Meadow to save their strength, to stay away from the noise and crowds, and to avoid the prying eyes of the Australians, as well as their sledging.

Noise filtered through the corridors of Wharfe House as the other oarsmen awoke and heaved themselves, groaning, out of bed. They had over six hours till the start time of the King's Cup final, at 12.30 pm. Time enough to shower, load up on a big breakfast, meet one last time to discuss their race plan, and then relax before taking the short, pleasant stroll across Henley Bridge to the Boat Enclosure. Inside the marquee they would change into their rowing togs and carry their boat to the staging deck.

By 7 am, spectators and soldiers were already streaming into Henley from the railway station. Load after load of dominion troops arrived, reminding veterans of the Western Front of the many railheads that they had been dumped at before making the trek to the field of battle.

Conspicuous additions to the trainloads of troops were the cream of British high society, English roses beautifully decked out with flower-adorned wide-brimmed hats and their prettiest dresses, with the common sense addition of mackintoshes and umbrellas. The gentlemen wore hats, boaters, coats and ties and carried their overcoats. On the waterfront, locals and visitors from up and down the Thames were already loading picnics and pastries onboard wherries, punts and skiffs, then rowing out to the booms, where they vied for the best spot from which to view the finish.

The beauty of Henley is that, win or lose, every crew wants to see it through to the end, even if they do so standing on the riverbank. Schoolboys, squads, soldiers and supporters who were billeted in and around the township were all intent on seeing the final day of racing. Would it be the Oxford University Army service crew or the AIF No. 1 crew? The Mother Country or the colonials? Gentlemen or convicts?

Carine Pennefather had arranged for the distinguished Mr John F. Cooper, a Henley local and secretary of the Henley committee of management since 1882, to meet her party outside the Leander Club. Mr Cooper was there waiting, right on time. He welcomed Carine and directed the bus driver to park on Lion Meadow. From there, Mr Cooper showed Pennefather and her lads where they could best watch the King's Cup and where to find the YMCA amenities marquee. The orderlies set to work carrying some of the legless diggers, while those who could wheel, hobble or shuffle on their own made their way to the marquee, and together they tucked into free tea and pastries. The Thames riverbank and Steward's Enclosure grandstands were now teeming with thousands of excited soldiers and spectators. Survivors of the Great War from almost every Allied army were arriving from the railway station or being bussed into Henley to see the Peace Regatta.

On the far side of the Henley course, the Bucks side, along the last 300 yards of the straight, were hundreds of small leisure boats, packed twenty deep in places, each crammed with spectators craning for a glimpse of the crews coming into the finish.

Behind the floating spectators, the Phyllis Court Club grandstand was filling with invited private members and guests. Further on, practically at the finish, the green lawn of Wharfe House was also filling with officers and guests of the AIF Rowing Section, including several Australian celebrities of stage and song. A wooden viewing platform was erected on the edge of the Wharfe House bank and filled up fast, celebrities and diggers jostling for space.

Along the riverbank next to the Steward's Enclosure, many of the Allied armies had erected their own makeshift grandstands from which they could cheer on the crews. The Steward's Enclosure was packed with the well-heeled of London, Oxford and Cambridge society, who strolled the green lawn in front of the grandstand and refreshments marquee. Standing prominently on the steward's lawn, guarded by a local Henley constable and a bowler-hatted regatta attendant, was a shelved glass cabinet in which many famous cups and trophies of the Henley Royal Regatta were displayed, including the revered silver Grand Challenge Cup for eight-oared rowing. This year, though, taking pride of place on the top glass shelf, was the impressive gold prize of the King's Cup.

At about 11 am, the Australian No. 1 crew, dressed for action in blue blazers, white shirts, flannels and shoes, began their stroll from Wharfe House to the Boat Enclosure. They walked as a team, accompanied by their mates of the No. 2 crew, across the narrow footpath of Henley Bridge, now brimming with spectators and motor traffic heading up and down Remenham Hill.

Henley was filling with thousands of diggers, some of whom cheered and clapped the crew as they jostled their way across the crowded bridge. Fellow soldiers ran up, clapped them on the back and wished them the best of luck. Coach Marshall led the team, pushing the crowd aside to make way for the oarsmen. They walked along the narrow brick lane that wound beside the Leander Club and led onto the towpath, passing the open waterside Leander boatyard. The Leander Club members, in hats and suits, or rowing caps and rowing club blazers, peered down at the Australian oarsmen – literally looking down their noses – as the diggers passed the boathouse.

It was cold, grey and drizzly, a not untypical English summer's day, so the Australians had taken their sweaters with them and together they headed into the Boat Enclosure to change. The Oxford University Army crew were nowhere to be seen. They had already walked down the towpath to the start.

Lieutenant George Goddard, a newspaper journalist from Queensland, was appointed Sports Control Board press liaison by Middleton and was on hand to record the triumphs, reckonings and atmosphere at the regatta.

> There were enormous crowds all along the banks & on the
> portion of the river allotted to the public. The colour effect
> during the brief spells of sunshine was something to remember.
> The transformation, when the showers came & everybody
> produced a mackintosh, was also remarkable.[2]

Inside the Boat Enclosure marquee, the AIF No. 1 crew had changed into their rowing togs. Draped around their shoulders were their pullovers, to wear down to the start and help them warm up against the chilly English summer's day. The golden rays (or bayonets) of the embroidered AIF Rising Sun crest proudly adorned their chests for the last time. One more race and it would all be over.

As they stretched and calmed their nerves, Gig reached into his kitbag and took out the small silk 'Dinkum Aussie' flag he had had made up and rigged it onto a thin flagpole about a foot long. They watched quietly as Gig fixed the flagpole into the small hole drilled just in front of Archie's bow seat.

Each of these oarsmen had rowed into war and now they were going to row out the other side. Some of them, after the King's Cup, would never step back into a boat again. Both Marshall and Middleton knew that the time for rousing pre-battle speeches was over. Now it was time to take in the atmosphere, forget the stakes at play and just go out for a row. This wasn't Gallipoli. No one was going to die. It was just a rowing race, and compared to everything they'd been through, a leisurely paddle at that. The crew went about their pre-race business, shook hands, quietly wished each other luck and then, on Clive Disher's call, laid hands on the boat.

Just on midday, they paused, waiting for a break in the crowd of people so they could edge through to the staging platform and put to water. They stood looking down the course, pullovers loosely tied around their shoulders, the little flag dangling upside down. If they craned their necks, they could just catch a glimpse of the quarter mile marker. The weather was still ominous, but the rain was holding off.

The Australians placed the boat on the water, tossed their oars over to the correct side of the boat, took their seats and threaded their oar handles through the poppet rowlocks, twisting the half-leather buttons under the twine and clasping their oar handles.

A throng of keen diggers then clasped the end of their blades and pushed them off, out into the Reach. As the crew drifted away, they tightened their stretchers, checked their slides, then briefly assumed a half-slide position to pose for an official AIF rowing crew photograph. They donned their pullovers and gently paddled down to the start. It took the crew fifteen to twenty minutes to reach the jumping-off point. Disher later wrote to his former rowing coach John Lang about how seriously they approached the final:

> We felt that day that we were rowing for Australia, and we were keyed up for it.[3]

The drizzle let up as the AIF No. 1 crew neared the start, providing a clear view of the Oxford University Army service crew drifting off the bank of Temple Island Meadow, awaiting their arrival. The two crews drifted on the Henley Reach at a respectful distance, wary of making eye contact as they prepared to do battle. Nothing was being said in the boat. The oarsmen were switching on, silently priming their bodies for the physical onslaught to come. Ahead of them lay over a mile and a quarter of no-man's-water.

Behind the Australians, the Henley umpire's launch puttered into view from behind Temple Island, carrying, among others, the official party of the Prince and Princess Arthur of Connaught; the coaches Colonel Norman Marshall and Colonel 'Tarka' Gold; the Henley race umpire officiating; Mr Fred Pitman, who was accompanied by Henley stewards as timekeepers; and a boatman. The petrol-driven launch *Enchantress* swung behind the crews and powered down the motor till the crews tapped towards the start.

The AIF No. 1 crew were to start in the Berks station and the Oxford University service crew in the Bucks station. Both crews paddled towards the dinghies moored in the Buckinghamshire channel alongside Temple Island. Once in position in their stations, they checked their run and then gently backed their boats down to the attendants reaching out from the dinghies, who grasped the stern of the boats, making sure to keep clear of the rudder and steering line.

Mr Pitman, wearing his Cambridge University rowing blazer and cap, stood at the bow of the launch. The Prince and Princess Arthur of Connaught sat to either side of him, followed by the coaches, Tarka on the Bucks side of the launch and Marshall and Ross-Soden on the Berks side, then other invited guests, the Henley boat race officials, and the timekeepers.

Casting a glance at his timepiece, with a minute or two before zero hour, Mr Pitman addressed the crews in a firm, clear voice. 'Gentlemen. When I see you are straight and ready, I will start you like this. I will say "Gentlemen, are you ready?" And then I will fire the gun. Get ready, please.'

As the crews came forward, nervously checked that their feet were secured in their stretchers and wriggled their backsides, the coxswains, with one hand raised, quietly ordered the bow or number 2 man of their crew to touch the boat around and straighten up for a clear line to the first right-hand bend, and into the boomed straight of the Henley course.

Freddie House relayed Gig's calls to Archie to 'touch it bow'. At the same time, in the umpire's launch, a steward loaded a blank round into the shotgun's breech, snapped it shut and handed it to Mr Pitman, who turned to Princess Arthur of Connaught and proffered a polite, 'Perhaps your Majesty may find it more comfortable to cover your ears?' Both crews now ready, Pitman turned to the oarsmen and called out, 'Gentlemen. Are you ready?'

When the crowd heard the starting gun, 'a silence fell for a while ... and all eyes turned down the straight mile and a half long reach'.[4] Both crews got away to a clean start. The first ten or so strokes are short, sharp and all about heaving the 130-stone-plus (825-kilogram-plus) dead weight of boat and manpower into forward motion, building momentum and translating that into sheer speed. Australia shot out of the blocks at a higher rate of striking than Oxford and edged in front even before they had drawn past the prow of Temple Island. The two crews battled it out into the bend but the Australians still had their bow in front at the half mile and reached the Fawley mark in a quick 3 minutes 25 seconds.

Berrisford, the Oxford stroke, asked for an effort from his crew and increased the rate, closing the gap a little between the two crews, but Disher responded by keeping his length and maintaining his rate of striking low. He asked Gig for more leg drive and finish from the engine room rather than increased rate. Scotty, Hauenstein and Middleton kicked in and gave the boat plenty of shove, turning muscle into motion as they cranked the watts out through the water.

This power meant the AIF No. 1 crew had drawn further ahead by the one-mile mark. An almighty cheer went up from the grandstands situated at the finish when the diggers saw the boat race official hoist up the large red '1' panel at the official mile mark post, signifying the crew in the Berks station was the first to pass the mile mark. Only a quarter of a mile to go.

Carine Pennefather and her cohort of walking wounded were watching the race and willing them on. A few of the boys had pushed forward to the riverbank but the diggers missing limbs were lost in the crush. Despite their injuries and infirmities, some had scrambled up trees 'you would have imagined could only have been safely negotiated by ants!'[5] They were literally hanging out of the branches for a better view, and yelling at the top of their lungs.

By now, Berrisford knew he had to throw everything Oxford had at the Australians and he wound up his Oxford crew to a very fast rate of 40 strokes to the minute along the Phyllis Court stretch. Disher was in the perfect position to read every desperate move the Oxford crew made. The risk of lifting the strike rate is that often the length of the stroke in the water shortens – particularly when fatigue sets in and the mind crumbles in panic. Disher kept his nerve and was now striking a lower rate than Oxford but maintaining the vital speed of the boat through the water.

There is sometimes a perception that a crew somehow rows faster at the finish because they 'draw away' – but perceptions can be deceptive. A crew has pretty much given their physical all by then. The reality is often that the other crews, even though they are moving rapidly up and down the slide inside the boat, tapping out a faster stroke rate, are often rowing shorter, fading away in power, and actually slowing down. This creates the misleading impression that the leading crew is drawing away.

To the masses of diggers cheering from the banks, it would have looked like the Aussie boat was suddenly accelerating on the water. Not quite – they were ploughing ahead, steady as she goes, while the Oxford crew's shortening left them slowing. They had fallen away to one length behind – but then steadied, hanging on with a dose of pure English grit. George Mettam's Scottish cousin Pollie, who had come to the regatta with Mettam's brother Frank, caused a moment of amusement among the well-heeled society crowd, 'calling on "George!" in her Scotch tongue!'[6] Disher recalled, 'They came at us, it is true, but we rowed home with the same old swing to the end, not quickening.'[7] As the AIF No. 1 crew neared 100 yards from the finish line, one length clear of Oxford, the roar from the diggers (and probably the Canadians and the New Zealanders) was deafening.

On the riverbank, Pennefather was ready and her orderlies lifted the legless boys out of their wheelchairs at the last moment and hoisted them onto their shoulders 'so that they saw splendidly!'[8] The AIF No. 1 crew crossed the finish line in a fast 7 minutes 7 seconds – the fastest time recorded for the eights throughout the whole of the Royal Henley Peace Regatta. The Perth *Daily News* enthused:

> They were physically the most powerful crew ever seen at Henley Regatta. They owed their victory to their racing experience and their marvellous uniformity. They were short in the water and had little grip of the water behind the rigger but had a powerful middle and finish to the stroke. What they did they did together and with great back force.[9]

Inside the boat, as they crossed the finish line, all the Australians knew was that it was over. They heard only a muted roar. A crushing weight had been lifted from their heaving shoulders. There was no fist pumping or splashing of water, no victory cries. This very public victory was, in the grand scheme of things, a pale echo of the larger contests they'd come through. Victory for the oarsmen had meant surviving a global catastrophe and living to tell a yarn or two when others did not.

The Australian crew looked across at the Oxford crew, who were slumped, with heads down. It is not difficult to imagine that the men of the AIF No. 1 crew sat stunned, exhausted, watching mute as thousands of diggers went wild on the riverbank. Then Fred House reached behind him and offered his outstretched hand to Archie Robb. What House and Robb had done, they had done together as proud Tasmanians. Tom McGill probably thought of his dead brother Norman. Scotty's thoughts may have turned to his dead brother, Edward – this one was for him. Hauenstein probably thought the job was done, and nothing would ever get him back in a boat again. He may have reached forward and patted Middleton on the back once or twice, and that would be it – an armistice of sorts. Middleton was probably still gasping for breath. He had survived the war and now he had survived the King's Cup. And it had been worth it. He had found a new home, and love. George Mettam was probably just chuffed. Being a late call into the boat he had done what he had to do to back up Disher. About the King's Cup race, George wrote:

> This was a much easier race for us although we rowed 17 seconds
> faster than the previous day ... The time 7.7 we considered
> remarkably fast considering the weather conditions. Many of the
> critics (and here, are not a few) think that had we been pushed
> the record of 6.5 would have been lowered. The 1912 Australian
> Olympic crew did the journey in 7.6 when they won the Grand
> Challenge Cup.[10]

Clive Disher couldn't believe it. He had not only rowed at Henley, the fabled home of rowing, but he had won, stroking an AIF crew and representing Australia. It was much better than college rowing. Gig Smedley just sat there facing the crew, with a broad grin on his face. Gig had all the time in the world to soak up the victory, and also to collect on his bets and partake in a chilled case of some very, very good French champagne. Victory at Henley was going to taste so sweet.

When Berrisford, the Oxford stroke, called for three cheers for the Australians, the noise exploded in their ears like a pin pricking a balloon. In the Oxford boat, MacNeil, sitting in the number 3 seat, probably cheered the loudest. The Australians returned a stout three cheers to Oxford, and Gig called for the crew to come forward for the last time. 'Half forward. Are you ready? Row.'

As the AIF No. 1 crew approached the Boat Enclosure staging platform, they were mobbed by hundreds of diggers, who ran to greet the crew and assist them off the water.

> When we got the boat alongside the ways we were overwhelmed
> by 'diggers' even to the rank of colonel, who wanted to help us out
> of the boat, and we were worried that they would tear the boat to
> pieces. We had at least 50 on each side helping to bring her in.[11]

In the crush, Gig was quick to souvenir the 'Dinkum Aussie' flag from the bow of the boat. The first thing Lieutenant Goddard had to do as press liaison officer was to push his way through to the crew and get the first official photograph of the King's Cup winners. Getting the crew free of the clamouring diggers was hard, but getting the crew free of ecstatic AIF superior officers proved even more difficult. The commanding officer of the AIF Administrative Headquarters, Lieutenant-General Hobbs, was delirious with joy, with tears streaming down his face. He grabbed Disher and hugged him as tightly as he could. A bemused Disher described the scene to John Lang:

> I draw a blank over the rejoicings. The 'digger' of whom there
> seemed to be hundreds nearly went mad. General Hobbs the
> Corps Commander almost cried down my neck and barely
> had voice to tell me he was the happiest man this side of
> the world.[12]

It was Australia's victory and any distinctions of rank or class were momentarily lost in the mayhem. Lieutenant Goddard hurriedly ushered the oarsmen to a corner of the Boat Enclosure as Lieutenant-General Hobbs wiped away a tear or two and collected himself. The diminutive Hobbs had been dwarfed by the oarsmen as he stood among them, posing for the photographer and looking as proud as punch. The oarsmen themselves hadn't quite taken it in and the photo captured stony faces and empty gazes.

Of course, for the English it was never a case of simply having been outclassed – heaven forbid! It was said that the Australians 'had the advantage of much longer training than the English crews, and in physique were superior to the oarsmen representing the universities'. *The Times* though gave credit to Middleton's bold crew changes, which had helped the AIF No. 1 crew find form:

> The winners were undoubtedly the best eight at the regatta,
> and the changes made a fortnight before the racing by bringing
> up three men from the second boat strengthened the crew that
> looked like going stale.[13]

For the rest of that afternoon, the English summer showers opened up and for the spectators it was a case of switching from brightly coloured fashions to dark wet-weather gear and black umbrellas, and back again. It didn't deter many from staying, though; they could see the standard of racing was high and the presence of so many 'foreigners' must have given the competition an international flair. Perhaps the showers and the Peace Regatta washed away the pain of war for a while.

The Australian oarsmen made their way across the Henley Bridge, back to their digs at Wharfe House, cheered and clapped along the way by the boozy diggers pouring out of the Angel on the Bridge Hotel. Once inside the grounds of Wharfe House, both AIF rowing crews shook hands and exchanged light embraces with two or three mandatory taps on the back before they stripped, showered and changed back into their flannels, shirts and rowing blazers.

Over the next few hours, they grabbed something to eat, watched the remaining races and chatted and mixed with the invited officers, diggers and notable guests on the trimmed Wharfe House lawn. All very much like a right royal English garden party with a touch of Australian style.

Throughout the afternoon Lieutenant Goddard got down to serious business, setting up both crews for formal team photos, group shots and casual snaps. The oarsmen had to wait till the racing was completed for the day for the Peace Regatta trophy presentations within the Steward's Enclosure. Middleton had issued strict orders about no drinking, so they had to remain 'dry' till after then.

The oarsmen particularly wanted to see the formidable New Zealander Darcy Hadfield in action against the Etonian old boy Lieutenant T. Nussey, a promising sculler aged only twenty, representing the Army of the Rhine in the Kingswood Sculls final at 3.30 pm. Lieutenant Nussey, whose form confounded the critics, probably knew he was up against it in the final, being outweighed by Hadfield by over 1 stone 6 pounds (9 kilograms). Everyone in Henley had watched Hadfield's muscular performances on the water during training and in the Kingswood heats. He was the epitome of strength and aquatic grace.

The Australians and the other dominions still felt there was a class system at play at Henley. A handwritten addition by an unknown Australian in one surviving Royal Henley Peace Regatta program disdainfully noted that Nussey's rank, 'Lieutenant', accompanied his name but that Hadfield's lower rank was omitted:

> Note the snobbery. Hadfield is a Sgt, but of course it would have been 'infra dig' for an officer to row against a mere N.C.O. so they left his rank out.[14]

During the afternoon, the sheepish and hapless publican from the Crown Hotel in New Street, true to his word, arrived at Wharfe House with the promised case of French champagne. Gig then presented his 'book' and duly collected the winnings for all the crew at the healthy odds of six to one. The champagne was quickly put onto ice to chill it in preparation for the crew's return to Wharfe House and a well-earned toast.

The Kingswood Sculls final started on time. Hadfield powered away, led by half a length at the quarter mile and had increased his lead by the mile. This was a race between a hardened war veteran who had been wounded in action and a young officer full of brio, with a military career ahead of him. Nussey had knocked out some serious Henley veterans, though they were all a bit older. Hadfield was efficient and powerful. His legs and arms were solid. Nussey was rowing wildly but had the fitness to just hang in. In the spirit of Henley, if a crew or sculler is dominating in battle, they follow an unwritten rule of gentlemanly sport and refrain from thrashing their hapless opponent by too large a margin – almost the complete opposite of the rules of engagement they had been fighting under for the last four years.

As Hadfield approached the finish, he kept a steady, measured two lengths in front of the thrashing, twisting Nussey, who, 'with his own extraordinary style', was never going to concede until the last stroke.[15] After Nussey crossed the line, he was spent. In a display of supreme sportsmanship, Hadfield casually flicked his scull around, paddled towards Nussey and then backed his single scull closer so that they could shake hands face to face on the water, in front of the crowd. What was said between them would remain a secret shared by a master and his apprentice. The spectators were impressed by Hadfield's sportsmanship. An all-round nice bloke, he would go on to win New Zealand's first medal in rowing at the 1920 Antwerp Olympics. Two of the four trophies for events open to the Allied Forces at the Royal Henley Peace Regatta were now heading to the Antipodes.

At about 4 pm, Carine Pennefather and her party realised they had squeezed in all the racing they could for the day and piled back into the motor bus. 'The day was wet and miserable but our victory warmed the boys' hearts,' wrote Pennefather, 'and the day was a great success.'[16] They motored across the bridge into the centre of Henley for afternoon tea at a high street restaurant before heading back to London. As they were getting back on the bus, Archie Robb, who was heading over to the Steward's Enclosure for the presentations, ran into them. It seems Miss Pennefather was quite smitten by her fellow Tasmanian:

> When loading up again Robb came up and had a chat to us about the race, in which he formed one of the crew. He looked quite calm and cool, and awfully nice in his flannels and dark blue sports coat with plain gold buttons and a large 'rising sun' and wattle embroidered on the pocket.[17]

The Oxford University Army service crew were depleted and deflated after their King's Cup duel. The big one had got away. Any other prize perhaps felt a little 9-carat in comparison – even if it was a grudge match against their old nemesis. The final event of the day, the University Race, scheduled for 6 pm, felt a little anticlimactic and by gentlemanly consensus Cambridge and Oxford agreed to a no row.

Hundreds of spectators and competitors gathered in the Steward's Enclosure for the trophy presentation. As the *Referee* reported:

after the luncheon interval it was fairly fine until the last race had been rowed. Then the rain came down, and there was a general rush for shelter. After waiting for some time, Princess Arthur of Connaught distributed the prizes in the rain.[18]

Princess Arthur of Connaught stood on a raised platform, sheltered by an umbrella or two. The victors, dressed in their team colours and blazers, paraded in line and were called upon in turn to be presented with their trophies. As Captain Disher stepped onto the dais, the Princess presented the King's Cup, shook hands, then presented a Peace Regatta medal – sitting within velvet in a smart red leather case – to each of the sodden oarsmen. The medals had been struck especially for the regatta. On one side, in relief, was a Grecian goddess holding a laurel wreath in one hand and a dove bearing an olive branch in the other. In the background were two rowing fours on an Elysian river.

The evenings seem to linger for eternity during the height of summer in England. When the oarsmen returned to Wharfe House, the extended twilight enabled a full evening of riotous laughter and many rowing 'war' stories. The house and lawn were full of young female admirers, generals, supporters and guests. Gig paraded the fluffy toy kangaroo mascot. General Birdwood's large Australian 'Gallipoli Flag' hung damp and unmoving on the tall flagpole above them. Gig distributed the winnings, and the French champagne was chilled to perfection.

The oarsmen poured the champagne into the King's Cup – 'we thought His Majesty might not like it if we used beer.'[19] Each drank from the Cup, spontaneously starting a tradition that would last another hundred years. This was the type of victory they had all long forgotten – though they knew that the real prize was in the hours, the work and the friendships that had enabled the victory. For years, success for the oarsmen had meant simple survival of a gruesome living hell, so this night among veterans of the bloodiest war the world had seen was infinitely precious. And the win wasn't just about sport; the King's Cup was also about the collective dead, the lost brothers and comrades – Norman McGill, Edward Scott, Thomas Whyte, Cecil Healy and Keith Heritage, to name just a few of the commemorated 60,000.

When the long evening at Wharfe House ended no one knows for sure. Nights like these are for those who earned them, not the history books. As the party wound down, Middleton wondered what to do with the actual King's Cup. Tired and relieved, he abrogated all official responsibility for a night and thrust the Cup at Lieutenant Goddard, telling him to look after it – or else. Goddard, no doubt wobbly on his feet, carried the gold cup up the stairs of Wharfe House and stepped over the rows of bodies sleeping a big night off, just like the old days of the Front. 'I hadn't the least idea what to do with the thing. I took it to bed with me,' he said.[20]

The oarsmen already knew the King's Cup wasn't theirs to keep, and it was certainly not going into any dusty trophy cabinet or carry case. Disher wrote the next day how one of the oarsmen – no one can say for sure who – had already 'suggested that the King's Cup be put up as the Interstate yearly trophy. Each state was represented in the crew except Queensland.'[21] From now on, the King's Cup could be held aloft annually by a new rowing crew, by fresh generations who weren't called upon to die for their King and country.

28

The Inter-Allied Regatta, Paris

The next day, Sunday 6 July 1919, the Australians roused themselves from bed, recovering from an intense night of celebration, cigars and French champagne. After almost five weeks of accommodating thirty or so ravenous oarsmen, cooks, masseurs and support staff, capped by a raucous party, poor old Wharfe House had had its fair share of wear and tear. Among an itemised list of repairs to the house was one for plate glass costing £19.11.[1] It would seem the oarsmen, letting their hair down after years of endless discipline, had had quite a night. The next morning, likely with a crew hangover, there was one last crew photograph off the edge of Wharfe House on the abandoned still water of the River Thames. The rowing squad spent the next few days tidying up and repairing any damages to the house before leaving for Paris.

It was the last day of the American-convened Inter-Allied Games at Pershing Stadium in Paris – although rowing events had been postponed. The American Games Committee – with Colonel Wait C. Johnson GS, the chief athletic officer of the AEF, as chairman – had generously rescheduled the rowing events to 17–18 July 1919.

The Americans had offered to ship the boats of the competing crews to Paris post-haste on board a waiting American cruiser.[2] The rowing squad had to derig the 60-foot-long single section onto a trailer with the oars, seats and riggers. The Americans would do the rest, allowing time for rerigging and a week or so of training on the River Seine to prepare for the Inter-Allied Games.

After giving all they had for the King's Cup, both Middleton and Hauenstein had flagged that they would not step back into the boat. The two 1912 HRR Grand Challenge Cup winners and Olympians made clear that their rowing careers were finally over. With experience came wisdom, and the elder statesmen of the crew probably knew when the creaking of their joints and their strained muscles were telling them to call it a day.

They would be sorely missed in Paris, where the crew would have to make do without their expertise and raw power. Disher wrote, 'Middleton won't be going unfortunately, and we are trying to persuade Hauenstein to go but he is pretty firm about it.'[3]

Why Hauenstein firmly declined is subject to conjecture but it is possible that his responsibility to his troubled brother Paddy, who was still in England, hovering around the edges of Wharfe House, was a deciding factor.

Middleton still had his many organising duties with the AIF Sports Control Board and decided his talents and efforts were better employed at a desk than in a boat. Also, now that the King's Cup had been won, there was also the possibility of seeing more of Marion and meeting her friends and family. How an older, burly, gruff, secular Australian would be received by the family of a Roman Catholic Irish peer remained to be seen, but Middleton was determined to present himself in the best possible light, and convince Marion's family that his intentions were completely honourable.

Captain Clive Disher wrote of the win to John Lang:

Well you will have heard the result long before you get this and
I hope you have not been displeased. John there is no prouder
person alive today than I am at the present moment.[4]

For an oarsman who had initially been indifferent to the whole concept, he had certainly changed his tune. Disher had rowed in an all-Australian representative crew that, for all its faults, troubles and idiosyncrasies, was undoubtedly the fastest Australian eight-oared crew at the time. A ragtag bunch of oarsmen had stumbled out of the war and formed a tight-knit unit in which the powers of discipline, will and dedication combined to create something state-based allegiances could rarely achieve.

His priority now was to further his medical training but the prospect of the Cambridge University service crew entering the Inter-Allied Games event – and the chance to right the wrongs of the Peace Regatta – was enough to change his mind and coax him back into the boat.

> The next thing is the race in Paris at the Yanks Regatta. I wasn't
> going but as usual feel principally because Cambridge have
> decided to go as it appears that Oxford have refused to row them.
> The course in Paris is with the stream and I believe the centre
> crew has untold advantage there ... I hate to think of Cambridge
> winning and so vindicating English Rowing.[5]

The rowing squad heading to Paris was a smaller squad than that which had triumphed at Henley. Middleton was out of there as soon as he could be, to get back to London. Many of the other oarsmen began to pay final visits to friends and family throughout England, hoping to catch an early boat homeward.

Major Audsley wrote:

> From all accounts, everybody is arriving back home now or on
> the way and the other day they came around and asked for those
> who wanted to go home directly after Henley ... You can bet
> your life that I put in to go home ... I reckon I have been away
> long enough.[6]

And so began the parting of many rowing squad comrades and friends, on their separate journeys homeward across the open seas.

The Americans, of course, went to extraordinary lengths to make sure the AIF oarsmen's stay in Paris was as comfortable as possible when they arrived – albeit sans boats. As Disher wrote to Lang:

> Packed up the Cambridge boat on Monday it was to have
> been taken by the Americans at 9am Tuesday by trailer to
> Southampton shipped on one of their cruisers to Havre thence
> by trailer here. All the boats the same way. However, they didn't
> leave Henley until late Tuesday afternoon and they are 24 hrs late
> now and no sign yet. In the mean time we all sit and wait.[7]

There was, however, some very nice accommodation in prefab huts that their American hosts had installed on the edges of the Bois de Boulogne, and plenty of good old American-style food whipped up by American chefs, and a motor car placed at the AIF oarsmen's disposal for sightseeing. As Disher recorded:

> The Yanks seem out to do any mortal thing they can for us. Paris
> is a wonderful place. To look at undoubtedly the finest city I have
> seen. It is really magnificent. Disappointed in the women. Had
> heard a lot about them but beyond being chic in a way afraid I
> can't say I like them better than the English women.[8]

Since the signing of the Treaty of Versailles, the public mood had changed throughout the Allied nations and hope for the future swept over the people. In Paris, they decided to celebrate 'Peace Day' on their significant national day, Bastille Day, 14 July. The French knew how to party and they had a lot to celebrate. Without their boats on hand, the AIF made the most of the delay and joined in with the Peace Day celebrations.

> There is to be a great day here on Monday and huge processions
> through the streets. Already the place is decorated. They know
> how to enjoy themselves there alright. For the first time since
> 1870 troops are to march through the Arch of Triumph.

To make sure the AIF oarsmen were settling in as arranged, and dismayed by the delays, Middleton took the step of flying across from England and supervising squad arrangements. When the boats from Henley did finally arrive, delivered by a delayed convoy of American motor trucks and trailers, there were only two and a half days to go before the Inter-Allied Games Regatta, and there 'wasn't much time in which to get together for a race'.[9] The AIF oarsmen crammed in a few sessions on the Seine but certainly did not have the time to fully adjust to the new crew combination, though they were not completely unhappy with their rows.

Harry Hauenstein also came across to Paris, not to row but to watch and perhaps do a little sightseeing.

Allied nations and colonies had entered the Inter-Allied regatta, and by American accounts, at least, it 'proved to be the largest and most successful service Regatta ever held'.[10] On the afternoon of Thursday 17 July 1919, the rowing event for eight-oared crews was to be decided by two heats of three Allied crews, and one heat of four Allied crews, with the first-placed crew of each heat advancing to a three-crew final the next day. The countries represented were Belgium, Czecho-Slovakia, Italy, Portugal, Canada, England, New Zealand, Australia and the United States. The elimination heats were held over a mile and a half on the River Seine, starting from St Cloud and finishing at Suresnes Bridge.

Australia was now crewed by Archie Robb (bow); Nip Newall (2); Lyn Davis (3); Scotty (4); McGill, who'd slipped into Hauenstein's seat in (5); Freddy House, taking over from Middleton in (6); George Mettam (7); Clive Disher (stroke); and the dependable Gig Smedley in the cockpit with the ropes. The crew missed the strength and power of the two big 1912 oarsmen but had plenty of racing experience together. Johnny Begg and Blue Penny were selected as emergencies, Harry Ross-Soden took over sole coaching duty, and Ossie Wood was appointed rowing squad manager.

In the first of the three eight-oared heats Australia led from start to finish, dispatching Italy, who finished second, with Czecho-Slovakia in third. The second heat saw Clarrie Healey's formidable New Zealand crew defeating Canada, who finished in second place, with Belgium finishing third and poor old Portugal 'catching a crab' and not even finishing. The final heat was the best race of the day, as America pushed the Cambridge service crew 'right to the end and for a little while looked like overhauling them' but Cambridge hung on for a thrilling win by a mere half-length over the once-again frustrated American crew.[11]

The stage was set for Australia, New Zealand and Cambridge in the final, and it had all the hallmarks of a great final between three talented and experienced crews. At the start, Cambridge were slow out of the blocks and were left behind by half a length. Australia burst out of the start ahead of New Zealand, who were striking a lower rate but keeping steadier rhythm and using their power and length to stay within touch. Over the next 600 yards, Cambridge began to find their rhythm and started to catch up to the two Antipodean crews, drawing level with Australia.

> For over a quarter of a mile Cambridge and Australia, side by side, rowed exactly together. The oars of both crews caught and came out of the water together. The extra reach of Cambridge was practically equalled in power by Australia's slashing stroke.[12]

Cambridge held their nerve and showed their mettle and doggedly drew away, inch by inch and stroke by stroke. The Australians, missing the power of Hauenstein and Middleton, could not wear down the plucky Cambridge crew, who crossed the line barely a third of a length in front of Australia, with New Zealand only three quarters of a length further behind in a well-contested final. As Disher wrote:

> We certainly were not disgraced and in some ways were very pleased with ourselves though certainly we should have like to have won. With our Henley crew I think we would have got it. We get a bronze medal for being second. The same as 1st but with different inscription of course.[13]

A respectable win, but not the triumph of the Kings Cup, by any means.

29

The *Euripides*

The men of the AIF rowing squad drifted away from each other during these last few months of 1919, as they prepared to return home. Their individual journeys mixed into the vast movement of men from base camps by road and rail to port, and then by sea. Some of the oarsmen took the opportunity to undertake apprenticeships or business attachments to prepare themselves for employment and their uncertain future back in Australia. Fred House delayed his return to Australia to further his study in motor engineering on full military pay from 8 September till 31 December 1919. His report for his course said he 'made the most of the opportunities afforded him'.[1]

When Disher returned to London, he immediately headed to Horseferry Road and signed up to further his medical training. He soon found himself comfortable quarters in the shadow of the Westminster Boys' School, overlooking the school cricket ground. He told Lang:

By next week I hope to have some photos ready to send you of the crews. The Cup is at present in the Queensland Government Office window in the Strand and looks A.1., also an enlarged photo of the crew. I fancy Sid [sic] told me he had had a copy

sent to each of the associations, but I am not sure. The official
photographic section has shut down and we can't get copies now
of any of their photos until we get back to Australia which is
a nuisance as by that time we probably won't be so keen about
them and goodness only knows where they will be obtainable.[2]

For a time, there had been the nagging question of what to do
with the actual King's Cup. It had now become the property of the
Australian government, much to the annoyance of the English rowing
establishment. In the short term, as Disher noted, the King's Cup was
proudly showcased in the prominent corner window at Australia House
on the Strand.

One midsummer afternoon in late July 1919, Major Middleton,
Captain Disher and Lieutenant Ross-Soden rendezvoused for a
clandestine trip, to visit Mr W. S. Robinson.

Last Sunday week Major Middleton, Ross-Soden and I motored
down to Bourne End for the afternoon and evening taking
the King's Cup down there for the Robinsons to see. It was
nearly 1am before we got home but it was a very pleasant run
and they gave us an excellent dinner besides taking us out on
the river.[3]

By August, Middleton was pushing George Goddard to collate
and write the official account of the AIF's various glorious competitive
endeavours on the sports fields, courts, boxing rings, ovals and arenas of
England and Europe. This account would be somewhat unimaginatively
titled *Soldiers and Sportsmen – An account of the sporting activities
of the Australian Imperial Force during the period between November
1918 and September 1919*. Goddard put his rapid journalistic skills to
work and it was completed by October 1919. In his introduction to the
book, Lieutenant Goddard wrote:

It is safe to say that there is in this old world no greater sport-
loving community that that of our own Australia ... over 200

handpicked Australians [competed] against the rest of the world,
to win occasionally, to lose occasionally, but always to command
the interest of the other two hundred thousand who were
awaiting return to 'God's Demesne'.[4]

In his office in Horseferry Road, Middleton was now settling
outstanding accounts, balancing books, organising official photographs
and auditing costs to report back to the AIF Comforts Fund, who had
generously funded much of the AIF Sports Control Board's work and
organisation.

Eventually most of the King's Cup AIF oarsmen – including Harry
and Paddy Hauenstein, 'Brum' White, Tom McGill, Roy Clark, J.
'Chung' Howieson, Harry Ross-Soden, George Mettam, Gideon 'Blue'
Penny, Alma Cox, Jack Cogle, Bub Jarvis, Archie 'Blond' Robb, Ossie
Wood, Duke Mullins, 'Ack Vie' Scott and Gig Smedley – along with
many other representative AIF sportsmen, were issued repatriation
orders to depart England on 6 September 1919 on board the HMT
Euripides under Captain P. J. Collins.

The HMT *Euripides* made nine return trips to Australia and three
return trips to America, carrying 7000 Yanks and 38,000 Australians
home from the war and covering 250,000 miles in the process.[5]
Onboard the ship, the diggers were given lectures in a variety of
subjects ranging from wool classing, repatriation schemes, and English
and Australian history, to boot-making, telephone engineering, algebra
and pottery. They also occupied themselves competing in boxing bouts
of all weight divisions, tug-of-war, deck quoits, crib, bridge, draughts,
skipping, and putting together concert parties, brass bands and even an
orchestra. When the *Euripides* pulled into Durban, South Africa, the
oarsmen had one more 'picnic' regatta at the invitation of the Durban
Rowing Club. A race for three coxed four-oared boats was held, with
two AIF crews against the locals. Somehow Harry Hauenstein was
talked into the No. 1 crew with R. J. Clark, Scotty, George Mettam
and Gig Smedley. In the No. 2 crew were Googly Cogle, Tom McGill,
Gideon Penny and Archie Robb, with a local coxswain. In a relaxed
day on the water, over a three quarter mile course, Harry's No. 1 crew

led from the start, but the No. 2 crew broke a foot stretcher and had to withdraw. And so ended the final rowing race for the AIF Rowing Section in 1919.[6]

Officially, the AIF disbanded on April Fool's Day in 1921. For years afterwards, the survivors of the Great War banded together in returned servicemen organisations, in an attempt not to relive the war but to finally end it.

Almost from the moment of winning the King's Cup, the oarsmen had wanted the Cup to be the trophy for the Men's Interstate Eight-oared Championship. But the Cup became part of the detritus of war and was quickly absorbed into the artefacts of the Australian War Museum (AWM).

There were moves from state rowing bodies – in particular the Victorian Rowing Association – to acquire the Cup as a trophy. Initial entreaties to the AWM for release were considered, but met with a flat refusal. Many people, from Prime Minister Billy Hughes to Governor-General Lord Henry Forster, were involved in the buck-passing; requests from oarsmen and state rowing associations were continually deflected. On 1 November 1920, the Victorian Rowing Association (VRA) noted in their minutes that the War Museum Committee, 'could not agree to the request to allow the King's Cup to be used as a perpetual trophy for the Interstate Race'.[7] Eventually Ted Kenny, the secretary of the VRA, took decisive action and decided that a petition to King George V himself was to be drawn up, and signed by Clive Disher, asking him to declare his intention for the King's Cup. The petition pointed out that 4097 oarsmen had served in the AIF and that the petitioner 'humbly prays that Your Majesty may be graciously pleased to make your wishes in regard to the disposal of the said trophy'. Meanwhile, counter petitions had been sent to King George V throughout 1920, outlining an argument for retaining the King's Cup for the Australian War Museum.

Eventually, on 13 May 1921, Winston Churchill, the original architect of the ill-fated Dardanelles campaign that had initiated Australian oarsmen into the Great War, wrote:

> His Majesty commends me to inform you that it is his wish
> that the Cup should be a permanent trophy and is competed for
> annually in the Interstate Eight-oar race of Australia.

Ted Kenny and Clive Disher finally secured the King's Cup on 29 July 1921. It was almost a year later, on 6 May 1922, that the Cup was finally presented to South Australia on the Parramatta River, Sydney, as winners of the King's Cup Men's Interstate Eight-oared Championship.

Over a hundred years, the King's Cup has evolved and developed to also include the Queen's Cup (ULVA/Queen Elizabeth II Trophy) for Women's Interstate Eight-oared Championships; the Noel F. Wilkinson Trophy for Men's Youth Eight; the Bicentennial Cup for Women's Youth Eight; the President's Cup for Men's sculling; the Nell Slatter Trophy for Women's sculling; the Penrith Cup for Men's lightweight fours; and the Victoria Cup for Women's lightweight quad scull. From a rowing victory won by battle-weary diggers of the Great War, the King's Cup has since come to celebrate inclusivity and diversity of women's and men's events at the highest standard of oarsmanship.

EPILOGUE

So burn my body there with all the arms I possess, and raise
a mound for me on the shore of the grey sea, in memory of an
unlucky man so that men yet unborn may learn my story. Do this
for me, and on my barrow plant an oar I used to pull when I was
alive and with my comrades.

Homer, *The Odyssey*

After the HMT *Euripides*, like a shuttle boat service, had disembarked
crew members and the oarsmen were demobilised, they returned to
their homes changed men, settling into a changed world. There were
few official or government support services, apart from repatriation
hospitals and war pensions. Generally, the repatriation approach was
for the men to get on with their lives: learn to hold down a steady job,
marry, raise a family. No one understood that traumatic stress–related
disorders would, over the ensuing ten or so years, stymie the efforts of
many returned servicemen and -women to get on with their civilian lives.

Harry Hauenstein's brother Paddy returned to his wife Grace and
three young children and together they welcomed a new baby son. He
was drinking more often, and struggled to find steady work to support
his young family. After four years of trying to make ends meet, and
with a business partner taking him to court for spending business money
before a construction job had even been completed, Paddy decided to rob
a bank in Hurlstone Park, Sydney. He jumped the counter and assaulted
the bank manager, Alexander Steele, trying to knock him senseless so as
to enter the strong room and make off with the cash. The bank manager
resisted and his desperate yells of 'Help!' brought his wife rushing,

screaming, onto the scene. Perhaps suddenly realising what he was doing, Paddy jumped back over the counter and made off empty-handed.

When Grace saw a dishevelled Paddy back at their Holden Street home, she asked what had happened. Telling her he'd fallen off a tram, he took a small envelope from his bedroom drawer and headed off to the park with his children. When the police arrived in the park, Paddy took off but was apprehended soon after. He made no trouble and went to the Canterbury police station quietly. He knew one of the arresting constables, Constable Wiblin, from his time on the police force. Wiblin asked him, 'What has come over you to come at this?'

Paddy replied, 'Well old boy, I am hard up against it ... and I owe money everywhere. I staked my lot on the throw of the dice and failed. So here I am. It will be all over soon.'

Paddy asked for a glass of water and, without anyone suspecting his plans, swallowed a white substance from the envelope. He told Constable Wiblin, 'It is all over, constable, say goodbye to the wife and children for me. I have taken a dose of strychnine ... Let me go. Do not try to save me.'[1]

Within ten minutes, foaming at the mouth, he died from strychnine poisoning on the Canterbury police station cell floor, leaving his wife Grace, a thirteen-year-old daughter and three other children, the youngest fourteen months. Grace told a journalist that Paddy had been 'depressed since his return from the front'.[2]

The major Australian newspapers, who had exhorted Australian sportsmen and oarsmen to 'swap oars for bayonets' and go to war, were now complaining that not enough was being done to support those they had themselves flippantly cajoled to fight.

Many of these returned servicemen and -women were damaged and struggling to find a place in an altered world that promised them very little. Paddy's sad fate is a classic example of the tragic stories of the survivors of war whose names are not inscribed on marbled or bronzed memorial walls.

Harry Hauenstein rejoined his wife, Eva, and together they settled into a nondescript life in Macdonaldtown, Sydney. A practical man, Harry used the illuminated commemorative oars from his

Interstate Championships, the 1912 HRR Grand Challenge Cup and the 1919 Royal Henley Peace Regatta as picture rails in his home in 11 Leamington Street.

Harry eventually put his practical Pioneer skills to work as a lift mechanic and worked for several years as a contractor. On the hustle for further contracting work, Harry wrote to Base Records, Melbourne on 1 October 1940 looking for a copy of his 'service discharge for certain employment', hoping to receive a duplicate copy to present to future employers.

Whatever happened then happened fast, possibly because Harry had ignored a lingering pain in his stomach or because a niggling pre-existing condition suddenly worsened. One month later, on 5 December 1940, Harry Hauenstein was admitted to Prince Henry Hospital, Little Bay, New South Wales and died from stomach cancer the next day.

Fred House returned to the Derwent Rowing Club after the war to stroke the club to two more state championship eights. He was selected as stroke of the Tasmanian eight, and his old AIF No. 1 crewmate Archie Robb was again backing him up in the number 7 seat in the crew that competed on the Brisbane River on 15 May 1920 for the first King's Cup (with the Cup itself still withheld and unavailable).

The Tasmanians struggled, rowing into third place behind the plucky working-class winners, the 'Cods' from Murray Bridge, South Australia; the Cods crew featured their old AIF crewmate 'Ack Vie' Scott. In 1921 the Interstate King's Cup race was rowed on the Tamar River, Tasmania and Freddy House was again selected as stroke – but business reasons prevented him from competing that year, with C. Deans stroking the Tasmanians into second place behind a historic, first-time King's Cup win for the Western Australians.

Fred House and Archie Robb remained good friends and always took a keen interest in rowing. One amusing Robb family tale tells of Fred and Archie, having spent a few long hours partaking of liquid refreshment, re-enacting the Peace Regatta final, both on their backsides, shuffling blindly around the loungeroom to gales of laughter from friends and family as they bumped into furniture, knocked over light stands and rolled about laughing.

259

Fred House married Ruby Miller on 22 May 1920, and ran a hire car business. He and Ruby had two sons, Roderic and Graeme. Both sons served in World War II. Fred and his sons all had a keen interest in fly fishing and hunting and spent many weekends in the high country of Tasmania at Great Lake.

When Archie Robb returned to Tasmania, he was discharged medically unfit with concussion deafness but found work at the Cascade Breweries as a maintenance fitter and turner; he stayed there for more than thirty years. He represented Tasmania twice after the war, in the King's Cup in 1920 and 1921. On 16 March 1927 Archie married Zoe Schott and they had two children, Helen and John. In 1962, Archie travelled to England to attend his daughter's birthday, but died suddenly during the visit.

Fred House wrote to Disher and broke the bad news to him:

From the brief news to hand it would appear that there was a birthday celebration (his daughter's) and, late in the evening Archie did not feel very well [and] was taken to a spare room to rest but he was gone twenty minutes later. A frightful shock to the family, but a marvellous way to finish.[3]

Towards the end of his life, Fred was concerned about his precious illuminated Royal Henley Peace Regatta oar and medallion and what to do with them. His wife Ruby wrote to Clive Disher that

He sent the oar to the War Memorial and is quite content to know it has a permanent home – as he said – the boys have modern homes and maybe the wives could have other [ideas] for decoration and he wanted to be sure it had a home in the years ahead.[4]

Fred House died on 21 September 1973 at the Repatriation General Hospital, Hobart.

Arthur Scott disembarked from the *Euripides* in Adelaide on Tuesday 21 October 1919, took a seat in a boat on Wednesday and incredibly won the Stewards' Challenge Cup (Senior Fours) at the Henley on Yarra, Melbourne on the Saturday 25 October 1919. Scotty returned to Murray Bridge and resumed work with the South Australian state railways, eventually becoming a locomotive engine driver. On 15 May 1920, he represented South Australia in the first King's Cup Interstate Championships on the Brisbane River, Queensland and his crew won convincingly, by four lengths.

Scotty continued rowing at an elite level, representing South Australia seven times. He also represented Australia, aged thirty-seven, in the Paris Olympic Games in 1924, as part of the 'Murray Cods' crew. But the Murray Cods struggled with finances, transport and dysentery in Paris and finished second behind Italy in their heat. They were then eliminated in the repechage, behind Canada and Argentina. There was conjecture that their long rowing style was better suited for longer races, rather than a 2000-metre short course. Scotty rowed well into his fifties and 'still rows a powerful oar, and his back is still as straight'.[5] Scotty never quite reconciled with his ex-wife Ada and son Walter and had little contact with them. Arthur Valentine 'Scotty' Scott died on 26 July 1966.

Albert 'Gig' Smedley also returned aboard the HMT *Euripides*, arriving in Sydney on 24 October 1919. Gig was a talented artist and had worked as a signwriter before the war. In 1921, he married Myra Lewis and together they had two children, Beryl and Leslie Albert.

Gig found a position with the State Electricity Board and moonlighted as a taxi driver. The war had undoubtedly shaped Gig's view of people, places and time. Whenever Myra asked him to drive her somewhere and said she might be some time running errands, Gig would reply that he had all the time in the world. Gig Smedley experienced some serious ill-health in his later years and was admitted to the Concord Repatriation Hospital. He died on 25 November 1965.

George Mettam returned from England, along with his brothers Harry and Frank, who had also survived the war, to their family in Perth. He continued to row and represented Western Australia in the King's Cup eight-oared event on five occasions. On 4 November 1924, George married Jessie Burns and together they had a son, David, and a daughter, Dee. Having trained as an accountant with the Agricultural Bank (WA) before the war, George eventually found work with Cresco Fertilizer & Co. George's skills and attributes were rewarded in due course when he took the position of General Manager of Cresco Fertilizer.

Rowing always had its claws in George, and he was actively involved in the Swan River Rowing Club and West Australian Rowing Club, both as a master oarsman and a coach to a whole new generation of oarsmen and -women.

Sadly, on 5 April 1967, George Mettam died of a heart attack after swimming out to rescue the occupants of an upturned boat during a regatta on the Swan River at Mount Pleasant, Perth.

Thomas McGill returned to Lewisham, Sydney and returned to work with the family haulage business, driving trucks delivering gravel and sand gravel. He represented New South Wales in the King's Cup from 1920 to 1922 but he was up against the talented South Australian and West Australian state crews and never made the podium. On 3 July 1926, Tom married Dorothy Lillian Rapp and they had two sons, Bruce and Barry. For many years Tom was involved in the Leichhardt Rowing Club and Old Oarsmen associations, frequently attended the rowing reunions and made a regular trip on the tram to Sydney Rowing Club for a quiet Sunday afternoon drink. Tom knew the significance of his win at the 1919 Royal Henley Peace Regatta and always said that there would 'only be one King's Cup'. Tom McGill died on 23 August 1979, the last oarsman of the AIF crew who won the King's Cup to pass on.

Captain Clive Disher remained in London studying advanced medical techniques at the London Hospital and the Children's Hospital in Great Ormond Street until he returned to Australia in 1920. He practised medicine as an anaesthetist for many years. In 1926, Harold Clive Disher married nurse Doris Parks and settled down to a busy medical practice of specialist anaesthetics at the Royal Melbourne Hospital. Throughout his life, Dr Disher always took a keen interest in Victorian rowing events, especially those related to Scotch College and Melbourne University Boat Clubs.

In 1935, Disher wrote to George Mettam:

I don't see or hear very much of the other members of the crew.
Sid [sic] Middleton and I used to write at intervals and then
mainly through neglect I think it died out. However, I saw him
when he was out about a year ago. He looked very well then, but
I believe was very ill on the way back to England. He married and
has a boy aged about ten or so now. I have never heard a word
about Harry Hauenstein since his brother committed suicide some
years ago. A.V. Scott seems to have disappeared from S.A. Tom
McGill I think married. Fred House runs a garage in Hobart,
and I hear of him also Archie Robb occasionally. Smedley drives
a taxi I believe in Sydney. Eric Harrison is in Parliament, Jack
Coghill I saw at Henley here 2 or 3 years ago. Newell, I haven't
seen for some years, but I believe is about Melbourne somewhere.
Ossie Wood seems to have retired. Harry Ross Soden I
see occasionally. We met last at the University Boat Race Dinner.[6]

In the same letter he wrote:

I have often felt that I didn't know you nearly as well as I wanted
to and that is meant to be a compliment in more ways than
one. You see I had a devil of a time at Henley trying to keep the
machine going and oiling friction parts. Many were the hours I
spent trying to do it and all the time wondering when I was going
to get the boot. Much as I admired Syd Middleton... he took an
awful lot of handling and Harry Hauenstein, well he added years
on to my life. I don't suppose I knew all the under-currents, but
I knew more than I wanted to have to try and handle. And this
all leads to me saying that I knew from the time you started at
'7' behind me that there was one man at least I needn't worry
about, someone who couldn't be disloyal however much he might
vary in his ideas. So, after many years George I am going to say,
'thank you' and sort of apologise for taking it all so much as it
were as a matter of course at the time. You have no idea what

weight you took off my shoulders and how much easier things
were after you got there. It was a good day for us when Nip
Newall suggested you at 7.

When World War II broke out, Disher, aged forty-eight, once again
enlisted for active service and was appointed assistant director medical
services (ADMS), 6th Division in North Africa, Palestine and Crete.
For his military service in places such as Bardia and Tobruk, Disher
was awarded a CBE in 1941.

Disher was tiring of war, and Doris had fallen ill back in Melbourne.
He retired from the army as an honorary brigadier in 1945. He wrote
to Mettam in 1945:

I have given up medical practice and am now a grazier on the old
family property which my grandfather took up in 1869. I like the
life immensely and have looked forward to it for years. I just felt
I couldn't face the worry of doctoring again.[7]

Sadly, Doris died in 1946 and Disher, childless, spent his remaining
years on the family property 'Strathfieldsaye' as a full-time pastoralist.
He wrote again to Mettam in 1961:

I hope all is well with you these days. It is quite a while since I
saw you or even heard of you. Personally, I keep reasonably well
but feel quite a lot older and don't go about over much ... Usually
when I am in town, I drift down to the river but rarely see anyone
I know so I just wander along and dream my dreams of days gone
by. I wonder if I am getting old in thoughts because I don't think
the crews are as good as they used to be. A lot of hard work goes
on, but much seems to be wasted and there is not much 'lift'
in the boats ... Perhaps we are forgetting to use our legs. We
certainly walked lots in the old days ...[8]

Captain Harold 'Clive' Disher died on 13 March 1976, the second-
last of the original AIF oarsmen who fought for and won the coveted

King's Cup. He left behind a considerable sum of money, which he bequeathed to higher education in his beloved Victoria.

Sydney Middleton stayed in England, following his heart. The love between Marion and Syd had remained strong. When Middleton was working in Germany for W. S. Robinson, gaining valuable business interests in the automobile trade, he wrote to her about those first days:

> When you say you love me most sweet heart I'm afraid I
> can't even attempt to prove you wrong but on your own past
> admission I can say I've loved you longest. I shall never forget
> Le Tréport ... at that time I thought I had banished all ideas
> of ever getting married completely from my dull brain, but my
> resolutions began to waver and be in danger right away and I
> watched every movement I was lucky enough to see you make
> sweetheart.[9]

In late 1919, Middleton received an OBE for his work on the AIF Sports Control Board. He reported to Marion:

> That most certainly means another trip to Buckingham Palace
> when I'm over there as I'd rather anything than be forced to get it
> in Australia where the whole sporting fraternity would laugh and
> rag me knowing my view of the OBE as they do.[10]

For a figure such as Middleton, who dominated and intimidated many around him in both war and peace, it was incredible that the diminutive Marion Streatfeild could tame his towering personality. Middleton suffered from numerous episodes of depression and he often found strength in Marion, who was his rock.

Middleton married Marion Streatfeild on 6 September 1921 at the Roman Catholic St Mary's Church in Cadogan Street, London. The product of a fervent Presbyterian upbringing in Pyrmont, by the end of the Great War Middleton had spurned all concept of religion; he now believed that a person's right to choose *was* his religion: 'though you think I have no religion I certainly have my own, and I am very very strong on it but never want it to force it on others (that's part of my religion).'[11]

Eventually Middleton, having worked in Coblenz and Hamburg, Bucharest, Rumania, and the oilfields of Baku, Azerbaijan, developed business and mining interests with W.S. around the world. Together he and Marion had one son, John Peter, who later served as a second lieutenant in World War II from 1944 with the 12th Royal Lancers in the Italian campaign. Middleton became involved in all sorts of sports organisations and often looked after the interests of visiting Australian rugby teams and crews in England. He often wrote articles about rugby for the newspapers. Eventually, in 1935, Middleton was accepted as a member of the exclusive Leander Club, Henley-on-Thames. Syd Middleton and Marion were happily married and lived in Iverna-Gardens, South Kensington.

Years later, Marion wrote to W. S. Robinson:

One lives with someone, listens to stories, mostly amusing of things which happened… and then it's too late and a wonderful war story from the inside, from a magnificent line soldier is lost. I saw him win at Henley later on the King's Cup and in Sept 1921 we were married … Everyone thought I was doing a very rash thing, as in those days people thought that all Australians over here … had left wives behind. So I took no notice of my relations backed my own judgement, the result 24 years of complete happiness + a memory of someone whose qualities and loyalty courage and integrity were higher than the average person one knows … although he wasn't good at sharing his feelings …[12]

And Clive Disher, reflecting upon Middleton's input and impact on the campaign to win the King's Cup at Henley, wrote to John Lang:

What I would like you … to publish in some rowing notes is the appreciation we all have had for Middleton's efforts for this crew. You can justly say it was his crew he made it in the boat and out of it and was our stronghold in all times of trouble … well I can

only say that Middleton is the only man yet that I have come in
contact with who dare hold a candle to Charlie in that line. It
required a very strong man to make this crew from the chaotic
state we were in ... but it needed a Middleton to get us out of it
once we were in it.[13]

After Middleton died suddenly on 2 September 1945, his funeral
was held at St Margaret's Lothbury. The Cambridge University service
crew coach and High Commissioner for Australia, Stanley Melbourne
Bruce, and the Oxford University service crew coach, Colonel Harcourt
'Tarka' Gold, were among the many high-profile mourners. It seemed
plenty of water had passed under the bridge between old rowing foes in
the years since the Royal Henley Peace Regatta.

Many years later, Steve Fairbairn was asked which crew he thought
was the best he had coached. With his photographic memory, out of
all the countless Cambridge, Thames, London and Jesus College crews
he had coached, Steve took great pride in the fact that he had had the
privilege of coaching the AIF rowing squad for 'over a month before they
won the King's Cup at Henley the year after the War'.[14] He answered:

The Australian Soldiers' Eight at Henley. They were just back
from the war and full of nerves, but they were the easiest lot
to coach. You could tell them what to do, and then hang your
megaphone up in the shed.[15]

Perhaps Steve's recollections of his time at Putney were happily
selective and had somewhat softened. He certainly did not hold any
grudges or bitterness toward either Harry Hauenstein or the obsession
of the Australians with their one true 'Australian rowing style', which
they held above all others, including 'Fairbairnism'.

In the years after the Great War, Steve wrote several books about
'Fairbairnism', which tried to articulate the elusive genie of rowing.
These books influenced oarsmen and rowing coaches all around
the world for generations. He also wrote an autobiography entitled
Fairbairn of Jesus. When Steve died in 1937, he requested that his ashes

be scattered underneath the stained-glass window of his beloved Jesus College Chapel, Cambridge.

The Oarsman's Song

The willowy sway of the hands away
And the water boiling aft,
The elastic spring and the steely fling
That drives the flying craft.
The steely spring and the musical ring
Of the blade with the biting grip,
And the stretching draw of the bending oar
That rounds the turn with a whip.
And the lazy float that runs the boat,
And makes the swing quite true,
And gives that rest that the oarsman blest
As he drives the blade right through.
All through the swing he hears the boat sing
As she glides on her flying track,
And he gathers aft to strike the craft
With a ringing bell-note crack.
From stretcher to oar with drive and draw,
He speeds the boat along.
All whalebone and steel and a willowy feel
That is the oarsman's song.

Steve Fairbairn

Notes

Prologue – Rowing into war

1 AWM PRO4722 (Folder 4 of 4PR), Whyte, Thomas Anderson, 22 January, 1915, Letter No. 10, p. 5

2 AWM PRO4722 (Folder 4 of 4PR), Whyte, Thomas Anderson (Private), Personal correspondence, p. 164

3 AWM PRO4722 (Folder 4 of 4PR), Whyte, Thomas Anderson (Private), Personal correspondence, 24 April 1915

4 AWM PRO4722 (Folder 4 of 4PR), Whyte, Thomas Anderson (Private), Personal correspondence, p. 95

5 AWM PRO4722 (Folder 4 of 4PR), Whyte, Thomas Anderson (Private), Personal correspondence, p. 80

6 AWM PRO4722 (Folder 4 of 4PR), Whyte, Thomas Anderson (Private), Personal correspondence, pp. 89

7 Register, Adelaide, Letter from Arthur Blackburn to Miss Eileen Champion, Friday 6 August 1915, p. 9

8 AWM PRO4722 (Folder 4 of 4PR), Whyte, Thomas Anderson (Private), Personal correspondence, p. 167

9 AWM PRO4722 (Folder 4 of 4PR), Whyte, Thomas Anderson (Private), Personal correspondence, p. 169

10 AWM: Item # RCDIG0000862, Diary entry, John Adams, C Company, 2nd Battalion (later MC and Bar), p. 49

11 AWM4 Item # 23/27/2, 10th infantry Battalion Diary, March–April 1915

12 AWM: Item # RCDIG0000862, Diary entry, John Adams, C Company, 2nd Battalion (later MC and Bar), p. 49

13 Register, Adelaide, Letter from Arthur Blackburn to Miss Eileen Champion, Friday, 6 August 1915, p. 9

14 AWM PRO4722 (Folder 4 of 4PR), Whyte, Thomas Anderson (Private), Personal correspondence

15 Letter from A. Blackburn to Miss E. Champion, Register (Adelaide, SA), Friday 6 August 1915, p. 9

16 NAA: B2455, Item Number 8388250, Service & Casualty Record, Whyte, Thomas Anderson, p. 10

17 'Soldiers' Letters: A Real Hero', Register, 6 August 1915, p. 9, Meleah Hampton, AWM

18 NAA: B2455, Whyte, Thomas Anderson, Series number: B2455, Barcode: 838825

1 The game is worth the candle

1 *West Australian*, 5 May 1915, p. 6
2 *Argus*, 3 May 1915, p. 6
3 *Adelaide Advertiser*, 1 May 1915
4 *Argus*, 3 May 1915, p. 6
5 *International Journal of the History of Sport*, vol. 14, no. 1 (April 1997), pp. 78–96
6 *Referee*, 21 April 1915, p. 16
7 *Referee*, 18 August 1915, p. 16
8 Ibid.
9 *Sun* (Sydney), 27 February 1927, p. 24
10 *Sun* (Sydney), 27 February 1927, p. 24
11 *Sydney Morning Herald*, 1 May 1935, p. 17
12 *Sun* (Sydney), 27 February 1927, p. 24
13 Greg Middleton, notes and recollections from grandfather
14 Match report, *Sydney Sportsman*, 15 June 1910
15 NAA: B2455, Item Number 5476366, Service & Casualty Record, Heritage, Keith, pp. 6–8
16 *Sun* (Sydney), 3 June 1917, p. 9
17 AWM4 Subclass 23/36 – 19th Battalion, March–September 1915, AIF Unit War Diary, p. 5
18 Middleton letter home, published in *Referee*, 29 September 1915, p. 13
19 *Referee*, 13 October 1915, p. 16
20 Middleton letter home, published in *Referee*, 29 September 1915, p. 13
21 *Gallipoli* (1981), director Peter Weir, screenplay Don Williamson (Village Roadshow, 1981)
22 *Statistics of the Military effort of the British Empire during the Great War*, 1914–1920, HMSO, London, 1922
23 Middleton, letter to W. W. Hill, published in *Referee*, 3 November 1915, p. 16
24 George Franki, 'Major Sydney Middleton', *Digger*, no. 46 (2014), p. 63
25 NAA: B2455, Item Number 8012773, Service & Casualty Record, Middleton, Sydney Albert, p. 11
26 Middleton, letter published in *Referee*, 15 December 1915, p. 16
27 T. A. White, *The Fighting Thirteenth,* Tyrrells Ltd. for the 13th Battalion, AIF Committee, Sydney, 1924
28 Middleton, letter published in *Referee*, 15 December 1915, p. 16
29 AWM 25/367/152, Report of Colonel J. Paton, V.D., Anzac Evacuation, 30 December 1915, RCDIG1075159
30 Personal correspondence to W. S. Robinson, 1961, Melbourne University Archives, Victoria
31 Keith Heritage, letter to his parents, *Ascanius* at sea, 6 January 1916 AWM 1DRL/0347

32 Personal correspondence to W. S. Robinson, 2 July 1958, Melbourne University Archives, Victoria

2   Hauenstein

1   NAA1000228546 Item # A471/3460/HAUENSTEIN Henry (Acting Corporal): Service Number – 3795: Unit – 12th Reinforcements, 2nd Battalion, Australian Imperial Force: Date of Court Martial – 22 January 1916
2   *Wagga Wagga Advertiser*, 3 September 1904, p. 5
3   *Sydney Morning Herald*, 25 September 1929, p. 19
4   *New South Wales Police Gazette*, 20 April 1904, p. 139
5   *New South Wales Police Gazette*, 4 October 1905, p. 359
6   *Referee*, article by 'Stroke-side', 28 June 1916, p. 15
7   AWM28 1/8/PART 2 1st Division, 16–22 August 1916, Part 2, collection R1599242
8   *Referee*, 28 June 1916, p. 15

3   The dying days

1   NAA: Middleton, Sydney Albert. Service and Casualty Record. Series # B2455 Barcode 8012773
2   Syd Middleton, letter to Marion Streatfeild, 18 January 1920 (Middleton Family Archives)
3   NAA: Middleton, Sydney Albert. Service and Casualty Record. Series # B2455 Barcode 8012773
4   NAA: B2455, Item Number 8012773, Service & Casualty Form, Middleton, Sydney Albert, Recommendation for DSO, 7 September 1918, p. 32
5   *Referee*, 30 October 1918, p. 1
6   TEXT TO COME
7   AWM Personal Files Book 21, 3 Oct – 24 Nov, Monash, Sir John KCMG, KCB p. 1, RCDIG0000572
8   AWM4 AIF War Diary, November 1918, 5th Infantry Brigade, Item # 23/5/41, 13 November
9   Address on 26 November 1918, Monash Personal Files, Book 21, 25 Nov – 31 Dec 1918, RCDIG0000639
10 Scribbled note, 6 December 1918, Monash Personal Files, Book 21, 25 Nov – 31 Dec 1918, RCDIG0000639
11 AWM4 Repatriation & Demobilisation Item No. 30/1/1 Part 2, Feb–Oct 1918, RCDIG1002984 (see picture section)
12 Scribbled note, 4 December 1918, Monash Personal Files, Book 21, 25 Nov – 31 Dec 1918, RCDIG0000639
13 AWM4 Repatriation & Demobilisation Item No. 30/1/1, Part 2, Feb–Oct 1918, RCDIG1002984

14   AWM4 Repatriation & Demobilisation Item No. 30/1/5, Part 4,
     Dec 1918 – Feb 1919, RCDIG1003354
15   Address on 26 November 1918, Monash Personal Files, Book 21,
     25 Nov – 31 Dec 1918, RCDIG0000639

4   Occupy the men
1   Robert Gerwarth, *The Vanquished*, Penguin, 2017, p. 57
2   Mario Isenghi and Giorgio Rochat, *La Grande Guerra 1914–1918*,
     Nuova Italia, Milan, 2000, pp. 463–64
3   Adrian Hyde-Price, *Germany and European Order: Enlarging NATO and
     the EU*, Manchester University Press, Manchester, 2000, p. 75
4   AWM4 Item 1/44/28 Part 1 General Staff, HQ, 2nd Australian Division,
     RCID1011386
5   Gerwath, *The Vanquished*, p. 63
6   AWM4 Formation Headquarters, Item No. 1/37/9, December 1918,
     RCDIG1009758
7   George Goddard, correspondence to his mother, 25 November 1918,
     pp. 2–3, Accession No. 2885, Item No. 2885/73 (State Library of
     Queensland)
8   AWM4 Formation Headquarters, Item No. 1/37/10, January 1919,
     RCDIG1009251
9   Lieutenant G. H. Goddard, *Soldiers and Sportsmen*, AIF Sports Control
     Board, London, 1919, p. 8

5   Battlefield to playing field
1   Greg Crowden, *Gold, Mud 'N' Guts: The Incredible Tom Richards Story*,
     ABC Books, 2001, p. 175
2   Address on 26 November 1918, Monash Personal Files Book 21,
     25 Nov – 31 Dec 1918, RCDIG0000639
3   Handwritten notes, Monash Personal Files Book 21, 25 Nov – 31 Dec 1918
     RCDIG0000639
4   Letter to W. S. Robinson, 2 July 1958, Melbourne University Archives,
     Melbourne
5   Goddard, *Soldiers and Sportsmen*, p. 8
6   Goddard, *Soldiers and Sportsmen*, p. 9

7   The Sports Section
1   Lieutenant G. H. Goddard, *Soldiers and Sportsmen*, AIF Sports Control
     Board, London, 1919, p. 13
2   Syd Middleton, letter to Marion Streatfeild, 27 December 1919 (Middleton
     Family Archives)
3   Ibid.

4   Lieutenant G. H. Goddard, *Soldiers and Sportsmen*, AIF Sports Control
    Board, London, 1919, p. 13
5   AWM Sports Control Board, 30 January 1919

8   The oarsmen of Pozières
1   NAA: B2455, Item Number 3002726, Scott, Arthur Valentine, Sern. 3598
2   AWM4 Item # 13/31/21 Headquarters 3rd Field Artillery Brigade, July 1916,
    RCDIG1014017
3   NAA: B2455, Smedley, Albert Ernest, Barcode: 8086628 (2nd Divisional
    routine orders)
4   AWM4 5th Infantry Brigade War Diary, June 1916, Item # 23/5/12,
    RCDIG1008455
5   AWM28 2/72 5th Brigade, 2nd Division, AIF, 18 July 1915
6   NAA: B2455, Captain Keith Heritage, Barcode: 5476366
7   *Examiner*, 7 October 1916, p. 8
8   AWM4 Engineers AIF Unit War Diary, Item # 14/13/6, 1st Australian
    Pioneer Battalion, August 1916, p. 9

9   Disher
1   AWM4 Medical, Dental & Nursing, AIF Unit War Diary, Item # 26/48/22,
    5th Field Ambulance
2   AWM 2018.8.337 RMO reports, March 1918, 4th Australian Field Artillery
    Brigade, January to November 1918
3   AWM 2018.8.337 RMO reports, 31 May 1918, 4th Australian Field
    Artillery Brigade, January to November 1918
4   Disher, letter to family, 8 January 1919, Melbourne University Archives,
    Melbourne
5   AWM4 AIF War Unit Diary, Artillery, Item # 13/32/35 HQ, 4th FAB,
    February 1919
6   NAA: B2455, Ross-Soden, Harry, Barcode # 8037956
7   Harry Ross-Soden, letter to Alf Ross-Soden, 20 February 1919
8   Harry Ross-Soden, letter to Alf Ross-Soden, 11 February 1919
9   *The Inter-Allied Games 1919*, compiled by Major George Wythe, edited by
    Captain Joseph M. Hanson, published by the Games Committee, p. 17
10 Ibid., p. 19
11 *The Inter-Allied Games 1919*, p. 56

10 Getting back into the boat
1   Kenneth Grahame, *The Wind in the Willows*, 1908 (reprinted Penguin
    Books, London, 1994), p. 8
2   Sir Theodore Cook, *Henley Races: A Complete Index of Competitors and
    Crews since 1839*, Oxford University Press, London, 1919, p. 1

3   C. T. Steward, *Henley Records 1919 to 1938*, Hamish Hamilton, London, 1939, p. 20
4   Steward, *Henley Records 1919 to 1938*, p. 20
5   *The Times*, 11 February 1919
6   Everard Wyrall, *The King's Regiment (Liverpool) 1914–1919*, vol. 3, E. Arnold, London, 1935
7   Sir Theodore Cook, *Henley Races: A Complete Index of Competitors and Crews since 1839*, Oxford University Press, London, 1919, p. xxiv
8   *The Times*, 2 July 1919
9   Original orders ex Sports Section, AIF Administrative HQ, 130 Horseferry Road, Mettam Family archives.
10 Harry Ross-Soden, letter to Alf Ross-Soden, 11 February 1919
11 Harry Ross-Soden, letter to Alf Ross-Soden, 20 February 1919
12 NAA: B2455, Ross-Soden, Harry, Barcode # 8037956
13 *Referee*, 26 March 1919, p. 1
14 Lieutenant G. H. Goddard, *Soldiers and Sportsmen*, AIF Sports Control Board, Horseferry Road, 1919, p. 12
15 Clive Disher, letter to family, 2 March 1919, Melbourne University Archives, Melbourne

11 Putney
1   Desmond Morton, '"Kicking and Complaining": Demobilization Riots in the Canadian Expeditionary Force, 1918–19', *Canadian Historical Review*, 1980, p. 338
2   *Indiana Gazette*, 25 January 1919, p.6
3   *Indiana Gazette*, 25 January 1919, p. 6
4   *The Times*, 24 February 1917
5   Major Alan Audsley letter to family, 30 March 1919, State Library of NSW Archives, c046150287h
6   The Australasian, newspaper, 'Rowing Notes,' Melbourne, Victoria, Saturday 17 May 1919, p. 12
7   Middleton, letter from Coblenz, Germany to Marion, 27 December 1919
8   AWM Sports Control Board Minutes, progress report, 14 March 1919
9   *The Times*, 27 February 1919, p. 5
10 AWM Sports Control Board Minutes, Progress report, 22 March 1919

12 Gathering the oarsmen
1   Lieutenant G. H. Goddard, *Soldiers and Sportsmen*, AIF Sports Control Board, Horseferry Road, 1919, p. 84
2   *New South Wales Police Gazette*, 17 June 1908
3   AWM AIF Sports Control Board minutes

13 Making the cut

1   Gideon Penny, handwritten recollections of rowing kindly provided by the Penny and Wurm families
2   Major Alan Audsley, letter to family, 23 March 1919, State Library of NSW Archives, c046150286h
3   Major Alan Audsley, letter to family, 30 March 1919, State Library of NSW Archives, c046150290h
4   Major Alan Audsley, letter to family, 30 March 1919, State Library of NSW Archives, c046150287h

14 The Australian style

1   Clive Disher correspondence to family, 19 March 1919, Melbourne University Archives, Melbourne
2   Clive Disher, letter to family, 29 March 1919, Melbourne University Archives, Melbourne
3   Clive Disher, letter to family, 29 March 1919, Melbourne University Archives, Melbourne
4   *Mercury*, 11 May 1935, p. 8
5   Clive Disher, letter to John Lang, 5 May 1919, Melbourne University Archives, Melbourne
6   AWM Sports Control Board minutes
7   Clive Disher, letter to John Lang, 19 April 1919, Melbourne University Archives, Melbourne
8   Clive Disher, letter to family, 5 April 1919, Melbourne University Archives, Melbourne
9   Clive Disher, letter to family, 13 April 1919, Melbourne University Archives, Melbourne
10 Clive Disher, letter to John Lang, 19 April 1919, Melbourne University Archives, Melbourne
11 Clive Disher, letter to John Lang, 19 April 1919, Melbourne University Archives, Melbourne
12 C. T. Steward, *Henley Records, 1919–1938*, Hamish Hamilton, London, 1939, p. 22
13 AWM, letter from Major Middleton to Lt-Colonel R. J. A. Massie, AIF Sports Control Board minutes, 1 March 1919

15 The boat

1   Christopher Dodd, *Bonnie Brave Boat Rowers: The Heroes, Seers and Songsters of the Tyne*, AuthorHouse, 2014, p. 54
2   AWM Major Middleton to Lt-Colonel R. J. A. Massie, AIF Sports Control Board minutes, 28 March 1919
3   Major Alan Audsley, letter to family, 14 May 1919, State Library of NSW Archives, c046150300h

16 Fairbairn

1 Major Alan Audsley letter to family, 21 April 1919, State Library of NSW Archives, c046150298h
2 F. Brittain and H. B. Playford, *The Jesus College Boat Club*, W. Heffer & Sons, 1928, p. 80
3 Brittain and Playford, *The Jesus College Boat Club*, p. 79
4 Steve Fairbairn, *Rowing Notes*, edited by Arthur Eggar, Mills & Boon, London, p. xiv
5 Brittain and Playford, *The Jesus College Boat Club*, p. 80
6 Fairbairn, *Rowing Notes*, p. xiv
7 Brittain and Playford, *The Jesus College Boat Club*, p. 83
8 Interview with rowing historian Chris Dodd, River & Rowing Museum, Henley-on-Thames, June 2018
9 Fairbairn, *Rowing Notes*. p. xi
10 Brittain and Playford, *The Jesus College Boat Club*, p. 87

17 Trouble in the boat

1 *The Times*, 21 May 1919, p. 5
2 Major Alan Audsley, letter to family, 4 May 1919, State Library of NSW Archives, c046150298h
3 Clive Disher, letter to John Lang, 19 April 1919, Melbourne University Archives, Melbourne
4 Major Alan Audsley, letter to family, 15 April 1919, State Library of NSW Archives, c046150286h
5 *Democrat and Chronicle*, 6 June 1919 , p. 34
6 *Ithaca Journal*, 29 April 1919, p. 2
7 Ibid.
8 *Wellington Sports*, 15 August 1935
9 *Boston Globe*, 28 April 1919, p. 10
10 Clive Disher, letter to John Lang, 15 April 1919
11 Clive Disher, letter to John Lang, 25 April 1919, Melbourne University Archives, Melbourne
12 Clive Disher, letter to parents, 27 April 1919, Melbourne University Archives, Melbourne
13 Clive Disher, letter to John Lang, 25 April 1919, Melbourne University Archives, Melbourne
14 Ibid.
15 Clive Disher, letter to parents, 27 April 1919, Melbourne University Archives, Melbourne
16 *Age*, 13 June 1919, p. 8
17 Clive Disher, letter to John Lang, 25 April 1919, Melbourne University Archives, Melbourne
18 Ibid.

19 Clive Disher, letter to parents, 27 April 1919, Melbourne University Archives, Melbourne
20 Ibid.
21 Clive Disher, letter to John Lang, 25 April 1919, Melbourne University Archives, Melbourne
22 Clive Disher, letter to John Lang, 5 May 1919, Melbourne University Archives, Melbourne
23 Ibid.

18 Anzac Day
1 Clive Disher, letter to John Lang, 24 May 1919, Melbourne University Archives, Melbourne
2 Clive Disher, letter to John Lang, 19 April 1919, Melbourne University Archives, Melbourne
3 *Weekly Times* (Melbourne), 19 July 1919, p. 17
4 Clive Disher, letter to parents, 27 April 1919, Melbourne University Archives, Melbourne
5 by D.T. Merrett, '"The School at War": Scotch College and the Great War', *Media Studies in Education* (1982) 24:1, 209–233
6 Major Alan Audsley, letter to family, 28 April 1919, State Library of NSW Archives, c046150295h
7 *Argus*, 29 April 1919, p. 5
8 Major Alan Audsley, letter to family, 28 April 1919, State Library of NSW Archives, c046150294h
9 Major Alan Audsley, letter to family, 21 May 1919, State Library of NSW Archives, c046150302h
10 *The Sunday Times*, London, 21 December, 1913 newspaper cutting, Rowing Assoc. of NSW records, State Library of New South Wales, Sydney
11 Clifford Thomas Steward, *Henley Records 1919–1938*, Hamish Hamilton, London, 1939, p. 21
12 Clifford Thomas Steward, *Henley Records 1919–1938*, Hamish Hamilton, London, 1939, p. 21
13 *The Times*, 25 April 1919

19 Mutiny in the boat
1 Clive Disher, letter to John Lang, 5 May 1919, Melbourne University Archives, Melbourne
2 Clive Disher, letter to John Lang, 18 May 1919, Melbourne University Archives, Melbourne
3 Major Alan Audsley, letter to family, 4 May 1919, State Library of NSW Archives, c046150298h
4 Clive Disher, letter to John Lang, 5 May 1919, Melbourne University Archives, Melbourne

5   Ibid.
6   *Age*, 13 June 1919, p. 8
7   *Daily Mirror*, 11 May 1957, p. 4

20 Picking up the pieces
1   *The Times*, 1 May 1919
2   *The Times*, 19 May 1919
3   Clive Disher, letter to John Lang, 18 May 1919, Melbourne University Archives, Melbourne
4   Clive Disher, letter to John Lang, 5 May 1919, Melbourne University Archives, Melbourne
5   AWM25 Barcode# 897/2 Item No. 319 AIF Sports Control Board correspondence – Middleton letter to Goodrich 8 April 1919
6   Clive Disher, letter to John Lang, 24 May 1919, Melbourne University Archives, Melbourne
7   Ibid.
8   Clive Disher, letter to John Lang, 31 May 1919, Melbourne University Archives, Melbourne
9   Clive Disher, letter to John Lang, 5 May 1919, Melbourne University Archives, Melbourne
10 Clive Disher, letter to parents, 24 May 1919, Melbourne University Archives, Melbourne

21 New digs, new coach
1   Major Alan Audsley, letter to family, 9 June 1919, State Library of NSW Archives, c046150298h
2   *New York Times*, 12 May 1919
3   *The Book of Athletics*, edited by Paul Withington, MD, Lothrop, Lee & Shepard, 1914, p. 347
4   *New York Times*, 21 May 1919
5   *Ithaca Journal*, 29 April 1919, p. 2
6   Clive Disher, letter to John Lang, 15 June 1919, Melbourne University Archives, Melbourne
7   *Oregon Daily Journal*, 29 June 1919, p. 20
8   *Charleston Daily Mail*, 3 July 1919, p. 14
9   The Honolulu Advertiser, newspaper, (Hawaii, USA) Sunday, 28 December, 1919, p.11
10 Clive Disher, letter to parents, 24 May 1919, Melbourne University Archives, Melbourne
11 Clive Disher, letter to John Lang, 31 May 1919, Melbourne University Archives, Melbourne
12 Clive Disher, letter to John Lang, 24 May 1919, Melbourne University Archives, Melbourne

13 Clive Disher, letter to John Lang, 8 June 1919, Melbourne University Archives, Melbourne
14 Major Alan Audsley, letter to family, 9 June 1919, State Library of NSW Archives, c046150298h
15 Alex Thomson, letter to Ossie Wood, Secretary of the NSW Rowing Association, 3 June 1914, Archives, Mitchell Library, State Library of NSW
16 5 November 1913, p. 20
17 Clive Disher, letter to John Lang, 22 June 1919, Melbourne University Archives, Melbourne

22 The two crews
1 Clive Disher, letter to John Lang, 8 June 1919, Melbourne University Archives, Melbourne
2 Clive Disher, letter to John Lang, 8 June 1919, Melbourne University Archives, Melbourne
3 Clive Disher, letter to John Lang, 15 June 1919, Melbourne University Archives, Melbourne
4 *Daily Mirror* (Sydney), 11 May 1957, p. 4
5 Ibid.

23 Six to one
1 *The Times*, 21 May 1919, p. 5
2 *The Times*, 2 July 1919
3 Clive Disher, letter to John Lang, 15 June 1919, Melbourne University Archives, Melbourne
4 Amateur Rowing Association of NSW papers, newspaper clipping, 'Rowing Affairs', 25 October 1913, Archives, State Library of NSW, Sydney
5 *Henley Standard*, 20 June 1919
6 20 June 1919
7 Clive Disher, letter to John Lang, 22 June 1919, Melbourne University Archives, Melbourne
8 *Henley Standard*, 20 June 1919
9 Clive Disher, letter to John Lang, 22 June 1919, Melbourne University Archives, Melbourne
10 *The Times*, 2 July 1919
11 Clive Disher, letter to John Lang, 22 June 1919, Melbourne University Archives, Melbourne
12 *Border Watch*, 20 March 1923, p. 4
13 Ibid.
14 *Ottawa Citizen*, 3 July 1919, p. 20
15 *Daily News* (Perth), 26 June 1937, p. 8
16 *New York Tribune*, 15 June 1919, p. 12
17 Ibid.

18 *Missoulian*, 19 June 1919, p. 8
19 *Fort Wayne Sentinel*, 2 July 1919, p. 12
20 *The Times*, 2 July 1919
21 *Daily Mirror* (Sydney), 11 May 1957, p. 4
22 *Sydney Morning Herald*, 14 May 1935, p. 16

24 The Marlow Victory Regatta

1 Clive Disher, letter to John Lang, 22 June 1919, Melbourne University Archives, Melbourne
2 Clive Disher correspondence to John Lang, 22 June 1919, Melbourne University Archives, Melbourne
3 Major Audsley letter to family, 22 June 1919 Mitchell Library Archives, State Library of NSW
4 Clive Disher, letter to John Lang, 22 June 1919, Melbourne University Archives, Melbourne
5 *New York Times*, 10 June 1919, p. 16
6 Clive Disher, letter to John Lang, 22 June 1919, Melbourne University Archives, Melbourne
7 *The Times*, 1 July 1919, p. 13
8 *The Times*, 1 July 1919
9 Eric Halladay, *Rowing in England: A Social History –The Amateur Debate*, Manchester University Press, 1990, p. 89

25 Tough choices

1 Clive Disher, letter to John Lang, 29 June 1919, Melbourne University Archives, Melbourne
2 *Sun* (Sydney), 3 August 1912, p. 6
3 *Western Times*, 8 July 1912
4 *Sydney Morning Herald*, 20 July 1912, p. 15
5 *Daily Telegraph*, 27 September 1912, p. 15
6 *Glen Innes Examiner*, 2 August 1930, p. 2
7 *Sun* (Sydney), 28 September 1912, p. 9
8 *Glen Innes Examiner*, 2 August 1930, p. 2
9 *Daily Mirror* (Sydney), 11 May 1957, p. 4
10 *Daily Mirror* (Sydney), 11 May 1957, p. 4
11 Clive Disher, letter to John Lang, 29 June 1919, Melbourne University Archives, Melbourne
12 Clive Disher, letter to John Lang, 29 June 1919, Melbourne University Archives, Melbourne
13 *Daily Mirror* (Sydney), 11 May 1957, p. 4
14 Clive Disher, letter to John Lang, 29 June 1919, Melbourne University Archives, Melbourne

15 Clive Disher, letter to John Lang, 29 June 1919, Melbourne University Archives, Melbourne

26 The Royal Henley Peace Regatta

1 Unidentified newspaper clipping, 4 July 1919 (Mettam Family Archives)
2 *Star Gazette*, 18 April 1919, p. 9
3 *Daily Sentinel*, 12 September, 1939, p. 4
4 *Indianapolis News*, 4 July 1919, p. 18
5 C. T. Steward, *Henley Records 1919 to 1938*, Hamish Hamilton, London, 1939, p. 25
6 C. T. Steward, *Henley Records 1919 to 1938*, Hamish Hamilton, London, 1939, p. 33
7 Letter to his mother, 8 July 1919
8 *Daily Mirror* (Sydney), 11 May 1957, p. 4
9 *Daily Mirror* (Sydney), 11 May 1957, p. 4
10 Clive Disher, letter to John Lang, 6 July 1919, Melbourne University Archives, Melbourne
11 *Referee*, 3 September 1919, p. 14
12 Clive Disher, letter to John Lang, 6 July 1919, Melbourne University Archives, Melbourne
13 George Mettam, letter to his mother, 8 July 1919
14 *New York Herald*, 30 November 1919, p. 25
15 C. T. Steward, *Henley Records 1919 to 1938*, Hamish Hamilton, London, 1939, p. 26
16 *Edmonton Journal*, 28 November 1919, p. 27
17 *New York Herald*, 30 November 1919, p. 25

27 The King's Cup

1 Carine Pennefather, letter to Mrs. H. P. Douglas, *Geelong Advertiser*, 1 November 1919, p. 7
2 George Goddard, letter to his mother, 14 July 1919, Accession no. 2885, Item no. 2885/82, State Library of Queensland
3 Fred House's recollection in the *Mercury*, 11 May 1935, p. 8
4 *Morning Post* (London), 7 July 1919, news clipping from Mettam Family Archives
5 Carine Pennefather, letter to Mrs H. P. Douglas, *Geelong Advertiser*, 1 November 1919, p. 7
6 George Mettam, letter to his mother, 8 July 1919
7 *Sporting Globe*, Wednesday 8 May 1935, p. 12
8 Carine Pennefather, letter to Mrs. H. P. Douglas, *Geelong Advertiser*, 1 November 1919, p. 7
9 *Daily News* (Perth), 8 July 1919
10 George Mettam, letter to his mother, 8 July 1919

11 Recollections of Fred House in the *Mercury*, 11 May 1935, p. 8
12 Clive Disher, letter to John Lang, 6 July 1919, Melbourne University Archives, Melbourne
13 *The Times*, 7 July 1919
14 Royal Henley Peace Regatta, official program, writer unknown, Museum of Sport, Melbourne, Victoria
15 *Referee*, 3 September 1919, p. 14
16 Carine Pennefather, letter to Mrs H. P. Douglas, *Geelong Advertiser*, 1 November 1919, p. 7
17 Ibid.
18 *Referee*, 3 September 1919, p. 14
19 *Smith's Weekly*, 11 November 1933, p. 34
20 *Smith's Weekly*, 11 November 1963, p. 34
21 Clive Disher, letter to John Lang, 6 July 1919, Melbourne University Archives, Melbourne

28 The Inter-Allied Games, Paris
1 AWM25, Notes on proposed organisation of AIF Sports in UK and France, Control # 897/6, item # 711575
2 Clive Disher, letter to John Lang, 6 July 1919, Melbourne University Archives, Melbourne
3 Ibid.
4 Clive Disher, letter to John Lang, 6 July 1919, Melbourne University Archives, Melbourne
5 Ibid.
6 Major Allan Audsley, letter to parents, 22 June 1919
7 Clive Disher, letter to John Lang, 12 July 1919, Melbourne University Archives, Melbourne
8 Clive Disher, letter to parents, 11 July 1919, Melbourne University Archives, Melbourne
9 Clive Disher, letter to John Lang, 12 July 1919, Melbourne University Archives, Melbourne
10 Inter-Allied Games, Paris, 22 June to 6 July, published by the Games Committee, p. 254
11 Clive Disher, letter to John Lang, 18 July 1919, Melbourne University Archives, Melbourne
12 Inter-Allied Games, Paris, 22 June to 6 July, published by the Games Committee, p. 254
13 Clive Disher, letter to John Lang, 22 July 1919, Melbourne University Archives, Melbourne

1 NAA: B2455, House, F. A. Lieutenant, Barcode: 5822180
2 Clive Disher, letter to John Lang, 27 July 1919, Melbourne University
   Archives, Melbourne
3 Clive Disher, letter to parents, 5 August 1919, Melbourne University
   Archives, Melbourne
4 Lieutenant G. H. Goddard, *Soldiers and Sportsmen*, AIF Sports Control
   Board, London, 1919, p. 3
5 *The Homing Aussie*, HMAT *Euripides* on-board magazine, p. 29
7 Victorian Rowing Association minutes, Australian Sports Club, 1 November
   1920, p. 63

1 *Sydney Morning Herald*, 21 February 1923, p. 13
2 *Register*, 22 February 1923, p. 8
3 Fred House, letter to Clive Disher, 5 September 1962, Melbourne University
   Archives, Melbourne University
4 Ruby House, letter to Clive Disher, 30 November 1969, Melbourne
   University Archives, Melbourne University
5 *Mail* (Adelaide), 16 November 1940, p. 18
6 Clive Disher, letter to George Mettam, 4 July 1935
7 Clive Disher, letter to George Mettam, 22 September 1945, Mettam Family
   collection
8 Clive Disher, letter to George Mettam, 17 October 1961, Mettam Family
   Collection
9 Syd Middleton, letter to Marion Streatfeild, 27 December 1919 (Middleton
   Family Archives)
10 Syd Middleton, letter to Marion Streatfeild, 24 December 1919 (Middleton
   Family Archives)
11 Syd Middleton, letter to Marion Streatfeild, undated, c. 1920
12 Marion Middleton, letter to W.S. Robinson, 2 July 1958, Melbourne
   University Archives, Melbourne University
13 Disher, letter to John Lang, 6 July 1919 (Melbourne University Archives,
   Melbourne)
14 Steve Fairbairn, *Rowing Notes*, Mills & Boon, 1926, p. xvi
15 *Argus*, 12 March 1921, p. 5

Map of the Henley course

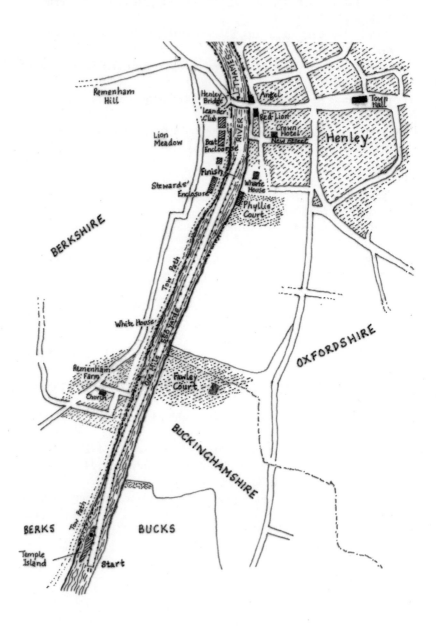

Index

Acknowledgements

I would like to thank numerous people who have generously provided their time and assistance in the research and writing of the story of these AIF oarsmen. The journey tracking down family descendants of the oarsmen has been an exhilarating ride in itself. It involved many random cold calls, letters and emails that allowed me to view and record previously unseen personal letters, clippings and family albums of the Royal Henley Peace Regatta that hadn't been publicly seen before. These were crucial in bringing human perspectives to the story of this regatta and the members of the AIF Rowing Section. Special thanks go to Paul and Sharon Smedley; Sonya Hayes; Lois Ross-Soden; Brian and Debbie Ross-Soden; Rupert Middleton and family; Lynda House; Dr Rob Walters, Henry Wurm; Coral Hauenstein; Russell and Ruth Perrott; Barry McGill; Greg Clota; John Robb; Helen Gay; Jan Ratcliffe; and Kim Mettam and family.

Special thanks is also extended to the staff and librarians of the Melbourne University Archives, the Mitchell Library, the State Library of New South Wales, Sydney; the National Sports Museum, Melbourne; the River & Rowing Museum, Henley; the Australian National Maritime Museum, Sydney; the National Archives of Australia, Canberra and Melbourne; and the Imperial War Museum, London, all of whom always guided me to the right files, people and/or original documents. Special thanks must also go to the helpful staff of the Research Centre and Media Office at the Australian War Memorial, Canberra; and specifically to Dr Meleah Hampton, who gave her time for interviews, researched the military records of the oarsmen, and provided essential background to the Battle of Pozieres and many military details.

There have been many rowing experts from Australia and around the world who shared their knowledge and expertise. Special thanks go to John O'Brien for bouncing off many ideas about the story; Barry Moynihan OAM from Leichhardt Rowing Club; Bill O'Chee; Keith Jameson OAM from Sydney Rowing Club; John Boultbee AM

from Sydney University Rowing Club; Lucy Benjamin from Rowing
Australia; Colonel Andrew Hine; Larry Writer; Rob Prescott; Owen
Nix; Göran Buckhorn; Geoff Armstrong; Thomas E. Weil; Andy
Anderson; the ever resourceful Tim Koch; Louis Petrin; Greg Denieffe;
Marilyn Wiscart; Donald Legget; Clare Sargent from Radley College;
Russell Sears from the Sports Heritage Trust, New Zealand; Julian
Ebsworth from London Rowing Club; and Jennifer Leatherby from the
Imperial War Museum, London, who organised a fantastic interview
with IWM historian Alan Wakefield.

Special thanks to the Stewards of the Henley Royal Regatta and
Leander Club, Henley, including Sir Steve Redgrave, Sir Matthew
Pinsent, Robert Treharne Jones and Daniel Grist, who provided their
valuable time and access to Leander Club and the Henley Royal Regatta.

Many people gave their time to be interviewed about the Peace
Regatta and my appreciation and thanks to His Excellency General
the Honourable David Hurley, AC, DSC, FTSE (Ret'd), the Governor
General of Australia; world rowing authority Chris Dodd; Peter
Mallory; Paul Thompson; Mark Blandford-Taylor; Dr Tony Wober,
who also skippered me along the River Thames at Henley; Dr Bruce
Coe; Natalie Patel; Dr Meleah Hampton from the Australian War
Memorial, Canberra; Dr Marina Larsson; Colonel Nicole Sadler;
and Dr Peter Stanley FAHA, from the Australian Defence Force
Academy, Canberra.

Special thanks for the generosity, dedication and commitment of
Howard Croker from Croker Oars, who hand-crafted eight replica
oars made from Canadian spruce as used by the original AIF crew; and
also John Driessen from Rowfit, who constructed poppet riggers; and
Michael Kemp from Vintage Wooden Rowing Boats.

Special thanks also to the service men and women of Australian
Defence Force Rowing Club, Canberra, in particular Brigadier Alison
Creagh, who enthusiastically assisted me in filming an historical
recreation of the 1919 AIF No. 1 crew in action on the waters of Lake
Burley Griffin, which allowed us to see poppet riggers and Canadian
spruce toothpick oars back in action, and has supported the story in
every possible way.

Special mention and thanks to Arwen Summers from Hardie Grant, who steered this story forward; Marg Bowman; Tricia Dearborn and the ever enthusiastic Liam Pieper, who all, I hope, learned a lot about rowing. I would also like to specially thank Meredith Curnow, who first tapped the story along.

I also extend much love and thanks to my wife, Felicity, for her encouragement and support, my daughter Chloe with her great love of Greek myths and ancient history; and my oarsman son Charlie, who rowed as part of the Australian Defence Force crew that competed in the centenary commemoration of the original King's Cup competition at the Henley Royal Regatta in 2019.

Special thanks to Charlotte Ingoldby, who has always been a welcoming and a treasured friend, and who has opened her house on my numerous travels to Henley and often been my Henley 'boots on the ground'. Also, to our late great friend, Shiplake local and former London housemate Mary Ferraira, who always enthusiastically supported me in my efforts to tell this story, but who sadly passed away before she could see the story of the oarsmen push off on the water. Mary would have loved this very Australian story.

Special thanks also to oarsmen Andrew Guerin, who first brought this story to my attention and has been a vocal champion of the story of the AIF oarsmen for many years. Without Andrew's dedication and commitment this story of the AIF oarsmen, the winners of the original King's Cup, would have slipped away without recognition; and thanks also to Barry Ryan, whose enthusiasm, support and assistance has been much appreciated. Both these individuals have been invaluable to me, and without their generous support the telling of this story would not have been possible.

Credits

Text

Page v
'A Brief for the Defense' from *Refusing Heaven* by Jack Gilbert, © 2005 by Jack Gilbert. Used by permission of Alfred A. Knopf, an imprint of the Knopf Doubleday Publishing Group, a division of Penguin Random House LLC. All rights reserved.

Pages 13, 48, 161, 257
Homer, *The Odyssey*. Translated by E. V. Rieu. London, England, Penguin Books, 1991

Images

Page 1
TOP LEFT Davis Sporting Collection, courtesy of Mitchell Library, State Library of NSW; CENTRE LEFT National Library of Australia, Trove, *The Referee*, Sydney, Wednesday 28 June 1916, p.15; TOP RIGHT Informal portrait of 47 Private (Pte) Thomas Anderson Whyte (sitting left) and 159 Sergeant John Rutherford Gordon sitting on one of the large stones of the Great Pyramid at Giza. Australian War Memorial P09576.002; CENTRE RIGHT The Sporting Globe, 22 April 1931, p. 1; BOTTOM Courtesy of the Smedley family

Page 2
TOP LEFT Captain Keith Heritage, MC. Darge Photographic Company collection of negatives, Australian War Memorial DAC51276; CENTRE LEFT Courtesy of the Perrott family; TOP RIGHT University of Melbourne Archives, 1976-0013-00126 Strathfieldsaye Estate Collection; BOTTOM Courtesy of the Smedley family

Page 3
TOP Courtesy of the Perrott family; CENTRE Davis Sporting Collection, courtesy of Mitchell Library, State Library of NSW; BOTTOM Courtesy of the Smedley family

Page 4
TOP LEFT Courtesy of the Smedley family; TOP RIGHT Courtesy of the Smedley family CENTRE AWM Repatriation and Demobilisation, AIF Item # 30/1/1 Part 2 RCDIG1002984, p.98; BOTTOM Courtesy of the Smedley family

Page 5
TOP LEFT Courtesy of the Middleton family; TOP RIGHT Courtesy of the Middleton family; CENTRE Courtesy of the Smedley family; BOTTOM Courtesy of the Ross-Soden family

Page 6
TOP University of Melbourne Archives, 1976-0013-00126 Strathfieldsaye Estate Collection; CENTRE LEFT Courtesy of Leichhardt Rowing Club; CENTRE RIGHT Source unknown; BOTTOM Courtesy of the Smedley family

Page 7

TOP LEFT Courtesy of the Smedley family; TOP RIGHT Courtesy of the Smedley family; CENTRE LEFT University of Melbourne Archives, 1976-0013-00126 Strathfieldsaye Estate Collection; CENTRE RIGHT Courtesy of the Smedley family; BOTTOM University of Melbourne Archives, 1976-0013-00126 Strathfieldsaye Estate Collection

Page 8

TOP Courtesy of the Middleton family; CENTRE University of Melbourne Archives, 1976-0013-00126 Strathfieldsaye Estate Collection; BOTTOM Courtesy of the Smedley family

Page 9

TOP University of Melbourne Archives, 1976-0013-00126 Strathfieldsaye Estate Collection; CENTRE Courtesy of the Ross-Soden family; BOTTOM Courtesy of the Smedley family

Page 10

TOP Courtesy of the Middleton family; CENTRE University of Melbourne Archives, 1976-0013-00126 Strathfieldsaye Estate Collection; BOTTOM University of Melbourne Archives, 1976-0013-00126 Strathfieldsaye Estate Collection

Page 11

TOP Used with permission from the Australian Army; CENTRE Courtesy of the Ross-Soden family; BOTTOM Henley, England 1918. A stand on the edge of the river reserved for Australian soldiers and their friends. Australian War Memorial H01231

Page 12

TOP Courtesy of the Middleton family; CENTRE LEFT Courtesy of Rowing Australia/Delly Carr; CENTRE RIGHT The Weekly Courier, 19 October 1916. Courtesy of Launceston Library Archives; BOTTOM Courtesy of the Ross-Soden family

Page 13

TOP University of Melbourne Archives, 1976-0013-00126 Strathfieldsaye Estate Collection; CENTRE Courtesy of the Smedley family; BOTTOM University of Melbourne Archives, 1976-0013-00126 Strathfieldsaye Estate Collection

Page 14

TOP Davis Sporting Collection, courtesy of Mitchell Library, State Library of NSW; CENTRE LEFT University of Melbourne Archives, 1976-0013-00126 Strathfieldsaye Estate Collection; CENTRE RIGHT Cook, Sir Theodore, *Henley races: with details of regattas from 1903 to 1914 inclusive and a complete index of competitors and crews since 1839,* London; New York: Oxford University Press; H. Milford, 1919; BOTTOM University of Melbourne Archives, 1976-0013-00126 Strathfieldsaye Estate Collection

Page 15

TOP University of Melbourne Archives, 1976-0013-00126 Strathfieldsaye Estate Collection; LEFT [headline] National Library of Australia, Trove, *The Sun,* Sydney. Thursday, 28 August 1919, p.5; [programme] Courtesy of Barry Moynahan; BOTTOM Courtesy of the Smedley family

Page 16

TOP LEFT Courtesy of the Middleton family; Top right: Used with permission, name withheld; CENTRE Courtesy of the Smedley family; BOTTOM Courtesy of the Robb family

About the author

Scott Patterson is a director and filmmaker based in Australia. He has worked extensively across film, television, advertising and the theatre during his thirty-year career. A keen oarsman himself, he is producing a documentary about the 1919 Royal Henley Peace Regatta, also entitled *The Oarsmen.*